PRAISE FOR

Joey Buran and *Beyond the Dream*

"My life has been forever impacted by Joey Buran. His sense of conviction and purpose in life are something of a contagious nature. He will inspire you to serve others, take chances, reach for excellence, achieve greatness and enjoy the journey God has set before you along the way."

—GARID BEELER
Senior Pastor, Vision City Church
Irvine, California

"The captivating story of a man whose life has influenced so many others. His constant encouragement, wisdom and life-giving words have inspired so many others to pursue their dreams. *Beyond the Dream* is a page-turner that takes you through every high and low life has to offer and leaves you with hope that never fails."

—SUSAN BRANCH
Former General Manager, Roxy America
Former General Manager, Billabong Women's Global

"For anyone growing up in Southern California with an association with surf culture, Joey Buran was a household name. I remember hearing about his legendary surfing years before my husband brought him home to dinner after they met surfing in Carlsbad. Joey enthralled us with his epic surf stories and adventures. Now that same thrill can be shared by anyone who reads his memoir, *Beyond the Dream*. Thank you again, Joey, for taking us on the amazing adventure of God's call and anointing upon your life."

—CHERYL BRODERSEN
Gracious Words Podcast
Author and Speaker

"The takeaway from *Beyond the Dream* can be life changing! Finding purpose and focus for your life is intentionally woven throughout the book. So many life lessons and great practical advice. A 5 out of 5 stars and an inspirational read!"

—LUKE CALDWELL
President, Timber and Love Home Design and Real Estate
HGTV Star of Shows *Boise Boys* and *Outgrown*

"In the many years I have known Joey, it has always been clear that God has given him a heart and vision for the youth of this generation. His passion for God has influenced many, including myself."

—JEREMY CAMP
Musician, Grammy Nominee
Multiple Dove Award Winner

"The beach-blond life force of Joey Buran hit me on my first visit to Hawaii back in 1978. I eyed him for the ease in which he found the tricky tubes at Rocky Point and then eventually to where our true surfing character was to be revealed down the beach . . . at Pipeline! Watching Joey win Pipeline Masters in 1984 lit a fire in me that pushed me for even greater successes in my own career. After Pipeline he just disappeared! What a blessing to now see the contributions of his life being defined and celebrated in his book *Beyond the Dream*. Thank you, Joey, for bringing your commitment and boundless energy to everything you do!"

—TOM CARROLL
Two-Time ASP World Surfing Champion
Three-Time Pipeline Masters Champion

"Joey Buran is an extraordinary individual whose impact on the world of surfing and beyond is unparalleled. As a Pipeline Masters champion and World Champion surf coach of the USA Surf Team, Joey's positivity and encouragement have been a beacon of inspiration to all who know him. His dedication in guiding others to reach their fullest potential is truly remarkable. He is a true role model, embodying a life of faith, service, excellence and humility. *Beyond the Dream* is an inspiring read and one that I thoroughly enjoyed!"

—**Greg Cruse**
Former CEO, USA Surfing
Team Manager, USA Olympic Surf Team, Tokyo 2021

"Loved the journey of this book! A reminder of the amazing ways God has used the life of Joey Buran over the decades. In *Beyond the Dream*, Joey takes the reader on a fascinating adventure from young local surfer to the top of professional surfing and then ultimately to a lifetime of serving God. Filled with tenacity, determination, discipline and humility, you can expect to be amazed by Joey's journey while being inspired and encouraged to discover and fulfill your own."

—**Pastor Jim Gallagher**
Senior Pastor, Calvary Chapel Vero Beach
Vero Beach, Florida

"Joey teaches life lessons and that surfing isn't everything, but that friends, family, education and other things beside surfing matter."

—**Kaleigh Gilchrist**
Two-Time Olympic Gold Medalist
Team USA Women's Water Polo

"It is such an honor to endorse *Beyond the Dream*! Joey's life and ministry have been nothing short of tried-and-true faithfulness. His steadfastness in surfing and ministry have inspired following generations to emulate his example, including my own. This book will encourage the weary while reminding all of us to pause and realize God's steadfast faithfulness throughout the highs and lows of our lives. Thank you for making such an impact on my life!"

—**Sarah Hill**
Executive Director
Beautifully Flawed Foundation

"*Beyond the Dream* is a compelling story of Joey Buran's passionate and relentless pursuit of his dream. An authentic tale of a champion who helped usher in the era of modern professional surfing which then became the meteoric growth of the sport and lifestyle billion-dollar industry. Having known Joey since he was 15, I have watched his journey in amazement. From one unimaginable dream to another, it is the ultimate ride and I am a fan! His story, accurate, honest and humble, is a completely relatable human journey filled with human struggles and unfathomable successes. This book is a page-turner and one that I could not put down!"

—**Bob Hurley**
Founder and Former CEO
Hurley International

"Like Joey, *Beyond the Dream* is a rip-roaring narrative where we see the anvil of God break down the desires, ambitions, pains and dreams of his life, all the while shaping them into a magnificent work of art. The California Kid is still riding high!"

—**Pancho Juarez**
Senior Pastor
Ark Church Montebello

"Joey Buran's multifaceted career from California Kid to Pipeline Master to Team USA coach and Calvary Chapel pastor unfolds in *Beyond the Dream*. A great read."

—JIM KEMPTON
Author, *Women on Waves*
Former Publisher and Editor, *Surfer* magazine

"In 1974, Joey Buran and I sat beside each other in the lineup at Tamarack Beach in Carlsbad. *Beyond the Dream* brings me to those early days. A profound adrenaline rush of Joey's journey to become the Pipe Masters champion, and his inspiring shift from surfer to pastor."

—JULIE MOSS
Author, *Crawl of Fame*
Member, International Triathlon Hall of Fame

"*Beyond the Dream* is an amazing story of God's glory through Joey's extraordinary journey. Breathtaking and life changing, this book will inspire and encourage many. A must-read book for anyone who wants to make the rest of their life the best of their life."

—KEITH RANDOLPH
President, Liberty Financial
Author, *100 Secrets to Success*

"For a kid from North County San Diego, to see our local hero Joey Buran on *Wide World of Sports* (with 30 million viewers) not only participating but dominating made me look at myself and say, 'Why not me?' Joey led the way for all of us, helping us truly believe that we could all make a difference on a global scale and that anything is possible."

—Stevie Salas
Lead Guitarist, Rod Stewart "Out of Order" Tour
Author, *When We Were the Boys*

"With Coach Joey it was always, snap, crackle, pop! First turn commitment, clean flow and a strong finishing turn. He was always positive and uplifting toward everyone!"

—Caitlin Simmers
USA Olympic Surf Team, Paris 2024
WSL Pipeline Champion 2024

"I was there on the beach the day Joey Buran won the Pipeline Masters and he was killing it! In *Beyond the Dream*, Joey does the surfing world as well as any sports enthusiasts a favor, giving us insight into the heart, mind and soul of a professional athlete at an elite level. Mahalo for writing with such candor and compassion, showing us the way to success on earth and in heaven!"

—Mike Stangel
Pastor Emeritus, North Shore Christian Fellowship
Former Chaplain, Hawaii Triple Crown of Surfing

"*Beyond the Dream* is about a surfing legend, but also so much more. It is packed with real-life wisdom and faith that go beyond the waves. Joey's storytelling hooks you from the start with life lessons tucked in every chapter. It's a book you will want to keep reading, filled with Joey's down-to-earth style, humor and a journey that speaks to anyone looking for more."

—Monica Swanson
The Monica Swanson Podcast
Author, *Raising Amazing* and *Becoming Homeschoolers*

"An enthralling ride of commitment and faith. Makes you feel like you just won the Pipeline Masters!"

—Shaun Tomson
World Surfing and Pipeline Masters Champion
Author and Motivational Speaker

"Joey has always been an inspiration in and out of the water. His accomplishments in the water as a kid growing up in California are nothing short of amazing. Even more impressive is his attitude, positivity and energy. His guidance as the coach of Team USA helped many of us to reach our goals. Thanks, Joey!"

—Nat Young
Two-Time Team USA Gold Medalist, ISA World Surfing Games
Winner, Numerous World Surf League Pro Surfing Events

BEYOND THE DREAM

BEYOND THE DREAM

From the King of Pipeline

to a Life of Serving and Inspiring Others

FOREWORD BY ROBERT YEHLING

INTRODUCTION BY KEN KEBOW

A MEMOIR

JOEY BURAN

Transformation Media Books
Saint Louis, Missouri

Published by Transformation Media Books, USA

www.TransformationMediaBooks.com
info@TransformationMediaBooks.com

An imprint of Pen & Publish, LLC
Saint Louis, Missouri
(314) 827-6567
www.PenandPublish.com

Paperback ISBN: 978-1-956897-44-9
e-book ISBN: 978-1-956897-45-6
Library of Congress Control Number: 2024940699

Front cover design by Katie Lee Grosskopf
Front cover photo by Brian Stephen (Hank Foto)
Back cover photo (background) by Aaron Chang
Back cover author photo by John Jackson

In dedication with love and gratitude to my incredible wife, Jennifer, and the amazing children God has blessed us with, Hannah, Leah, Timothy and Luke. We have been on this journey together for over 35 years now, and I never cease to be filled with joy and amazement as I consider the experiences we have all been able to share through many seasons of life.

Beyond the original family, this book is also dedicated to our sons- and daughters-in-law, Nathan, Jakeh, Isabella, Arika and the wonderful grandchildren who have come along with them.

I love you all beyond words.

CONTENTS

FOREWORD

ROBERT YEHLING

I had not heard from Joey Buran in some 30 years when he called me one afternoon in October 2023. This might come as some surprise to those who knew how closely he and I had worked together in the surfing world in the 1970s and 1980s, he as a surfing superstar and me as a reporter and later event promoter. However, our life paths diverged widely as we both left the sport. Life can be funny like that.

Yet, when Joey called, I knew what I'd heard through the grapevine: He had finally written a draft of his long-awaited memoir, and needed help enhancing and refining it into final book form. After writing, cowriting and editing books for more than a quarter century, I was winding down my career, but when certain people knock . . .

Joey was knocking. I couldn't believe my good fortune.

I beamed as we spoke, my smile as wide as an ocean. It was so good to hear from him, so joyous to feel his energy and boundless positivity, to see his eyes dancing and that "super stoke" pouring from him. It felt like no time had passed as we caught up on the past decades, our victories and our challenges, our triumphs and tribulations. Our conversation was open and free-flowing, warm and engaging, two friends from the surfing mecca of Carlsbad, California, since 1976 rekindling a kinship interrupted by life.

As Joey got to the business at hand, a tear came to my eye. I gulped, not quite sure how to tell him that I might have trouble taking on what I considered one of the best literary wingman assignments of my career: I was fighting stage 4 prostate and bone cancer, just recently removed from yet another hospital stay. Do I tell him now? Do I wait until I get knocked asunder by the next wave of this insidious disease? Do I act like all is okay and pray and hope nothing happens in the five months it would take us to bring this book to final form?

Then, as Joey kept updating me, I thought about his amazing life. After his Herculean achievements as one of the greatest surfers in the world, capped by winning the 1984 Pipeline Masters title, surfing's greatest event, Joey lost his drive and purpose. He went through a tough spell. What did he do? Did he hide from it? Did he cower, try to wish it away or pretend it wasn't there? Did he decide to cash in his chips and conclude he'd enjoyed his greatness, done enough for the world, and would just slog through life?

NO on all counts. Not by a long shot. Joey got off the mat. He took full accountability of himself, and embraced the greater purpose in his life, one that had been nudging at him for years: to serve and inspire others through his walk with God. He found happiness and joy in life again. He became a minister, and then a nationally respected minister. He found the love of his life, and he and Jennifer began a family that now fills his days and nights as a father and grandfather. He helped countless thousands navigate life through his ministerial work at the influential Worship Generation, buoyed by his boundless positivity and wisdom. And when he returned to surfing after a long absence, the gifts showered upon him: 1998 World Masters Champion. Coach of the American, British and Chilean national teams. Gold-medal-winning coach of Team USA in the 2017 World Junior Surfing Championships, a prelude to the Olympics.

So, I walked through Door Number One. I buckled my seat belt and told Joey about my health situation, leaving no stone unturned. His response, delivered with a huge smile on his face and eyes that could light up a blacked-out city? "Then I guess we need to get busy."

I can picture a generation of surf stars from Australia to California, Hawaii to South Africa nod their heads. They had to face this positive, affirmative force in competition more than they ever liked. In my case, it was a call to rise above my health situation and bring forth his amazing story for the world to see.

A depth of energy filled my body that I hadn't felt in a while. I felt the burning desire to help my friend bring his story to a world that remembers him very well for his wave-riding exploits, even as he continues to fulfill his higher purpose—as I realized he was doing by making sure I was going to come along for this ride with him.

When we got off the phone, we both had tears in our eyes. Our friendship was rekindled. I felt renewed energy to fight to live. And Joey had his wingman back, this time as an editor-advisor for *Beyond the Dream.*

We worked through the winter, bringing back the stories of our shared years in the surfing world at its most amazing developmental stage in the US. It was a great collaboration, for the simple reason we both lived through it. Quick memory snapshots broke out into stories. We were able to see the significance of periods of time, and how they shaped two generations culturally. Through it all, Joey got to see a side of me he'd never seen—the book writing and editing side—and I continued to be regularly blessed by his presence as a minister. Our friendship grew deeper by the meeting, not a common occurrence when you're working on a book together. Work sessions between author and writer-collaborator often get intense, contentious, even messy. That never happened with us. We were just so thrilled to live out this grand blessing of getting to work together one more time. And to do so with a shared goal in our work: ramping up to a sustained excellence in sharing Joey's story. This whole book felt like a peak experience as we enhanced Joey's original manuscript.

Now, the work is done. *Beyond the Dream* is much more than a surfing memoir, though that is certainly how it looks in the first half. It is the open-hearted, open-minded, deeply honest account of a singular man in our world who achieved greatness against all odds as an athlete, then again as a minister, but most of all, who turned his light, energy and wisdom into helping and guiding the lives of so many people—the ultimate form of service. Not many public figures who are the subject of worldwide acclimation can make such an adjustment to these levels of humility, but Joey did it. This book is a must read for all women and men who want to see how a truly soulful, healthy man brings all his blessings, gifts and tools together, supported by his rock-solid family, to make the world a better place. It is also a lot of fun.

This is both a joyous and bittersweet moment for me. I can't think of a greater full-circle way to close out nearly a half century as a professional writer than by working with the subject of some of my very first articles as a 17-year-old sportswriter. While I must lower my pen for health reasons, my friendship with Joey will forever live on. In fact, in one of the greatest gifts I have ever received in my life, he is at my side in a ministerial way while I pass through the advanced and final stages of cancer.

Enjoy *Beyond the Dream.* It is one heckuva ride, from cover to cover.

Robert Yehling
Award-Winning Author, *Voices*
Coauthor, *Crawl of Fame* and *When We Were the Boys*
Dolly Gray Award–Winning Coauthor, *Just Add Water*

INTRODUCTION

KEN KEBOW

In the world of surfing, there is no greater compliment than watching other surfers actually leave the water and break away from their own wave riding to watch someone else surf. It rarely happens. Rumor has it this happened consistently with Phil Edwards, one of California's earliest and most admired surfers. I'd speculate this happened with Hawaiian guru and Pipeline legend Gerry Lopez as well. However, the list of surfers that other wave riders would stop catching waves to watch is a very short and exclusive list.

Joey Buran is on that list. Other surfers felt it was more worthwhile to stop riding waves, get out of the surf, settle in on the beach, and watch and learn from Joey. I was one of those surfers. And regardless of the condition and shape of the waves, it was always worth watching Joey Buran catch waves.

My hometown, Carlsbad, California, is a beautiful beach town about 30 minutes north of San Diego. Life revolves around the beach in Carlsbad. It did when Joey Buran hit the surf scene in Carlsbad in the 1970s, and it still does. Families come to Carlsbad, become surfers and ocean lovers, and create generations of world-class surfers. Living in Carlsbad is more of a "lifestyle" than just a place to call home. Maybe you need to live there to understand what I mean, but it is an amazing place and was especially an incredible place to grow up.

Ask Joey and he'll tell you that 1973 was his "official new surfer" year. It was the year Joey bought his first new surfboard (a $30 beauty from Offshore Surf Shop and Barbie Baron), his first new wetsuit from Hansen's Surf Shop—and received his first new nickname—"Da Sandcrab!"

What I remember most from those wonderful days watching Joey surf was his ability to find a "tube" or the inside of the wave, regardless of the surf. Whether the wave was a small two-footer or a ten-foot monster big enough to swallow a family home, Joey Buran would get barreled! From the gentle mush of California summer waves to a six-foot grinder from a solid south swell, Joey Buran was "in the tube." What was amazing was his ability to find a tube where it didn't exist. Joey and his traveling magic show! I still don't know how he did it!

Joey almost never fell off his board. He just didn't fall. It was like his feet were superglued to the deck of his surfboard. The guy's balance was extraordinary.

And it wasn't just surfing. I remember one of the nights as teenagers we all went to the Escondido Skating Rink on a Saturday night and, even though it was Joey's first or second time on roller skates, he was skating backward in record time.

As for skateboarding, the other emerging beach sport of our youth . . . not only was Joey an exceptional skateboarder but one Saturday in 1976, there was Joey Buran, at the opening of the Carlsbad Skate Park by the Carlsbad Raceway, rumored to be the first skate park on earth. And there's "Sandcrab," with no shirt (and no pads unlike many of the other skaters) skating the grand opening of the park with the heavyweight skaters of the day—Gregg Weaver, Tony Alva, Ty Page, Tom Sims—and not only holding his own but looking right at home skating with the world's hottest skateboarders.

The Sandcrab never fell off anything!

Joey and I became friends in junior high and more so in high school at Carlsbad High. That's where I venture to say Joey met one of the most instrumental people in his life . . . David Barr. A year younger than Joey, David would meet him every Saturday morning near Carlsbad High School, both on their skateboards or bikes, often before it even got light, to go surfing. Sun or rain, epic surf or junky waves . . . it didn't matter. In the words of David Barr, "It was all about surfing."

Joey told me those mornings "were some of the most fun times I've ever had surfing. No pressure, just the innocence of youth and really great memories."

It continued in the summertime with all-day "sessions." In case six hours of surfing in the morning weren't enough, Joey and David would often scrounge up a couple of nickels, hitchhike or skateboard to the local Thrifty's, where ice cream was five cents a scoop, sugar up with a delicious Thrifty's cone and head back to the beach for a full afternoon of surfing. They couldn't get enough!

The relationship between Joey and David was like Rocky and his coach Mickey in the *Rocky* movies. (Joey loves sports analogies.) With each of them playing either role in the relationship at any time, they used humor, their competitive natures, and hours and hours of time together training to push each other to be the best surfers possible. And, like turning Rocky Balboa into a world-class fighter, this routine and their camaraderie turned two young Carlsbad surfers into future champions.

Joey and David pushed each other. They supported each other. They taught each other and they inspired each other. They developed a competitiveness that saw them usually land in the top two slots of any youth surfing competitions for years to come. Basically, they dominated California's youth surfing competitions. From there, they vaulted to world-class status. For more than five years of their lives, Joey and David were the top California surfers on the IPS World Surfing Tour.

A competitive fire burned in Joey's belly, partly pure DNA and partly stoked by his thousands of hours spent surfing with his "closest friend and fiercest rival" David Barr, that helped him truly excel. The talent was already there, but Joey's competitive determination and competitive desire made the difference. There was no better competitor than Joey. As you'll learn in *Beyond the Dream*, Joey's ability to watch, listen and learn in a surf competition environment, studying the best surfers and developing his own contest strategy, was an essential key to his tremendous success. Just like any athlete at the top of his game, Joey never stopped refining his God-given talent and nurturing his knowledge of the sport and his competitive instinct.

Like all of us who started surfing at Tamarack, Joey endured all the heckles and threats and "stolen waves" from the older and "wiser" locals, who made sure all us "grommets" paid our dues, whether it was climbing the Tamarack staircase or out in the waves. And being "spastic, having a wide stance like David Nuuhiwa [a famous Hawaiian surfer] and a loud mouth" (Joey's words about himself, not mine), made him the continual target of the local surfers' ridicule and harassment. Joey moved quickly up the pecking order of local surfers with his incredible talent, passion for surfing, and his enthusiasm and energy about the sport.

Moving from the slower waves at Tamarack a mile north to Carlsbad State Beach, Joey's tube-riding became legendary in the stronger, more powerful and "hollower" waves up at State. Long before he became the King of Pipeline, Joey was the master of the challenging and tubular waves at State Beach. And, in my humble opinion, no other surfer to this day has ridden the tubes at State Beach better or more frequently than Joey Buran.

As Joey says himself in the following pages, "Tube riding was my calling." And indeed, it was.

It wasn't long before Joey became "larger than life," winning contest after contest and ultimately getting dubbed the "California Kid." And, after a long slumber of the mellow California surf culture kicking back and grooving on the waves, Joey put the Golden State back in the surfing spotlight.

There was a great deal more to the world of surfing, competitive and otherwise, than just the California coast. I remember Joey telling me, when the waves were ten-plus feet at a great left break called Spot or "Spotland" just south of Tamarack, Joey would go out and hear the voice of ABC's *Wide World of Sports* Jim McKay announcing the Pipeline Masters Surf Competition and saying, "There goes little Joey Buran, screaming down the face of a Pipeline classic." Joey would actually "rehearse" surfing in the Pipeline Masters.

This "rehearsing" was much more than just hearing voices in his head. Joey has this amazing ability to visualize and project his success. You couple that with extreme self-confidence and a belief that he could never fail, and Joey succeeded, at a very high level, in most everything he's attempted and undertaken in life.

That confidence was on display one night when Joey came over one late afternoon and picked me up in his parents' car. We parked on the dirt cliff on the west side of the Pacific Coast Highway that now is a beautiful, manicured walkway. Joey told me he "borrowed" his college savings bonds and decided he would "quietly" take off for Hawaii and make his mark, without his parents knowing. He told me his plan (it's in the book so I won't give it away) with as much confidence and conviction as he'd ever shared with me. While I don't remember exactly how I felt, I'm sure I told Joey it was a great plan. After watching a classic Tamarack evening glass off, Joey drove me home. Exiting the car, I said goodbye and good luck to Joey as he departed. Suddenly, Joey stopped me, and with a serious look on his face that hinted that he was truly on the cusp of saying something prophetic, he said, "Don't forget to tell all the girls I said goodbye!" Here is Joey, sneaking away to Hawaii with "borrowed" savings bonds to pursue his dream of surfing Hawaii with no advance notice, and he wanted me to make sure the Carlsbad High School girls knew he was thinking about them. Pure teenage Joey!

It turned out his "borrowing the savings bond" plan worked out incredibly well. Again, not wanting to ruin the story you're about to embark on in this book, let's just say his gutsy trip to the North Shore of Oahu helped cement his surfing future. In fact, when Joey made the finals of the Pipeline Masters in 1978 at the age of seventeen, Pipeline legend Rory Russell pulled up next to him in the parking lot in front of a very angry surfing day at Pipeline. Rory, also a contestant in the finals and one of Joey's surfing heroes whose pictures adorned his bedroom walls at home, said, "You're going to die out there today."

Joey didn't die that day. Rather, he came back six years later to secure his status as a Pipeline Masters champion, one of the most coveted honors in our sport.

Joey and I lost touch with each other as our lives went in different directions in the '80s and '90s. I kept up on Joey's successes while talking with other surf buddies and occasionally ran into Joey on the beach at Pipeline as he was competing and I was videotaping the Pipeline Masters. It was always a quick "Hello" and "How's things?" as we were both preoccupied with the reason we were there (Joey to compete and me to film). I do remember at one point we got together after Joey decided to change the direction of his life and give his life to God in 1987 and, after leaving California for more than a decade, went on to be the founder of successful churches in Virginia Beach and Burlington, Vermont. While Joey always had a strong faith, that passion was now his driving force in life, as much as, if not more than, surfing once was.

Joey married a wonderful woman he met at community college named Jennifer George in 1988 and started a family with amazing kids and now grandkids and, from all signs, he seems happier than he's ever been.

I'd always wanted to see Joey delivering his message at the Worship Generation up in Orange County, where he is the senior pastor. Since I'd never heard him speak to his congregation, I made plans to drop in on one of his services after an event I attended one Saturday evening at nearby Fountain Valley. It was the same Joey I've always known and loved . . . passionate, convincing, inspiring and still using great sports analogies to make his message relatable, understandable and rock solid. It was a joy and pleasure to hear him spreading the good word in a different venue with the same passion and conviction he felt as a young surfer 45 to 50 years previously.

In Joey's words, his life is now "positively impacting people's lives with faith in God, building bridges and encouraging people to know that God has a great plan for their lives." Joey was the California Kid, the Pipeline Master—and now, his life beyond the dream, a pastor serving a much-higher calling and inspiring others through his service.

Beyond the Dream shares a beautiful story of Joey's journey from his "Sandcrab" beginnings to surf star to family man to spiritual leader in an incredible story that you could never make up. It's a story of a person who never gave up, who pursued and accomplished his dreams and, in doing so, made the world of surfing as well as the world at large a much better place.

What I remember most is Joey's influence on so many surfers in our area. He pushed people to surf their best, to do better and try harder and always be the best in the water they could be. It's a mistake to underestimate the positive effect Joey had on surfers and competitive surfing nearly five decades ago. And now he's using his talents to inspire, excite and enthuse people to live a spiritual and giving life. Regardless of the endeavor, Joey always rips!

Our little beach town of Carlsbad has never forgotten Joey Buran and, fortunately for us, Joey Buran has never forgotten Carlsbad!

KEN KEBOW is an Emmy Award–winning documentary filmmaker from Carlsbad, California. His documentaries, which include several surfing-related films, can be found on various streaming networks.

PREQUEL

There is no sport in the world quite like surfing—part athleticism, part lifestyle, and all about our personal relationship with the ocean. And there is nothing in surfing as magnificent as the tube, the hollow opening that occurs when a breaking wave pitches forward. Tube rides are sometimes transcendent experiences; they certainly are memorable.

Virtually every proficient surfer in the world yearns for tube rides. They become the stuff of dreams, of searches thousands of miles long over six continents, of paddle outs in everything from tropical to near-freezing waters. We gravitate to them like metal gravitates to magnets.

Then we drop into a whole new world. As the lip of the wave cascades over our heads, time seems to stand still. A few seconds can feel like eternity. My mind moves into hyperfocus and my spine tingles, especially in big waves. I lock into the present moment, surrounded by tightly compacted water and an eerie vacuum-like sound, looking inside out at the beach or reef on the other side of the world. The board accelerates as the wave thrusts me toward the opening, which is growing more and more narrow. *Will I make it out? Will the wave engulf me?*

When I emerge from tube rides, often with bigger waves "spitting" me out, I feel a sense of exhilaration nothing else in sports has ever given me. Many regard it as a deeply spiritual experience. Many others spend the rest of their days talking about the barrels they scored, the tube prevailing over any other kind of wave they surfed that day. Most longtime surfers can recall their finest tube rides decades later, as they truly are historic times and markers in their lives. Tube rides are that impactful.

On a magical day on Oahu's majestic North Shore, I was out to score more points than the other world-class surfers in the water.

Within their sports, athletes are often remembered for a specific aspect of their game or achievement. Tennis great Roger Federer ruled with his relentless baseline consistency. Nolan Ryan had his 100-mile-per-hour fastball. Tom Brady conquered the football world to the tune of seven Super Bowl victories. And Tiger Woods owned professional golf for 15 years by simply dominating golf courses and opponents alike with his complete game.

Tube riding was my calling.

And within that, one tube in particular: the most beautiful and most challenging in the world, Banzai Pipeline. Now, on December 17, 1984, it had really happened: I had just fulfilled my lifelong goal and dream of winning the premier event in all of pro surfing, the legendary Pipeline Masters, on a day when Banzai Pipeline was dressed in her Hawaiian finest and gave me the waves I needed to beat the best surfers in the world. In doing so, I fulfilled a proclamation I'd made to my mother 11 years before, while watching Gerry Lopez conquer all pretenders in the 1973 Pipe Masters: "I'm going to win that contest," I told her, just as sure of my calling and destiny as the day God called me into a greater mission nearly 15 years later.

Every time I recall that moment, I break into a silly smirk of a smile. I still do, a half century later.

When I told Mom what I was destined to achieve, I was 12, a newcomer to surfing and to Southern California. I hardly knew anything about surfing, other than it called to me in a way competitive swimming and Little League baseball, my other sports, did not. When I was seven, I had watched *The Endless Summer*, Bruce Brown's classic movie about the quest of Robert August and Mike Hynson to search the world for the perfect wave. Their journey leaped into my soul; I wanted that too! But it took another five years to follow my father's Marine Corps career to a town, Carlsbad, California, where I would again feel that inner leap.

Now, just over a decade later, after thousands of sessions at my home surf in the Southern California towns of Carlsbad and Oceanside, and elsewhere, along with countless contests and a decorated amateur and professional career, here I was, the newly crowned King of the Pipeline. Mission accomplished. It was as if an entire lifetime had come down to this very image.

Yet there I was, 30 minutes later, alone on the beach being soaked by a tropical deluge. The light was fading, the skies an ominous gray, the rain squall pushing through after holding off long enough to finish the contest. The only sound I heard was silence. An engulfing silence. I looked out to the water, and saw North Shore veteran Billy Stang, my close friend and one-time mentor at Tamarack Beach in Carlsbad, paddle out to his favorite break and mine, knowing that just a half hour earlier, he'd seen me win the most prestigious contest in the world.

Quite a moment shared between friends.

Just a few minutes prior, I had been under the warmth of late afternoon Hawaiian sunshine with hundreds of people cheering me on and congratulating me as the new King of the Pipeline. I was there on the winners' podium with the eyes of the entire surf world upon me, video and still photographers shooting away. During the postevent interview, my normally talkative self, one that had helped me carve out a distinct voice in the surfing media, had summed up not only the day but my entire life with the simple phrase "Dreams Come True!"

Yet here I was, all alone, standing in the midst of a typical North Shore rain squall, my mind seeking to grasp the reality of the day and the significance of this quiet moment. I was cold, exhausted—and triumphant. *It had really happened.* I had just fulfilled my lifelong goal and dream of winning the premier event in all of pro surfing, the legendary Pipeline Masters. And yet, I felt strangely and deeply unfulfilled inside. How could that be? Something much deeper and greater was missing. I had announced my retirement from professional surfing to start the US Pro Tour of Surfing, but even as my skeletal team and I were getting that together, before I flew to Hawaii for my final event as a regular on the Association of Surfing Professionals (ASP) World Tour, I felt like something was missing.

I could have never known that in that quiet moment of fading light, rain and solitude, my life was in the process of being clearly divided, pulled apart by a simple question: "What are you going to do next? What is your next great calling, a calling greater than this?" I'd spent 11 years completely focused on doing whatever it took to become a Pipeline Masters champion. I never knew why I felt such certainty I would attain the goal—I was a kid from Cleveland, Ohio, who spent most of the first 11 years of his life in Virginia, not exactly the typical home of a surfing champion.

But the biggest question churning beneath the realization of my dream, the question that really unsettled me on the beach at Pipeline, was "Why do I feel such profound emptiness inside in what I've just accomplished?" In the surfing world, what I did was big-time, a validation of all those years of traveling the world tour and surfing in contests from South Africa to Japan, Brazil to Australia, Hawaii to California and the East Coast. In my heart of hearts, it wasn't the answer.

Little did I know my life was about to paddle forward from the theme of "Dreams Come True" to a new life "Beyond the Dream." A life that has risen from obscurity to surfing greatness, from deep darkness to great light. A life that has reflected divine purpose and plans throughout its journey. A life of being inspired and hoping to bring inspiration to others.

1

PADDLING OUT

2007: Banzai Pipeline, Oahu, Hawaii

Ahhh, Banzai Pipeline. Hello, old friend.

I grabbed my board, looked down the beach, saw the palm fronds waving in the light trades like hula dancers, inhaled the distinctively Hawaiian plumeria scent, and paddled out—but not into the middle of the lineup. I stayed off to the side, in the safe zone, close to the exit point where I shot out of the many momentous, spitting barrels that defined my career and my place in surfing history. *Once upon a time, a half lifetime ago . . .*

It seemed strange sitting off to the side, but let's face it: I wasn't the California Kid anymore. So much time had passed—30 years since catching my first Pipeline wave, almost 25 since being crowned King of the Pipeline, and 10 since last competing as a trials qualifier by winning the ASP World Masters Championship. So much time. I'd retired from competition as the seventh-ranked surfer in the world, started and run the US Pro Tour, come back to be a top-ten surfer on that same US Pro Tour, become a pastor, started two churches on the East Coast, surfed only on a very limited basis over the next 10 years, jumped back into the water, coached a local surf shop team and Billabong's team, become the ASP World Masters Champ . . . and now, started as the head coach of Team USA.

Here I was a 46-year-old man unsure how far to tackle Pipeline, how much to test her on this, my first time seeing the wave in three years.

Plus, I wasn't alone this time. Very little of this week-long trip to the North Shore was about me. Along with me were members of Team USA, a dozen of the finest young surfers in America that I'd brought to Pipeline, partly at their urging, partly at my invitation. We showed up to train for our upcoming world competition, and what better big-wave training to test the mettle of these kids than giving them a day of 8-to-12-foot spitting barrels at one of surfing's most heralded spots? The Vatican of our sport, the one spot surfers revere in a truly religious way? These young men and women possessed the same fire and hunger that compelled me to split from home and surf the North Shore 30 years before. But now, they wanted to join a Pipe Master, their coach, in the water. Rather, they wanted me to join them, to see me surf in my old element—and to give them some pointers in the process.

They wanted to see if the old guy still had it.

I wasn't convinced—at first. After paddling out, I stayed in my safe spot. The girls on our team, not yet ready to tackle Pipeline, tackled the snappy waves of Ehukai Beach to my right, while my boys sat on their boards exactly where I really wanted to be, where I knew every movement, every read, every way to drop into the wave—at center peak of first reef. Where the most heralded tube rides in surfing history were born ... and still are.

I paddled a few strokes toward the kids, then paddled back. Paddled toward them ... and paddled back. I watched the speed, steepness and sheer explosive power of Pipeline, thought of how only those with cat-like reflexes and agility truly succeed there, and where I realistically stood on that scale. I thought of baseball players who lose their fastballs with age. Or golfers who know where the next drive needs to go, 300 yards down the fairway, but can only drive it 275. Or an aging Michael Jordan driving down the lane, wanting to launch for a slam dunk from the free-throw line as young Michael Jordan did ... only to pull up for a 15-foot jumper. Every time my ego brought up the truth, "I delivered out here; I really delivered," common sense and a basic desire to survive tamped it down with "hardly any people surf Pipeline when they're 46. I've got a wife, children, and I want to live to see them graduate college and get married."

I thought about the ten years I stepped away from surfing, ten years that could've made me a strong middle-age big-wave rider, ten years I spent living and ministering in Vista, Virginia, Vermont—Vermont!—and working room service. I laughed about it.

Then I heard Kolohe Andino, Nick Rupp and Nat Young, a few team members, yell out, "Coach Joey! Coach Joey! You've gotta go out! Over here!"

I took it all in, wanting to impress them, allowing them to convince me to paddle over into the impact zone, where some of the greatest rides in surfing history have happened. Where legends are made. And where wipeouts are fierce, sometimes even fatal. *But I'm not here for Joey Buran. I'm here for the team, to coach, to advise*, I reminded myself.

A nice inside wave popped up, one I could catch from the safe zone. I paddled, caught it, and zipped across the face toward Ehukai, feeling the speed, feeling my spirit again connecting with this place and all that it had given me. Which included the pedigree, reputation and background to be coaching our national surf team, and the knowledge of this wave to teach them how to ride it.

As I kicked out of the wave and turned my board around, it hit me: *I've gotta do this. It's 8 to 12 feet, I know how to surf these waves, I've gotta do this.* I was a past champion, and I didn't want to embarrass myself with the team by staying inside. That's the risk I took—to not be a kook in their eyes. I wanted to show them not only that I could catch a wave, but that I was better than or as good as them. Most of all, I didn't want them to be forced to watch some grainy graybeard footage from 1984, as if I were in a century-old silent movie, to see how their coach once surfed Pipeline before he became too old and incapable to handle it.

So, I paddled over to join my crew at the main take-off point of what we surfers call waves of consequence. The day was sunny, the water that iridescent Hawaiian turquoise blue that takes your breath away, the waves so inviting. But the Lord be with you if you wipe out, because you could really get hurt. On these waves, you cannot double-clutch, and act like you *really don't* want that wave. You put out that vibe at Pipeline, and one of two things will happen: First, if you catch a big wave and second-guess yourself, you're likely to get seriously hurt if your body or head smashes into the razor-sharp coral reef just four or five feet below the surface of the water. Or, you simply won't catch any waves, as the locals will squeeze you out. You have to fight for every wave, and commit in the strongest sense of the word.

I packed all of this knowledge with me when we boarded the plane from California. My team members owned the skills to surf Pipe and the fearlessness borne by youth to make the drop on waves more powerful than they'd ever surfed, but I could show them firsthand what surfing Pipeline was all about in this training session. A sideline-stalking, clipboard-carrying coach I was not.

As I made my way to the high-risk zone, I noticed how the waves were doubling up. *A combo swell.* Two swells from slightly different directions were converging, rising up in the middle, creating sets that, while not much bigger in size, packed much more power and energy than single-swell waves. In a sense, it was like two storms meeting to create a superstorm. The added power amped up the risk factor considerably; people got killed in these combination swells because of double-ups, including elite surfers.

This situation gave me pause. I had about eight teenagers under my watch in this lineup, under my direct responsibility. Some, like Kolohe Andino and Nat Young, were already professional surfers in a sense despite being teenagers, Kolohe in particular due to the money he was receiving in endorsements from the Target store chain and Billabong. Others were true amateurs. My East Coast kids, like Fisher Heverly and Nick Rupp, received clothing and a little travel per diem from their surf shop sponsors, but it didn't matter—they all ripped, and I could see they all took well to Pipeline.

Still, I had to consider their safety. I feel like coaches of teen surfers, more so than any other sport, need to trust and rely on their athletes' abilities to gauge danger, risk and their limitations. I watched them closely while in the safe zone, as well as the girls surfing to my right on the steep, snappy Ehukai sandbar, which was throwing down powerful five-footers itself. I watched them, realizing they also were figuring out what they could and could not do. You had to really *want it* to surf Pipeline well. Our kids possessed the skill level to ride smaller Pipe, for sure, and there was only one way to know if they could handle the bigger waves, where size, power, risk and danger factor were all magnified. The ocean has its own law that connects with our common sense when it needs to: "This is it for me."

The ocean polices itself. You will see far fewer surfers in 20-foot Pipeline than the 8-to-12-foot day we received, a near-ideal day considered a green-light special that draws many surfers. When the outer reefs break, the waves exceeding 20 feet, the crowd thins to a selective few. Pipeline is one of those spots where a surfer will not embarrass himself or herself by saying, "This is not my wave."

My team was no exception. While most of the boys sat on the main peak on this combo swell day, a couple preferred inside waves. The girls focused on the Ehukai lineup, immediately north of Pipeline. They all made good, responsible decisions, part of what I loved about taking on this Team USA coaching challenge.

Soon after paddling over to the main take-off point, I caught a wave and made the drop—and accelerated like a bullet train. *Whoa, whoa, whoa,* I thought, feeling the speed, calculating how good I would do in a barrel. I didn't get into the tube this time, but I did pop out the back. I paddled back to the lineup and to the crew. Stoked from that quick speed run, a thought far more certain and daring sprinted across my mind, stemming from my faith in God and in my abilities, which had always teamed with innate confidence and self-assurance to create my successes in life: *I've got this. I'm going to get a barrel next time I paddle for a wave.*

That's where I messed up. Right in the impact zone. By going against all the knowledge accumulated from 15 collective seasons of paddling out at Pipeline.

A really nice, big set rolled in, reaching its breaking point at first reef. In the high-risk zone. A wave of consequence. I paddled into the first wave—and double-clutched. I pulled back. The next wave, a 12-footer, broke like a liquid guillotine into 4 feet of water, crashing down on my head, then exploding. I looked over at the guy next to me, a Hawaiian kid, his face lit up with the same look of terror I was feeling. We threw our boards aside and dove toward the coral reef bottom, trying to squeeze underneath the detonation but above the numerous lacerations that awaited us if we hit that reef.

I cleared the worst of the turbulence—barely. I retrieved my board, turned to paddle back out and realized I was still caught inside. The next wave broke in front of me and then seized me, throwing me around like a ragdoll. Once again, I took a huge breath after being tossed in the surging whitewater, grabbed my board and started paddling. This time, I made it around the third wave—by a whisker. I was exhausted and out of breath. I could feel my conscience going off: *How many times have you averted disaster in waves out of your range, Joey? Laniakea, Sunset, Pipeline . . . how many times does the ocean have to remind you?*

It didn't have to remind me anymore. "Oh God, oh God, I'll never do this again," I said, over and over, both a plea and a promise as I paddled toward my crew—who had watched my attempt to roll back the clock and become King of the Pipeline again. "If you get me out of this situation, God, I'll never try this again."

The ocean made it clear. Many years before, I had a dream to win the Pipe Masters. I told my mother—then anyone who would listen. That dream came true. Now I was beyond that dream . . . time for me to support the dreams of the team and many others.

I reached the lineup, stunned from the experience. I'm trying to shake off my latest near-death moment on the North Shore while my team members are going, "Hey, Coach, what happened?" Like it was no big deal.

Well, it was big enough for me. I paddled over to the safe spot, taking what amounted to a walk of shame, but not overly concerned with how they viewed me now. I made a mistake by stepping into the mouth of the proverbial monster, and only the grace of God and some past knowledge helped me avoid serious injury from being caught inside.

We'd been in the water nearly two hours. The boys caught set wave after set wave once they figured out the drop and adjustments to the bullet-like acceleration once planting in the barrel. They surfed great, they surfed fearlessly, and they had both a wonderful life experience and a fantastic training session.

As for me? I caught an inside wave, rode it to shore, and stepped out of the water. Later that night, at dinner, we all had a good laugh about Coach Joey's return to Pipeline, about how I looked like kind of a kook out there . . . but also, how stoked they were to receive the opportunity to surf there, to be on Team USA, and to have such supportive teammates. I found in our dinner conversation everything I love about the stories we tell after surf sessions, and everything I love about coaching young men and women, whether American, Chilean or British riders, whether newer teams or world championship crews—or ministering to others in the Worship Generation, my defining project as a minister.

The smiles on their faces, their joy and laughter and chatter at the table made it clear: Not only would they remember this trip for the rest of their lives, but it would impact their lives in some way.

It certainly impacted mine. I never surfed Pipeline again. My season of riding my favorite wave was over, but I feel as much love for Pipeline now as on the day we met, through television. The day my beating heart and her two-story barrels intertwined.

2

GOD, COUNTRY—AND WATER

How does a kid from Cleveland, Ohio, by way of Virginia, take center stage as a driving force in the ascension of professional surfing in the United States? And how does a disruptive, vocal, undisciplined, average-at-best student who can't sit still through a Catholic Mass walk out of his adolescence with the skills and drive to become one of the world's top surfers, and then shoot for and win the world's most prestigious surfing event? While kindling a strong enough personal relationship with God that it later informs his life to the point of helping others strengthen their relationship and their faith in the Almighty?

My journey feels very much like the punch line of the nursery rhyme we all learned as kids: "Life is but a dream." A dream being the sleep-time version of the twisting, turning, up-and-down walk called life where surprises are constant and we never end up where we thought we would be when we started. Walking with God is no different; these experiences give us wisdom, stoke our inspiration, deepen our faith and strengthen our resolve to give part or all of our lives to serve others.

At least, that is how I got from Cleveland to today.

On March 21, 1961, this California Kid began his life journey in Cleveland, Ohio, in the nation's industrial belt and alongside not the Pacific Ocean, but Lake Erie. Yep! You heard it correctly. I entered the world as the second son born to Phil Buran and Dianne Ottman. My older brother, Phil Jr., preceded me in this journey by about three years. Almost six years after my birth, my younger sister, Barbara, was born, making me a middle child. This is the family God gave me and it was within this family that I was molded and shaped to find my own personal relationship with God, become a champion surfer, and then pivot to serve men, women and children from all walks and statuses of life as a minister.

Both my parents were from the Midwest, where loyalty, deep roots, hard work, family and faith matter. A lot. They still do. My mom was born and raised in the heart of Cleveland, while my dad hailed from Madison, Wisconsin. A career US Marine, Dad was stationed as a recruiter in Cleveland during the early Cold War era following the Korean War. He has always been friendly and easygoing, so in the process of making new local friends in Cleveland, he met my mom. Struck by her beauty, wit and charm, he successfully courted her, and to the dismay of her many suitors in Cleveland, he won her heart. After a relatively short courtship, they were married when both were in their early 20s.

My dad stood out among his peers as a particularly hard worker and a very loyal man. Those Midwest roots ran long and deep within him. The Marine Corps was a perfect fit for this man who liked simple things presented with order and fairness. It ran in the family. It's worth noting that his father, Fred, served alongside the Fourth Marine Division in the South Pacific with the Red Cross during World War II. The string of Buran men who wore the uniform carried further back than that, with military veterans who also served in World War I and even the Wisconsin Union Regiments way back in the Civil War. All of this military background strongly infused patriotism and civic duty into my dad's worldview.

By the time he was in high school, my dad was participating in the local Junior ROTC program, which carried through to the ROTC program at the University of Wisconsin. After graduating, he joined the Marine Corps as a young officer, then he went on to serve our nation over the next 22 years. His military service included deployments in the Korean War (Bronze Star), the Cuban Missile Crisis, and the Vietnam War (Bronze Star and Purple Heart). His many tours sent him abroad routinely, at which time my mom would return to Cleveland to be with her family. This was the case with my arrival; I was born in Cleveland while Dad was serving in Okinawa, Japan. Similarly, my sister was born while he was deep in Vietnam, preparing for what became the Tet Offensive.

For as long as I can remember, I held tremendous respect for my dad, the US military, and from that, our country. Years later, during my pro surfing career, I often sought to have red, white and blue incorporated in my surfboards and wetsuits, while also attaching USA flag patches and stickers to my wetsuits and surfboards. My patriotism was absolute, then and now, and I thought about the freedoms my dad and fellow servicemen and women secured for us whenever I flew to surfing tournaments in South Africa,

Japan, Australia, Hawaii or other locations. My position was not popular during the late 1970s and 1980s, when plenty of animosity still stirred over our participation in the Vietnam War. Especially in the otherwise laid-back California beach scene, where soul surfing and freedom of expression played out in our long hair and loosely fitting beachwear. It was a far different time and culture than our military-friendly society of today.

Then again, I always marched more to the beat of my heart and God's plan for me than what others may have had in mind.

While Dad's side of the family provided Phil Jr., Barbie and I with a sense of patriotism, it also introduced us to a moderate form of the Christian faith—half of my spiritual genealogy, as it were. My dad's family considered themselves as Liberal Protestants and were very much involved in the influential Congregational Church in the heart of downtown Madison. The church was well attended and greatly influenced by the liberal academia of the nearby University of Wisconsin. That being said, although while growing up I knew my dad confessed to believing in God, I also knew he kept his views private. Very private. He rarely spoke openly of where he stood with God, never particularly active within the Congregational Church—or any church or denomination. What Dad sought through religion was peace in our lives and peace in our home . . . which meant that Mom was in charge of the religious upbringing.

My mom came from a family of Irish immigrants. It was only natural that her side of the family was made up of devout Catholics. She grew up attending the prestigious girls-only Beaumont Catholic School on the East Side of Cleveland for all 12 years of her primary and secondary education. The youngest of three children, she was expected to get straight As—and did. She committed herself early on to excelling in her schoolwork, to being organized and to embracing a lifelong love of learning. My dad often referred to her as the "Belle of the Ball," and for good reason: She was attractive, the smartest girl in the school, a cheerleader and the Homecoming Queen.

After they fell in love, my mom guided and then persuaded my dad to become educated in the Catholic faith to the extent that it allowed him to accomplish his goal of marrying her. That was common practice in the Midwest in the post–World War II years. Whichever member of the marriage held the strongest religious views, the other member followed suit. From then on, throughout the entire time of my parent's marriage, he presented no resistance to Catholicism serving as the religious and moral compass of our household.

Accordingly, my earliest childhood "religious" memories are all connected to Catholic churches, Masses at base chapels, and a very Catholic influence on Christian holidays and events. This not only applied to Easter and Christmas, but also the Feast of the Ascension, and personal milestones such as baptism, First Communion, and confirmation, the first three of the seven sacraments. As I grew older, with this strong religious foundation, whenever the topic of God and religion came up, I always felt a sense of religious identity and security whenever I declared myself to be "Catholic."

Which did not mean I was a keen observer of the rules, a great student or an obedient child. Far from it.

My older brother was, by everyone's admission, my parents' favorite growing up. Phil Jr. was an easy child to parent, his disposition cheerful and happy, obedient to authority, good in school, and laid back. Not surprisingly, the status as an ultracool California soul surfer and even floral nursery owner lay in his future. In his early years, he attended a Catholic school, where he thrived. Likewise, my sister also attended Catholic school for her elementary school years. She, too, was quite bright and respectful of those around and over her.

Then there was me, parked in the middle of my two siblings. Not really parked—revving like a race car engine in an uncomfortable idle would be more like it. My disposition stood in complete contrast to theirs in both behavior and academic excellence. Like them, I grew up believing in God, sometimes praying to God and even considering myself accountable to God. However, that being said, you could've never concluded I held much, if any, sincere personal faith, based on the clear and convincing evidence of my overall behavior. From my earliest childhood, I pulled pranks and stirred up situations to provoke my brother and bring out, well, his worst. Beyond that, I lied, stole things, was disruptive and below average in school, frequently out of control, never stopped talking, and couldn't sit still to save my life (especially during Sunday Catholic Mass). I also refused to do any kind of schoolwork at home.

All of my behavioral issues made me the frequent recipient of my mom's wrath, which regularly featured wooden spoons, brushes, and belts for my innumerable spankings. We lived in a far different disciplinary world in the 1960s, when these were acceptable forms of parental punishment so long as our parents didn't really hurt us. She was a master at grabbing the small amount of hair near the front of my forehead, which she would grip firmly before leading me to the nearest convenient place for corrective discipline. Yes, it's true, I brought out the worst in my mom as well! While this type of regular discipline wasn't a parenting practice I would carry into my own family, I look at my mom's punishment of me with one set of eyes. I don't remember any spankings I did not deserve, and surely deserved more than I got! Her objective was not to hurt me, but to set me straight, to persuade me to toe a more obedient line.

Education was no picnic either. At no time did I ever really enjoy it. Oh, I learned reading, writing, and arithmetic, and always was very age capable at these and other basic academic skills. Yet, I routinely came home with C and D grades on my report cards. They were more reflective of my lack of effort than my actual potential. I had yet to find something that would capture my attention so greatly that I would harness my energy and funnel great effort into achieving something big. The classroom did not cut it for me. I simply hated the daily requirement of school buses, sitting in crunched-up desks for six hours a day, always having to be quiet and, especially, homework!

In all the difficulties I caused my mother (my dad never seemed to be nearly as upset), it is worth noting that I believed I would never get away with any of my disobedience before God. Even in these tender-age years. Somehow, deep down, I figured the day of reckoning would come at some point. Until it did, though, I carried on as a disruptive, disobedient, happy and overly energetic child who very much enjoyed growing up within the security of my family and the religious stability of regularly attending church.

In 1969, while Dad was stationed at the Marine Corps base in Quantico, Virginia, my mom came up with the bright idea to have me join the Devil Dolphins swim team (ironic team name for a young Catholic boy to join, right?). Our team consisted of military dependent sons and daughters who lived on Quantico.

Around the time I turned eight, I began spending my after-school days boarding a school bus that took me to swim practice, where I swam back and forth in a 50-meter pool for about two hours in the late afternoon. That introduced some pretty strong discipline and order into my life. It was quite effective in dispelling my abundant energy, a win-win for all as I enjoyed it as well. Much to the joy of my mom, I dragged myself home tired and ready for an early bedtime.

Joining the Devil Dolphins also achieved something else: It introduced me to the water, to swimming great lengths, to the feeling of how the water moved across my body and pushed outward with every stroke I swam. I felt a strong, natural comfort in this new environment, especially the relationship between how I moved as a swimmer and the way the water itself moved.

Soon thereafter, I began competing and found success, quickly becoming one of the very best swimmers in the state for my age group. Of course, my parents were quite proud of me, as my ribbons and medals gave them something to positively affirm for me in my life. More importantly, I affirmed within myself that I was truly good at something with which I had fallen in love: moving in the water at a high rate of speed. Well, as fast as an eight- or nine-year-old can move. It was also a fun time as I enjoyed traveling and competing throughout the state of Virginia, and palling around with my teammates.

In the summer of 1970, when I was between third and fourth grade, our family moved from Quantico to Charlottesville. My dad was ready to pursue his master's degree at the University of Virginia while still serving in the USMC. It was an uneventful year, but life was significantly different in our new neighborhood, as we no longer lived on a Marine Corps base. The following year, Dad was stationed at another overseas post, in Okinawa, leaving my mom in Charlottesville with the three of us.

I continued to swim competitively and accomplish successful results, frequently spending weekends with just my mom at swim meets. That wasn't all. Sometimes, we would drive up to Myrtle Beach, South Carolina, or down to the Florida beaches, where I started riding the small, smooth waves, bellying into shore on rafts and tubes and soft boards. I never stood up, but I felt an incredible sensation of movement in the water, not by propelling myself with crawl strokes, but by the force of an incoming wave. Well, not so much propelled as guided forward, since the East Coast waves on these days were small, even tiny, not like the California waves awaiting me in my future. Not to mention the booming surf of Hawaii.

While living in Charlottesville, we attended one of the local Catholic churches right by the University of Virginia campus. It was in this church and in this season of life, my late childhood, that I began to hear the messages and scripture and understand what was being said in Bible studies. We were dismissed from attending traditional Catholic Mass, and walked to a residential house across the street where we were taught Bible studies using the *Good News for Modern Man* translation. I recall this very clearly, as those popular paperback Bibles featured distinctive pictures to accompany the stories of Jesus. At the same time, I was enrolled in a weekly Bible study during regular school hours. This study was taught off campus at a nearby residence and led by a young college-age teacher. Once again, our version of the Bible was the *Good News for Modern Man* translation.

These religious experiences left a positive impact on my life and helped me develop a personal perspective toward God. Rather than engage in the large-group call-and-response liturgy of the Catholic Mass between parishioners and the priest, we were encouraged to talk about what the scriptural passages meant to us, how they might work in our lives. I enjoyed this approach, feeling like my voice and view mattered in the class, and in my life as well.

What I didn't know was that I was beginning to learn and understand the value of having a relationship with God during a period of time now widely known as the Jesus Revolution. I was also taking the first steps toward thinking for myself, away from classrooms and Masses in big churches. Instead of being shushed for speaking out of turn in a full school class, or marked down for misbehaving or not doing my homework, I was encouraged to offer my viewpoint. That encouraged me to become more engaged in the classes, focusing my attention more toward valuable lessons than my usual subject of concentration—the next recess, lunch or the end of the school day. My mom wasn't in our Bible classes either. I appreciated the independence. The first phase of forging a path for ourselves in life is thinking for ourselves and then figuring out what we are good at, followed by the interests that completely capture our attention, and what we have to offer through them. This is especially true in ministering. I was already taking baby steps long before knowing what they added up to.

I can see all of these things now. Then, I was just a kid who liked going to my Bible classes.

What I also didn't know is my dad was heading home with news that would change my life—and take all of my swimming skills into a different arena entirely.

3

GOIN' TO CALIFORNIA

Not long after Dad walked through the door from Okinawa, he sat the family down with some news: "My next tour will be at Camp Pendleton, California," he said, smiling widely.

"Where is Camp Pendleton?" I asked.

"In Southern California. Along the beach between Los Angeles and San Diego."

I almost burst out of my skin, I was so ecstatic. Southern California? The land of sunshine, palm trees, movie stars, beaches? And ocean? And soon, me? I thought of the movies and TV shows based in California I'd seen, the daydreaming I'd done, how the weather always seemed to be sunny and warm, the people nice and tan, long hair and smiles and fun on the beach ... the stuff of my dreams.

I didn't know what to expect for my future, but I was eager and excited to enter into it!

Soon, we flew into the west, arriving in the massive chaos of Los Angeles International Airport. LAX. We got our bags and drove 80 miles south to our first home, Oceanside. We passed cities like Huntington Beach, San Juan Capistrano and Dana Point before getting to Oceanside, also passing near surf spots whose names I would become familiar with soon enough: Huntington Pier, Salt Creek, T-Street Pier, Cotton's Point, Trestles, Church, San Onofre, Oceanside Harbor and its two jetties, Oceanside Pier, and then ...

Buccaneer Beach. Across from that, our first home.

When we got out of the car, I saw the palm trees. "We're here! Surfing! The beach! The ocean!" I exclaimed, hardly able to contain my enthusiasm.

I was happy to the point of being giddy. As soon as the car stopped, I hopped out and ran into the middle of our front yard, got on my knees, and kissed the ground. I literally kissed the grass in the front yard. I could smell the salt air and I heard the sound of the waves across the street at Buccaneer Beach. Lots of waves, one set after another breaking well offshore and then running into shore. We had safely arrived and I would now be growing up in California!

And with that, the journey of the California Kid officially began.

Shortly after our arrival, as Phil and I were still unpacking boxes and shaking our heads at our unspeakable fortune, my mom signed me up for the Oceanside Swim Team. She wasn't going to give me time to idle around on the beach, which was probably a good idea. Though I had other intentions. My guess as to why she took me back to the pool so quickly? I never asked her, but I think she took one good look at the bustling SoCal lifestyle and its many options, its many distractions, and being a mom, realized if she didn't involve me in an organized activity I cared about, who knows how I would turn out?

So I was off to swim practice at a new pool, the newest member of the 11-to-12-year-old team at Brooks Street Pool. It didn't take long for me to see the difference in ability of California versus East Coast swimmers, how much stronger the California kids were; later, I figured half the people in the pool probably swam in the ocean too. Or more than half. I was no longer one of the very best swimmers on my team. Plus, I'd just moved up to the 11-to-12 age group. I loved the feeling of winning from all the meets I won in Virginia, but unless I improved a lot, I wouldn't be feeling it again.

At least not in the pool.

Something else changed. My interest in swimming began to wane. I couldn't figure out why, other than all the new things I wanted to see and try as a Southern California newcomer. I remembered scenes from the great 1965 surf film *The Endless Summer* and various movies—maybe it was the *Frankie & Annette* beach blanket movies, maybe the *Gidget* TV series, maybe a mashing together of all—that featured surfing. As I continued going to swim practice and cranking out laps, getting faster but not caring as much about how far it would carry me in competitions, I began wondering how I might learn to surf.

Within weeks, we moved again, across Buena Vista Lagoon to the town next to us, Carlsbad. Our new two-story house on Westwood Drive in the small blue-collar community was two miles from the beach, easy enough to reach on a bike and eventually a skateboard through the uncrowded streets.

Carlsbad was an amazingly cool place to grow up. Our neighborhood and those adjacent were filled with kids around our ages, the schools were nearby, there were fields, farms, ranches and avocado groves, and a village-like downtown area—and eight miles of coastline. Beautiful coastline. A coastline full of sandstone bluffs, dirt trails, stands of bamboo, wide sandy beaches and great waves, with people surfing them. Pop music superstars Jim Seals and Dash Crofts may as well have written their seasonal anthem "Summer Breeze" while sitting at Tamarack Beach. Or Cherry Street. Or State Beach. Or Southside, Terramar, Hole in the Wall or the state park campgrounds, all names for Carlsbad surf spots. What a great feeling!

Most of the families were military families, ranch families, or what they call today neighborhood families. Not many people had money, but everyone had fun and the freedom to move about our very safe new hometown. We rode our bikes all over the streets and neighborhoods without parents or anyone else worrying every minute about our safety.

When we got home from school, our parents would say stuff like, "Homework done? Good. Go out and play and don't come back until dinner." Except I didn't do homework. I look at my family today and the way I was in my teenage years and think, *how ironic.* I am surrounded by straight-A students and college graduates, from my wife, Jennifer, on down.

As for me? Well, the struggle was just beginning, and those Carlsbad surf spots and the waves pumping into them were pulling at me—hard.

During the summer, after dinner, our parents often broadened our already sweet freedoms with comments like, "Go out and play and make sure you're home when it gets dark." Then we'd grab our bikes and lay them in neighbors' front yards and hop fences, sip water from garden hoses and enjoy what truly did feel like endless summers. Our neighbors' parents watched over us as if they were our parents while we ran through their front- and backyards, or played with their kids inside ... it was like an invisible network, everyone watching over each other's kids. And older boys let younger boys know if they messed up, like older brothers handing it to younger brothers, regardless if they were brothers or not.

What an awesome town!

Imagine being able to release your kids to such unbounded freedom now. I look back at this with both fondness and sadness. Ours was an upbringing very hard to replicate in today's world, a sign of very different times, for sure. And Carlsbad was different from any of the other towns and cities in which we lived, a cozy, modest community of 15,000. Not so much today:

A half century later, Carlsbad is an affluent international resort destination and business magnet of 115,000, but a resort destination with excellent surf spots.

Clearly, the word got out.

Finally, my first of those seemingly endless Carlsbad summers was interrupted by the beginning of the school year. Sixth grade arrived. I couldn't wait to peddle my brand-new bike down Westwood Drive, Basswood Avenue and Monroe Street to Magnolia Avenue and Magnolia School. My parents had bought it for the occasion, and I thought it was cool because it had brake lights and blinkers!

I pulled up to the school, feeling cooler than cool with my bike—and quickly found out I wasn't. Rather than earning instant acceptance and admiration, my future classmates who didn't know me ridiculed me. Elementary school playgrounds can be tough places, especially when you're new. To add injury to insult, they also made fun of my southern accent. I didn't realize that I spoke differently than anyone else, but they certainly did. I pushed through it, pretending to not care too much about what others thought of me. Something in me kept telling me that when you care too much about what others think, you become what they want you to be. I wanted to be myself, to do my own thing, walk my own way.

But it bugged me. A lot. I wanted to be noticed, not ridiculed and then ignored. Later that evening, I begged my dad to take off the brake lights and blinkers. He looked at me oddly, like *what a strange request*, but he willingly consented. He wanted to be sure my brother, sister and I were comfortable in our new home and schools, especially since this was our fifth move in a half dozen years, the plight of many military brats.

What a memorable first day of school in California!

Soon enough, I began to realize that many of the sixth-grade boys at Magnolia who surfed were seen as the coolest students in class. They were already kings of the hill for being sixth graders, the highest achievable grade in elementary school, but they also strutted into class and onto the decomposed granite playground for recess with something else—long hair like the boys on the popular TV show *The Brady Bunch*. And their own cool language. I found myself quickly learning words like *stoked* and *far out* and *tube* and *drop in* and *unreal* and *bitchin'* and *dude*, concluding that the more I spoke their language, the more I would be part of their group. Even better, most of the sixth-grade girls thought they were cute!

I watched how they got along with the girls, how confidently they walked in and out of classrooms, slid back on their desk chairs to nearly a prone position, their corduroy- or Levi's 501 jeans–covered legs stretched far beyond their desks, the two-foot icon on the chests of their striped Hang Ten shirts validating who they were. Surfers on top of their world, day-dreaming of riding waves after school and on weekends. Some even filled up their Pee-Chee folder covers with drawings of waves breaking and peeling. I watched with intent, keen interest, and more than a little longing and jealousy.

That's what I want to be. Exactly. How do I get into that group? I asked myself, over and over.

I'd never really been inclined to join groups before, but this was different. These kids were the coolest of the cool, the group I just *had* to join, whatever that required. They looked cool and talked cool, and much of the school's social scene revolved around them. *What would it be like to have a scene revolve around me?* I wondered, more than once, my attention to these details something I'm sure my teachers would have preferred seeing in my schoolwork.

Good luck with that!

I didn't need any more convincing: I was going to become a surfer! I felt so sure about this decision, the strongest choice I'd ever made. Then my competitive drive took hold. I didn't merely want to become a surfer, or even a good surfer—but the best surfer in Carlsbad! I would accomplish this, I figured, by paddling out and grabbing every wave I could and showing all these guys how great I could surf.

Just one thing: I needed a surfboard and to learn how to ride waves on it.

A week before my 12th birthday in March of 1973, it happened. My mom took me down to Offshore Surf Shop, just across the street from Tamarack Beach, to buy my first board. I walked inside, smelled the distinct perfumed scent of surf wax, and noticed a few things that made a huge impression on me: the racks of boards and wetsuits, owner Barbie Baron's competition trophies, and the latest issue of *Surfer* magazine. An overwhelming feeling moved through me like a quickly rising tide: *This is my new world.*

I found a board that looked cool, a six-foot-three model built by a local shaper named Mike Gilligan. Best of all, it fit my mom's budget. We handed over $30—and it was mine. I was so excited!

When I got home, the first thing I did was pretend I was surfing on my bed. I'd been watching some of the surfers in Carlsbad, and figured I knew what I was doing. I was an excellent swimmer and decent Little League baseball player ... how hard could it be? I even begged my older brother, Phil, to rock the mattress, which he did. I pulled myself up, stood and surfed the mattress. I really was surfing!

Well, not quite. Within a few days, I was off to Tamarack Beach to rip it up. My first session on that Saturday began with an immediate mistake before I ever carried my board into the water. I had stripped the wax off my board because I thought surf wax looked ugly—I had to look good. Especially when I ran into some girls from my sixth-grade class. I'd spent weeks bragging to them that I was a really good surfer. Time to prove myself. But there was a problem: Fiberglass surfboards are very slippery, and the wax gives your feet traction.

With no traction and tons of bluster, I paddled out to prove myself. I proved something, all right: I had no idea what I was doing. I could not stay on my board, even when paddling. I slipped off the side, over and over, embarrassing myself, imagining the girls on the beach chattering and laughing about the kook in the water who talked about how great of a surfer he was but couldn't even *paddle*, let alone stand. Luckily for me, the girls never made fun of me, and much to my relief, it seemed as if they hadn't even watched me, their eyes focused either on their conversations or tuning their transistor radios . . . or the guys out there who *could* surf.

On my second session, I walked into the cold water with no wetsuit, waxed-up surfboard in hand. I paddled around, trying to figure out how to surf. It looked pretty easy for the other guys in the water who were experienced and knew what they were doing. But for a beginner like me? Not easy at all. Surfing is very hard to learn, and even harder to master. Nobody just goes out there and starts ripping it up. You have to be dedicated, put a lot of time in the water, and not get discouraged by waves beating you down. You fall *a lot* before getting up and staying up. I couldn't and wouldn't allow myself to get discouraged by the other surfers, even those mocking or harassing me. It takes a lot of desire to stick with it—and I burned with that desire. When I set my mind to something, I never gave up, quit or even let up until I succeeded.

But success was as fleeting as a dream you try to remember. What separates surfing from any other sport is its constantly moving surface. Ocean currents are moving, the waves are moving, breezes are usually blowing, the whitewater of the breaking wave is frothing and roiling, and the board beneath you is moving. It's like playing chess on a four-dimensional board that shifts back and forth while you try to keep track of the pieces and your next move. The sport to which I like to compare surfing is golf, with its wide variety of course and hole designs, and weather conditions that can change at a moment's notice. So it is when you're catching a wave and sitting on top of the world, as the Beach Boys sang it.

Or, more accurately, standing up.

Then there's the matter of paddling into a wave and standing. It requires a delicate dance between body balance, board positioning in the wave, picking the right wave, standing, and then assuming a stance to stay on your feet as the wave propels you and the board forward. Or to the left or right, once you gain some basic stand-up skill. If falling is a measure of failing, well, get ready to fail often, just as I did. It takes a long while to stand up and consistently surf waves to the shore, and longer to negotiate them to the left or right on their open faces. Even the best surfers fall, usually while trying a maneuver that seems unearthly to the mortal sportsman.

As the spring of 1973 progressed, so did my surfing. I moved through the stand-up phase, grew accustomed to the feel of the board beneath my feet and the ocean, caught wave after wave, rode them in my wide, squashed-down stance, and eventually turned myself into the best whitewater surfer in Carlsbad. Notice I said *whitewater*. Any real surfer knows that excellence happens on the open faces of the wave, where accomplished riders move like acrobats and perform maneuvers that, like I said before, draw *oohs* and *aahs* from beachgoers and TV viewers alike. Many of whom surf very well themselves.

I wasn't anywhere near that level of proficiency yet. I looked like a real kook. But still, I paddled out in water as cool as 55 degrees, without a wetsuit. I still had a wide stance, no style whatsoever, and couldn't figure out how to catch a green-faced wave at its peak. I watched surfer after surfer take off, snap off a bottom turn, and gracefully glide down either the right or left side of the green open face, whichever was open. Like the guys on TV.

As for me? I could only turn around, catch the whitewater, stand and crank off little wiggly turns. For all the wrong reasons, you just couldn't miss me at Tamarack Beach—even though I thought I ripped and told everyone as much.

Ummm, not quite.

Another thing I noticed was some of the older surfers at Tamarack had nicknames, cool nicknames, handles that described their personalities, how they surfed, or some other aspect of who they were. I quickly realized a nickname was a symbol of respect. In fact, surfing predates all other sports in assigning colorful nicknames and single-name references to those who were especially good. Anyone in the sport only has to utter the name "Duke," and we all know who is being talked about—Hawaii's Duke Kahanamoku, the man who turned surfing into a world sport, and also won Olympic gold in 1920 as a swimmer. A surfer-swimmer. Which I was.

Sure enough, because of calling attention to myself, I picked up my first nickname. All because of a basic need for warmth. Because I didn't have a wetsuit, I lasted about 20 minutes at a time in the frigid springtime water before hypothermia set in. Once I couldn't take it anymore, I surfed or bellied on my board back to the beach and rolled in the warm sand. Since I was small and burrowing in the sand, some older surfers started calling me Sand Crab. Or in Hawaiian, Da Crab. Truth be told, I looked like a two-legged crab when I surfed too. This remained my nickname throughout most of my teen years. Even after my first name switched from Joe to Joey, and ABC's *Wide World of Sports* announcer Jim McKay and *Surfer* magazine dubbed me the California Kid, locals would come up to me and say, "Sand Crab!" They still do.

Interestingly enough, my first feature story was a piece in the inaugural issue of a regional surf magazine, *Breakout*, in 1979, when I had become the top US mainland surfer on the world tour. The cover didn't read "California Kid" (which probably would've sold more copies). Nor was it "California's Joey Buran." It was simply entitled, "Da Crab!" *Breakout* was published in Carlsbad, and publisher George Salvador, a fine journalist and surfer who liked being edgy and distinctive in his approach, decided to bring readers back to my most local roots.

Even today, some 45 years later, the nickname takes me back to the pure joy of my youth and the innocence of a time and place that seems so long ago. Sand Crab is forever linked with my memories of growing as a teenager, surfing the breaks from Black's Beach in San Diego to Oceanside Harbor's North Jetty, before big crowds filled the lineup and the population of the coastline exploded to what it is today.

Meanwhile, I had another sport to tend to. Swimming. I continued competing for another year, mostly because my mom encouraged me to. However, my heart, soul, focus and entire spirit were parked in whatever waves the ocean served up that day. Still, I pushed to be the best in the pool. I didn't know any other speed. In the summer of 1973, I competed in the regional AAU Junior Olympics, posted my best times of the year, then officially retired at age 12 from my five-year swimming career. In that final swim meet, I reached a couple of finals and returned home with ribbons and a sense of completion for that season of my life. I didn't feel like I quit too soon. In my performance and desire to be the best, I walked away feeling I achieved something I would later share with others as a pro surfer and minister—giving maximum effort until the last drop. A very important life lesson.

Best of all, my mom was happy with my final performance. With my swimming career behind me, I would now be able to focus all my attention and energy on my new passion … surfing!

I'm a sportsman, and like all people who grew up playing sports, I have my heroes. It's not an idolatry thing, not by any means. Having a hero is a good thing when that person exemplifies what you hope to achieve in your walk of life. We all are capable at excelling at something, and finding the people who are already achieving at that level often gives us the role models we need to push us forward. My admiration of the heroes of my youth comes from how they approached their sport or craft, how they embodied it in their actions, and how they threw their hearts and abilities into what they did while setting an example the rest of us could follow.

In surfing, that meant one person: the great Gerry Lopez, the first Pipeline Master and the undisputed King of Banzai Pipeline. I wasn't the only surfer enamored by the coolest of them all; just about every wave rider on planet Earth looked up to Gerry Lopez. And, like me, just about every teenage surfer taped or pinned his poster on the wall of their bedroom. I'd seen him on ABC's *Wide World of Sports*, and I'd seen him in the hot new surf movie showing in film houses and school gyms, *Five Summer Stories*.

I wanted to be like Gerry. I wanted to be King of the Pipeline.

Gerry surfed with a smooth, classic, graceful style that spoke to his deep Hawaiian roots. He was a goofy foot, standing face to face with the breaking Pipeline wave, just like me. He looked as cool as you can with his fairly long dark hair and surfboard with the distinctive Lightning Bolt logo, provided by his sponsor. He looked like a superhero. He picked up the biggest waves and dropped farther into the gaping tube than anyone else, his fearlessness just as epic as his style. These were not just small-wave openings either; Mack trucks could drive through Pipeline barrels. Not joking.

The strength of Gerry's surfing was tube riding. Tube riding has long been considered the highlight of surfing. As I mentioned earlier, when a surfer positions himself or herself under the pitching curl of the wave, often disappearing from the view of the beach, that person is tube riding. The trick is to skillfully ride out into view again, onto the open wave face. In the early '70s, nobody rode the tube as skillfully as Gerry Lopez.

Which meant I would work and will myself to become a great tube rider too.

However, what I loved most about Gerry was that he was a professional. He was paid to surf! I didn't know if surfing had a professional tour yet, or even events that offered prize money besides the two on TV—the Duke Kahanamoku Surf Classic and Pipeline Masters—but I knew already that I wanted to be a professional surfer. Like Gerry. He was everything I wanted to be!

History favors change agents and trailblazers, something we only learn years after things begin to change. With that, the timing of events couldn't have been better for me. There really was pro surfing, and it was in its infant stage, hardly recognized as a legitimate sport. But it existed, in Hawaii and in Australia.

Not everyone was convinced pro surfing would become a thing. One of my teachers at Valley Junior High School told me with complete confidence that surfers would never be professional, and I would never be paid to surf. I might not be the best person to tell that what he wants to do is something "you will never be able to do." Not the right guy at all.

Well, for those of us who know what we want and are singularly focused on attaining it, those aren't disqualifying words. They are motivating words.

These comments drive me even more to make it happen. They bring out my fight, my belief I can get it done, and my deepest faith that if it is in God's plan for me, it *will* be done. And it happened: Despite my teacher's bold declaration of what my future wouldn't include, by the mid-1970s, pro surfing events began to appear worldwide, and I saw my opening.

Once I could surf well enough.

Then came the day in 1973 that launched into motion the next 11 years of my life: the day I watched Gerry Lopez win the Pipeline Masters on ABC's *Wide World of Sports*. The weekly sports anthology drew 30 to 40 million viewers on Saturday afternoons, since we only had three major TV channels then—NBC, ABC and CBS. ABC had been covering the Pipe Masters and Duke Kahanamoku Surf Classic for several years, introducing America to Hawaii's fearsome waves and the fearless men who rode them (women's surfing greats Margo Oberg and Lynne Boyer would soon follow). The combination of idyllic setting and weather in December, warm water, giant waves and fearless watermen was too much to resist, especially for this grommet (an Australian term for youth surfer).

To this day, I still cannot fully explain it, but after watching Gerry win the event, I turned to my mom and said, "I am going to win that contest someday!" Now, we all know that it is quite natural for 12-year-olds to watch something impressive and say they will achieve it. Nothing unusual in my declaration to my mom. However, I *felt* it would become true. I *knew* in my mind, body, and spirit—and I truly believed it!

More amazingly, I *knew* I had found my life purpose, my calling. From that moment on, I never once doubted that I would someday win the Pipeline Masters and, like Gerry Lopez, become King of the Pipeline.

I've often looked back at that day and asked myself, *Why? Why did you say this? Why did you so firmly believe it?* But I did say it, and I believed it.

Even though I was still only riding whitewater waves, without a wetsuit or a surf leash, and rolling in the sand to stay warm, I knew my journey had begun.

That journey took a quantum leap about five months later. On a warm summer afternoon in Carlsbad, between sixth and seventh grade, everything began to click in the water. In what might have been the most significant session of my life, and a career not yet started, I managed to catch three green-faced waves in a row, and make moves on them. *That's it! I've cracked the code! I can really surf!*

Afterward, I pedaled my bike home at breakneck speed, my board tucked beneath my arm, probably the most stoked 12-year-old on planet Earth. My stoke level would have tested any Richter scale!

Well, there was another super-stoked kid in town, a year younger than me. He, too, stood out at Tamarack for being a young, hungry surfer with a style so refined for his age, just as eager to excel as me, just as destined to bring his game to the world stage.

Finally, we met. His name was David Barr.

4

MEETING DAVID BARR

Life is such a beautiful thing when we embrace the blessings it brings us. I often think of the many incredible opportunities my careers as a professional surfer and minister have sent my way, and then review the all-important follow-up side of these opportunities: What did I do with them? Did I make the most of them?

I couldn't articulate or wrap my mind around these truths when I was 12, but I did continue to hold a personal faith in God after we moved to Carlsbad. I viewed the best things that happened in my young life as blessings; I mean, what else would you call moving to Southern California? Or being a kid dropping into a surfing-rich town like Carlsbad when you're proclaiming to the girls in class that you're going to be the best surfer around? Even when I couldn't quite surf yet?

My next favorable turn of events happened in the summer of 1973. I was an intensely competitive kid who wanted to be the best, but I wasn't the best swimmer in Southern California. Only *one of the best.* So I turned my attention to baseball, my other sport. In any small town, there is *that kid*—the pitcher and best hitter on the Little League team, the quarterback on the Pop Warner football team—who carries the mantle, usually right through high school. Sometimes beyond. I wanted very much to be *that* kid in baseball, but again learned that in California, I was only average. As for Pop Warner football, my dad really wanted me to play, so I headed out to practice that first week with my pads on, and came home with my pads draped over my shoulders.

"How was practice, Joe?" Dad asked.

"Fine," I said, every day.

Not really. On the first day of practice, I got hit—hard. I decided football was not a team sport for me, so I faked it until I finally quit.

I never had a chance to be *that kid* in baseball or football. No one else did either. *That kid* was Bill Yehling, an exceptional pitcher, shortstop and hitter for our Western Auto Little League team. Whenever he pitched, I stood in the outfield thinking, *Thank goodness I don't have to hit against him.* I saw how players on other teams approached the plate to hit, their eyes filling with fear. In football, he was the quarterback with a gun for an arm. The dude could really sling touchdown passes and run for one first down after another. But baseball was his signature sport. Bill was so good that he ended his Little League career by throwing a perfect six-inning game. Eighteen up, eighteen down—fifteen by strikeout. Then he went to Carlsbad High and set the San Diego County career earned-run average record, which stood for 25 years.

Our coach at Western Auto, Max Isbell, was a championship coach. He'd won the last two Carlsbad Little League titles, and we nearly made it a three-peat. Max was a great teacher, brash ... and pretty wild. Decades later, Max and I ran into each other in a wonderful way, when he came to a Worship Generation church service after hearing me on the radio. Now an accomplished musician, Max sang the legendary Lynyrd Skynyrd song "Freebird" at our mutual friend Richard Norman's funeral service a few years ago. Afterward, Max gave me a nice compliment: "You were only average in baseball, so what you became in surfing seemed unbelievable to me."

It's always fun to exceed others' expectations! One of life's beautiful treasures, connecting and reconnecting with people who made a difference in our early lives and now having a chance to make a difference in theirs.

While watching Bill Yehling, and seeing him fairly often since our friend groups orbited each other's, I determined to be *that kid.* Only I was going to stamp my claim with my surfboard, not a blazing fastball or an arm that could throw 50-yard TD passes as a 12-year-old. Bill also surfed, but he preferred free surfing to competing. He scored his victories on the baseball field, not the waves. I always looked up to him, only to find out much later in life that he also always looked up to me. Not long ago, we chatted on FaceTime, the first time we'd seen each other since we were teenagers. It was like no time had passed ... except for the hairlines and growing wrinkles, of course!

Like Bill, I loved competition. I craved it. It felt very important to me to be the best at something. I wanted to be a game changer. "Be the best you can be" wasn't good enough. After Little League, I focused exclusively on surfing. Only one problem: No one else in Carlsbad seemed to care about competition. The locals didn't surf to win, or even do radical maneuvers on waves.

The only exceptions were Barbie Baron, the young owner of Offshore Surf Shop, where I bought my first board, and Randy Laine. Barbie, who is about 15 years older than me, excelled in the Western Surfing Association (WSA), a real trailblazer at a time when few girls paddled out, the most memorable being a redhead with quite a future ahead of her, eventual Ironman Triathlon Hall of Famer Julie Moss. Barbie was the best girl in our area, one of the best on the West Coast, and a true trailblazer in the industry. She was one of very few women who owned a surf shop in a time when our sport was very different in women's representation and status than it is today.

Back to Julie Moss. Even though I didn't know Julie that well, I admired her constantly upbeat spirit, even on the days when the guys in the water hassled her and other girls for being in the lineup. Which happened here, there and everywhere. She had a "you can't do anything to bring me down" way about her, such a relentlessly optimistic vibe, and she loved being in the ocean and always trying to outdo herself... sure signs of a future competitor.

Julie has surfed pretty much ever since—but surfing isn't where she made her mark on the world stage. Triathlon is. In what has to be one of the coolest small-town claims to bragging rights ever, the sleepy little Carlsbad of the late '70s and early '80s can proudly state that, in a span of three-and-a-half years between December 1978 and spring 1982, we had not one but two locals featured prominently by legendary host Jim McKay on ABC's *Wide World of Sports*—me for making the 1978 Pipeline Masters Finals as a 17-year-old, and Julie for her immortal crawl across the finish line of the 1982 Ironman Triathlon Championships, which made her a global star and elevated triathlon to world sport status. As well as put the idea of endurance sports and fitness in the minds of 40 million viewers. To think we both grew up surfing Tamarack and other Carlsbad spots at the same time ... must've been something in the water. Something really special.

I knew about another kid in Carlsbad who was also progressing in his surfing at about the same pace as myself. His name was David Barr. We were like salt and pepper, me with my shocking white-blond locks, he with dark hair. We began to hang out together, and by the autumn of '73, became best friends and surf buddies who pushed each other every day. We wanted the same thing—to compete. And win. And be the best.

Today, when I look back at meeting Barr, I see one of the most important people to ever enter my life. I believe a lot of things would not have happened without his constant presence during those formative years. Such is the sovereignty of God, not only to give us what we might need to move forward, to improve, but to put the perfect person in our lives to provide that friendship and push.

For the first few years of our friendship, we awoke in the wee hours, and met up on Saturdays around 4:30 a.m., long before daylight. We tucked our boards under our arms and skateboarded to the beach together. We arrived at the beach when it was still dark, waiting for the first light of day to brush the eastern sky, so we could be the first surfers in the water. Together we embarked on our dawn patrols (surfer-speak for early sessions; how I love the terminology!) and surfed the gentle waves at Tamarack Beach while hooting and hollering for each other. And constantly comparing each other's waves. We supported each other and pushed each other, and *voila!* Our rides on the open faces grew longer. We became bolder in the way we twisted and turned on the open waves, continually expanding the possibilities available to us. Our surfing abilities rapidly improved.

What I learned, and still find interesting, is that David and I were total opposites in almost everything, which made us ideal complements for each other's careers. By the autumn of 1973, we were already talking about our careers. Out of the water, David was a pretty quiet, yet confident kid, preferring to let his surfing do the talking. On the beach, my personality was outgoing, loud and confident. Then I had to paddle out to constantly prove it.

Our surfing styles and the types of waves we preferred were polar opposites. David was a right-handed regular foot, loved long point-break waves, and already possessed a smooth style and beautiful flow in his surfing. He would ride waves until they petered out. Or he did. As for myself, I was a left-handed goofy foot, a tube rider with an aggressive style, and I surfed as if the next wave was my last. I lived for tubes, for short, punchy rides where I could put my aggressiveness on display. While David would be stoked with six great, long rides in an hour or two at Jeffreys Bay in South Africa, I'd want six waves in 15 minutes at Salt Creek. He was like a Russian ballet dancer; I was more like a punk rocker.

Despite these differences, we held a few things in common. First, we dreamed of becoming successful pro surfers. Also, we both possessed the inner drive and commitment to get it done—and the latent talent, which really began to show itself. Funny how "talent" and "luck" merge in our lives whenever we work hard and devote ourselves to a goal, open ourselves to receive blessings, and then work even harder. From watching movies and reading surf magazines, and watching the few WSA (Western Surfing Association) contests we could get rides to, we became familiar with contest skills, the maneuvers that score points—and we rapidly improved at those too.

Throughout those early teenage years, we became fiercely competitive toward each other, at a level that could create bitter rivalries for those who aren't friends. However, we maintained a beautiful and mutually beneficial friendship. For the next few years, we showed up at California junior surfing events—and dominated. Either one of us or the other won our division. In 1982, he joined me on the world tour as the other California-based surfer ranked in the IPS Top 30. Together our passion for surfing, combined with friendship and rivalry, carried us to the very top of California pro surfing and onto the world stage. Even to this day I just cannot imagine the success of my career without the friendship of David Barr.

Our friendship was not on my mind on a Saturday in the summer of 1974, though winning was. On an early morning, the sun still hours away from burning off the marine layer, I entered the military dependents contest at Church Beach, near the newly built San Onofre nuclear power plant. How poignant, in retrospect: debuting at a break called Church! I sized up my competition, and even though I was smaller than most others, I knew how hard I had worked. That had to count for something. Like winning.

The contest provided a memorable experience—in a different way. Instead of serving notice that the next great competition surfer had arrived, I fell off on my first wave, lost my board, swam to the beach to retrieve it, paddled back out, and struggled the rest of the way. I finished dead last. I easily could've hung my head, given up, wondered why I told so many people how great I'd become, and just resorted to soul surfing like everyone else.

Except I didn't. My life goal of winning the Pipe Masters could not have been further away on the horizon. That didn't matter. Though I'd done poorly, I was filled with an unstoppable drive and purpose to fulfill my dreams. I now know that to be the presence of God working through me. I shook off the loss, and watched how the winners surfed, the maneuvers they pulled off to reach the victory stand. Then a friend drove me home.

David and I put in hour after hour, sometimes at Tamarack, sometimes at other Carlsbad breaks . . . and sometimes far down the road from the classrooms we were supposed to be in. We kept our boards at Tamarack, left school after our second-period classes, picked up our boards, hitchhiked southbound on Pacific Coast Highway to where the waves were bigger. That meant the South Carlsbad State Park campgrounds, or farther south to epic waves at Swami's Point and Black's Beach, a couple of surfing-crazed 13- and 14-year-olds. In our eyes, Swami's was like Sunset Beach, and Black's was like Pipeline, and surfing these waves made us feel like we were in Hawaii.

I found all my happiness and joy in surf sessions, and my desire to compete in contests. I surfed in as many as I could. They were still considered uncool by the older soul surfers, but I didn't care what the Tamarack surfing locals or anyone else thought. I had a dream and I was determined to hold onto it, and I sure wasn't going to let anyone take it from me. I knew then what I know now: The only one who has to believe in your dream is you.

Progress came fast. By the summer of '75, I began to win smaller events and make finals in bigger events. That same summer, in my return to Church Beach for the military dependents event, I was a bigger, stronger 14-year-old with a growing collection of moves in my bag besides tube rides—which remained my signature maneuver while I held on to my ultimate dream of winning the Pipeline Masters.

This time around, I didn't finish last. I advanced in one heat after another, eventually finishing second. The kid who beat me, Danny Smith, later was a nuisance in many world tour surfers' sides when the Stubbies Pro International Tournament came to Oceanside. His big brother played catcher for the Minnesota Twins; Danny caught the surfing bug to go with those athletic genes, and he knew how to compete—as I learned.

On my way home, a friend who had driven me up said to me, "Next year, you have to win."

To which I replied, "I will!"

And I did. That's how I was in my early teens, calling the shots with plenty of bravado, like boxer Muhammad Ali saying, "I'm the greatest!" Or Mr. October, Reggie Jackson, knowing he was going to hit a home run in the World Series.

As I steadily moved up the WSA ratings, I received an invitation to the prestigious USA Surfing Championships in July 1975—just two years after meeting David Barr, and two years after finally unlocking the mystery of how to surf open-faced waves. It was a quick ascension toward the top, as I see it now.

The event was scheduled to be held in September at South Padre Island in Texas. However, I needed some money to help my parents pay for the trip. That summer, I worked my first job in the tomato fields in Carlsbad, near Agua Hedionda Lagoon, where one of the world's newest watercraft sports, jet skiing, was developing quickly. My routine was simple and stripped down to the bare necessities: surf Tamarack in the morning and hitchhike the two-mile distance to work, then spend eight hours separating green tomatoes from red ones. Those fields are now covered by Legoland Theme Park, but profound memories remain of that first job. I saved my paychecks, and it allowed me to travel on the first major surf trip of my life.

By early September, I boarded the plane and headed off to Brownsville, Texas, to pursue my pro surfing dream! The Gulf Coast of Texas seemed like an unusual place to hold such a major contest with the much more wave-rich East and West Coasts available, but the United States Surfing Federation rotated sites each year. It truly was a national championship, and I was there, on my first surf trip outside of Southern California.

Once again, just like my first contest at Church Beach, I didn't start well. Trouble struck before my heat, when I broke my board while warming up. That could have been the kiss of death, but surfing is a very community-oriented sport and lifestyle with a lot of brotherhood and mutual support attached. Which is what happened. I borrowed a board from top San Clemente amateur Gary Ziegler. Instead of finishing last and watching from the beach, I advanced all the way to the finals, where I was outfoxed for waves by three more-seasoned competitors. I finished fourth out of the six finalists.

Now it was time to get to business. Rather than fly home and bask in the glory of making the US Surfing Championships finals, my mom started up her car and we drove to every surf shop in North San Diego County, trophy in hand, looking for a sponsor. My surfing obsession was becoming more and more expensive, beginning with surfboards, wetsuits, wax—and board leashes that were now all the rage. For those that had them, no longer did we have to swim all the way to shore if we lost our boards. As for boards, I now realized that different wave conditions called for surfboards of different lengths and dimensions; generally speaking, the bigger the surf, the longer the board.

My first introductions to surf shop owners did not produce the results we'd hoped. I was rejected for sponsorship by all of them. Pro surfing was still in California's future, though it had gathered steam in Australia and Hawaii, along with South Africa and the US East Coast, where a 12-event world tour now existed that paid prize money. New stars arose on the wings of paid sponsorships and media coverage. The North County shop owners were still in soul surfer mode, and certainly didn't see the value in assisting a 14-year-old with one national trophy to his credit.

Maybe they felt that way, but I wasn't about to let anyone interfere with my dream. I suggested to Mom we try going north, in hopes of finding better luck, since I knew most of the kids I competed against were Orange County locals. She agreed to drive 20 miles north to the other side of Camp Pendleton and San Clemente, home of great surf spots like Trestles and Cotton's Point.

And Natural Design Surfboards. Who stood behind the counter but Jeff (Midget) Smith, the owner? I was so ecstatic to see him! He was the Good Samaritan who witnessed my plight in Texas, then arranged for me to borrow the board from Gary Ziegler that I used to finish fourth. So he knew exactly what I was riding to enable me to win the trophy I was lugging under my arm.

Once again, I stirred up the nerve to ask, "I'm looking for someone to sponsor me. I'm going to surf every contest I can to be the best surfer around."

It didn't take Midget long to figure out that the burning intent in my eyes—and the surfing his eyes had seen in Texas—matched my words. "Yes, I'll for sure sponsor you."

I almost cried, I was so elated. Someone believed in my dream enough to sponsor me? Not only that, but he sounded truly stoked to be doing so!

My Natural Designs sponsorship and Midget's unwavering support was the final major piece I needed to take the next step. We all benefit from the support of others, whether or not we realize it, but I was smart enough to realize just how much he was helping me, how much of a rock of support he was in my young life.

Consequently, by 1977, I established myself as the number-one junior surfer in California. I peeled off a two-year undefeated streak in all the major WSA events. All the while, I had plenty of fun. Sometimes too much fun. Like the time Midget and I left in his Country Squire station wagon on a road trip to Houston, the Gulf Coast, Freeport and Galveston to deliver and promote his boards. As we were driving through the seemingly everlasting Texas landscape along the endless Interstate 10, a radio announcer came on and said the waves were good.

Midget had fallen asleep and handed me the wheel, even though I didn't have a license. Never mind. The surf was up—and I needed waves. When he woke up, he rubbed his eyes, turned to the dashboard and saw the speedometer: 100-plus miles per hour. That needle was *way* over the red line! "What are you doing?" he asked, admonishing me to throttle down the speed.

Even though the station wagon was chock-full of boards, I couldn't help it. I wanted to surf. We arrived safely, I paddled out . . . and the surf was a tiny one to two feet. No matter. I surfed, and helped Midget promote and deliver the boards. It was a hugely successful trip.

Midget gave me an instant education on how a caring sponsor operates. Besides helping me with the equipment and accessories I needed—which included proudly displaying a Natural Designs sticker on my Natural Designs board—he became like a big brother to me. He helped me with contest strategy, told me many great surf stories and taught me nuances of the sport. Including some of its business side. Plus, like David Barr, he knew how to tolerate my boundless and at times annoying enthusiasm, and never ran out of patience. Beyond that, he was probably the second person on the planet who believed me when I said (which I did quite often), "I am going to win the Pipeline Masters!"

For all of those reasons, we became the best of friends. He was like a big brother to me, not the last I had in the surfing world, but certainly the first. My mom loved Midget like a son, and trusted him implicitly. He was so good to me.

As the 1977 season progressed, David Barr was nearly always at my side on the victory stand, finishing in second place at these same events. He pushed me harder and harder in every final, and while I won them, I can say today, that without his quietly supportive friendship and the constant push he gave me as a coach of sorts in competition, I would not have enjoyed that level of success. While many in the world raised their eyebrows, it came as no surprise to me a few years later when David also became one of the world's finest surfers. He wanted it as badly as I did.

However, just when my close friend and rival David was fast-tracking with me toward the top of the national amateur ranks, he and the entire Barr family received a crunching blow—one that resulted in him falling behind me on our career trajectories. David's mom was diagnosed with cancer, a death sentence in those times. Throughout our friendship, I used to blame David when we got in trouble, and he used to blame me, so David's mom was never sure what to make of me. But she was sick, and it affected him very, very deeply.

Shortly before she died, I visited Mrs. Barr in her bedroom. A Bible sat next to her. She looked at me, her face thinned down by the cancer about to take her life, and said to me, "I'm praying for you, Joe Buran." Of all the conversations she and I had, this is the only one that stuck to me like glue—and still does.

Years later, one of my early in-the-water big brothers and mentors, original world tour pro surfer Randy Laine, told *Breakout* magazine, "One of the biggest reasons why Joey went to South Africa and did well and turned pro so young, and David didn't, was that David's mom had cancer. It set him back a couple of years."

Sadly, 30 years later, Midget lost his fight with cancer in 2008. A few years after that, his daughter asked me to officiate her wedding. Many of the San Clemente people I knew from my amateur surfing days were there; it was a wonderful gathering and celebration, and I know Midget was there in spirit, flashing that awesome smile on all of us, his daughter most of all.

As 1977 drew to a close, I noticed a significant sea change in the quality of wave riding at almost every surf spot in California. Rather than spotting one or two kids as driven by competition as David and me, we now paddled out to a whole new generation of rippers preparing themselves to be a part of the dream of pro surfing, a dream so new even their big brothers and sisters couldn't imagine it. The world tour was now in its second year, and one-off pro events in California, Florida and the East Coast were popping up and becoming part of the circuit, along with more-established Australian and Hawaiian contests.

I looked around, breathed deeply and closed my eyes. I was determined to make sure that I would be the one leading the way. I would show the others when the next set wave came through and I paddled for it. Wave hog that I was, I knew one thing: It would be mine. Both the wave and the victory.

5

THE OCEAN CAN BE A SCARY PLACE

Throughout my life, people have often asked if I was afraid or felt fear when I surfed really big waves the height of two- and three-story buildings. *Yes! Of course!* For all of us who challenge the bigger waves of the sea, there are occasional moments when we no longer feel in control of our situation. Each moment is terrifying for a world champion or a Pipeline Master, just as it is for a recreational surfer. I have been beaten up, injured, overmatched, thrown around like socks in a washing machine, tombstoned onto the ocean bottom and left holding my breath for 20 seconds or more, which seems like an eternity when you're violently held under water against your will.

What do I do in these situations? Trust my instincts and abilities and sometimes pray the ocean will release me from her grip. And, I would add, say a much longer prayer of thanks when I escape the grip of the sea and make my way to shore. I've said a few of those, for sure.

To push yourself as a surfer, especially as a professional surfer, there comes a time when we find ourselves in dangerous, potentially life-threatening situations in the ocean. Events are held in the world's most renowned big-wave locations like Teahupo'o, Banzai Pipeline, and Sunset Beach, along with specialty competitions in legendary huge-wave arenas such as Waimea Bay, Tavarua, Jaws, Mavericks, and the biggest of all, Portugal's Nazare. They test the mettle and fear levels of even the most brazen big-wave conquerors . . . let alone those of us who take them on only occasionally, sometimes because we have no other choice.

I'm reminded of a story I read in the 2015 biography of freestyle surfing phenom Clay Marzo, *Just Add Water*, in which his mother, Jill, recounted Clay's first foray into monster surf—a day with 20-foot faces on the outer reef of Ho'okipa, on the north shore of Clay's home base in Maui. Clay, who was diagnosed with Asperger syndrome in 2007, two years after winning the prestigious NSSA Nationals with a dominating performance, is one of the most insane surfers on earth. Clay goes off in the world's biggest waves, where he faces rocky reefs, hard-packed sand, and bottoms with very little ocean in between those surfaces and his boards. Sometimes, he even dry docks—landing in nothing but wet sand or dry reef. "Clay tries and pulls off stuff I'd never think of doing," said 11-time world surfing champion Kelly Slater.

Clay took a long look at the 20-foot waves growling like hungry beasts well beyond the place where surfers typically ride its waves. In Hawaiian measurements, it was 8 to 10 feet. The Hawaiians measure the backs of the waves, not the faces, meaning their measurements sound half as large. But a 20-foot face is a 20-foot face in my book. Clay paddled, and paddled ... and disappeared from view. For a few heart-stopping minutes, Jill didn't know whether Clay was waiting for a wave, in the grips of one, or in a fight for his life. Clay eventually pulled into view, speeding along on a massive set wave. He then paddled out and stopped her heart a few more times before calling it a day.

The kicker of this story? Clay was 13 at the time. "I was pretty afraid of those waves," he later admitted. But he still paddled back out and conquered his fears.

My first showdown with my mortality in the water came in the autumn of 1977, during my second trip to Hawaii. Now 16, I was one of the two or three best amateur surfers in America, just about ready to begin my pro surfing career. I'd surfed quite a few double-overhead days in California, but a big day in Hawaii is a different reality entirely. It starts with the bottom contour of the ocean. The bigger waves in California hit a mile-wide shelf before they break after being sent thousands of miles by storms. With few exceptions, such as Maverick's near San Francisco, or the Cortes Bank 90 miles off the coast of San Diego, the shelves dissipate their power to a degree, along with their size.

Not so in Hawaii. On Oahu's fabled North Shore, surfers who tackle giants confront walls of water that have traveled 5,000 miles from the Sea of Japan across open, deep ocean. The first shelves or reefs these waves encounter are the ones sitting beneath their surfboards. Their power is relentless and explosive; when they break, they sometimes look like a detonation—and feel like one too. Even the "smaller" 6-to-10-foot waves contain an energy much more powerful than anything all but a select few breaks in the world can match. Anything over 10 feet in Hawaii changes the playing field; anything over 15 feet changes it again.

I'd experienced Hawaiian waves before. Here's the story, one I'm not proud of today, shared only to show how obsessed I was with my dream of making it in Hawaii. What did I do? I stole $500 in savings bonds my dad was collecting for my college education, hopped on my bike, rode to our local bank . . . and cashed them. The bank didn't ask for my ID, my age, nothing. College? I wouldn't even stay in school. Surfing was my college.

Even though school had started six weeks before, I still hadn't shown up. I faked going to school every day, books and all. My parents thought I was in school, and the school thought I was still in the hospital, where I'd been for the first one and a half weeks of the fall semester. My scheme was perfect for those six weeks; I surfed every day, but both the school and my parents were starting to wise up. I knew the gig was almost over.

So I ran away to Hawaii. My friend, Carlsbad surfer Anthony Mata, drove me to San Diego International Airport. I bought a ticket for a PSA flight (PSA was a major airline then) and walked onto the plane. Again, with no ID check. The 1970s were easygoing beyond belief, and we didn't have to worry about the security procedures of today. They didn't exist.

When I arrived in Honolulu, I boarded a bus for my destination. But it was the wrong bus; I was clueless. I took the Circle Island tour with a load of tourists, stopped at Sunset Beach, and stayed at the house of Nick Benuska, a surfer I knew through Midget Smith. Mom now knew I was there; I never learned how she found out.

I ran out of money, and I called my mom. She then paid for my flight home.

Before that, I surfed early-season Pipeline . . . a dream come true. I paddled out on a Stinger surfboard, and soon caught my first Pipe wave—still one of the best of my life. A perfect ride. *This isn't so hard,* I thought. On the next wave, though, Pipeline initiated me properly, treating me to a horrible wipeout. Like I said, no one escapes punishment out there. Especially a cocky 15-year-old riding waves on his college savings account.

Finally, I flew home, and Mom met me at the gate. Her first words were the most crushing I could imagine, delivered with the anger she felt toward me: "Your father and I are getting a divorce." The first thing she said! My heart sank in my stomach. I knew Mom and Dad were having problems, but a divorce? I didn't say a word as we drove home.

The next day, I had to go with my parents to Carlsbad High School and face the music for being truant for now two months. I begged them to let me attend the continuation school, La Palma High, and school principal Bill Rouse agreed it was the best idea. I loved to read, but I hated being in class. I also hated doing homework.

It was the right solution for me. A great fit. I could read books, take notes—the same way I learn today—give reports, and work my schedule around the surf conditions.

But one thing for sure: I never pulled a fast one on my parents again.

The following year, I returned to the North Shore, this time with my parents' blessings. Shortly after arriving, I went from having a really fun time surfing 6-to-8-foot waves at Laniakea to suddenly thrashing for my life in the water, without a board, in a dangerous rip current in 12-foot waves. All within 20 minutes. Talk about fear! This happened on the back end of a two-hour surf session, when I was tired, fatigued and hungry.

Laniakea requires you to paddle about 200 yards to get to the inside of the breaking lineup. Simply put, it's way the heck out there! On a bigger day, say in the 8-to-15-feet range, the outside take-off spot can be a quarter to a half mile from the shore. On this particular day, I was still unfamiliar with the potential damage and chaos Hawaii conditions could create. Earlier, I drove up from Honolulu with the great pro Dane Kealoha, one of the world's five greatest surfers, equally efficient in small and big waves. Since Dane lived with Town & Country Surfboards owner Craig Sugihara, and Craig invited me to stay with them, well, they were stuck with me. Dane would usually give me a few tips about a surf spot before we paddled out, but after that, I was on my own.

There were plenty of people in the water, at least 30 surfers spread throughout the lineup. I pulled off a few good rides during my two-hour session, but trouble finally arrived: My surf leash broke on a wipeout, the wave so potent it snapped the polyurethane leash. I was now without my board. Since I was situated more toward the inside of the lineup, good fortune prevailed over possible disaster: I was able to safely swim to the beach.

When I got to the beach, I could not find my board. As I looked around, a local Hawaiian surfer pointed to the left of the lineup. Right there in the rip current bobbed a white surfboard, moving toward the west, about 100 yards off the shore. *Funny*, I thought. *Same color as the board I borrowed*; Craig had lent me the board, since my California boards were too short, and longer, leaner equipment was necessary to surf big North Shore waves. I began to head back into the ocean to retrieve the board.

Not the smartest move. As I stroked farther into the ocean, I found myself amongst waves that had jumped in size to 10 to 12 feet in Hawaiian measurements. It took no more than ten minutes to realize I was in a bad situation. I was no closer to the board than when I started to swim toward it, but now, like the board, I floated at the mercy of the dangerous riptide, headed toward the open ocean. The surfboard would float forever. As for me? Eventually, I would run out of gas.

The riptide carried me into the large lineup just south of Laniakea, known as Himalayas, which no one was surfing that day, its name an apt description of the waves' sheer size and power. Not to mention an intimidating presence. I was now about a quarter mile from the nearest surfers.

I was in trouble. No one could see me.

Quickly, I abandoned my quest to retrieve the board and redirected my thoughts and attention to returning to the safety of the beach.

As I began to swim toward shore, I realized that I was making no headway against the riptide. Instead, the rip was pushing me farther out to sea. The thought entered my mind that I was in grave danger, a truly life-threatening situation. I almost freaked out, but managed not to panic, which would've resulted in the kiss of death by drowning.

Instead, my instincts and survival skills took over. Along with some divine providence. I knew I had to stay calm and keep my wits. So, I gathered my thoughts, and reminded myself that I was a champion swimmer as a kid, and I could do this. About that same time, I looked toward shore and noticed the same Hawaiian who had directed me to the board watching me on shore. He was holding up a surfboard! I looked closely, survival adrenaline replaced by anger: *He had my board!* The one I was chasing belonged to someone else. This local had hidden my board and tricked me into entering this dangerous situation to fetch not my board—but his! Not cool, on any level. Welcome to Hawaii, *haole* boy.

Still, he knew I was in danger. His basic sense of goodness and common sense prevailed. Within moments, he jumped on my board and paddled out to help me. It took him about ten minutes to get to me. He arrived not a moment too soon; I was exhausted, down to my last few crawl strokes. When he arrived, we didn't say much to each other.

After resting on the board for a few seconds to catch my breath, we began to paddle and swim toward the shore. He was on the board paddling, while I was holding on to the single fin, stroking with my free arm. Together, we were able to break the grip of the powerful riptide and make it back to the safety of the shore. How long did it take? Probably ten minutes or a bit less. It felt like an eternity.

Once safely back on the beach, I don't remember anything the Hawaiian local said. We were both so relieved, me that I had survived and he that I had not drowned at his expense after his purposeful deceit. Shortly after the local rescued me, Dane came in from his surf session and we drove past Haleiwa and off the North Shore, through the pineapple fields and to Pearl City as if nothing had happened. In reflection, I'm not even sure if I told him. I was just happy to be alive.

My first brush with the dangerous North Shore surf, the sheer horror of being caught in the ocean in a powerless situation, was certainly not my last. A few years later, I survived another near-death experience, this time at world-famous Sunset Beach, where ABC's *Wide World of Sports* broadcasted the Duke Kahanamoku Surf Classic throughout the 1970s.

On a stormy, rainy day, all the elements of terror came together perfectly. The surf had surged from 10 to 15 feet, then to 15 to 20 feet in less than an hour, a sight to behold in and of itself. I'd never seen a swell jump that quickly. I paddled out on a six-foot-nine midsize big-wave board designed for waves in the 10-foot range, but within an hour, the ever-increasing waves made me feel like I was riding a kid's board. Most of the other surfers in the lineup were on boards seven-foot-six or longer. The surf piled atop itself so fast that huge whitewater walls began to wash out the deep-water paddling channel to the left of the breaking lineup. The 40 to 50 surfers were no longer bobbing fairly close together on the main peak where typical big Sunset broke, but were spread out over a 300-yard area. Even the best big-wave surfers started dodging the huge waves.

By now, daylight was becoming an issue, the stormy sky turning an absolutely medieval purple, the swells massive and billowing like walls of water sent from another planet. Less than an hour of light remained.

A familiar feeling crept over me: *Get out of here.*

I was determined to get back to the beach as quickly as possible. I was cautiously confident in these circumstances, again because of my swimming capabilities, but vulnerable to the situation. Catching one of these larger waves on my smaller board would be a fool's errand at best, a brush with disaster at worst. My ocean exit strategy was simple: to wait for a lull in the sets, paddle inside the outer reef and its sharp-fanged 15-to-20-footers, and catch a smaller wave in the 12-foot range to get back to the beach.

Then I paddled furiously for the first smaller wave of an approaching set—and just missed it. *Ahhh!*

I turned around and found myself in no man's land, caught right in the middle of the impact zone. I looked up into the jowls of multiple 20-foot waves about to break on my head and enjoy a helpless Californian for dinner. Between the sheer power and surge force of these massive mountains, I stood no chance to hold on to my board and push through. I had to throw my board to the side, dive deep, and hope my surf leash would hold.

It did not. *Snap!*

Just like that, I huffed and puffed for breath about a half mile out at sea on the very outside of Sunset Point without a board, in 20-foot waves, the dark and stormy clouds suggesting about 45 minutes of daylight remaining. It was a serious situation, and I was on my own.

I whipped up a new plan: start swimming toward the beach, while letting the giant waves push me in the same direction. Only, there was a problem. While this plan works perfectly at Pipeline, which breaks within a few yards of the beach, it does not always work favorably at Sunset Beach. The greater challenge at Sunset is that all those tons of violent water beating on you have to go somewhere. That somewhere is the deep-water channel that runs parallel to shore, about 100 yards from the sand. As the giant waves dissipate in the deep water, they create a dangerous current that turns into a fast-moving river running parallel to the beach. If you visualize a small river ripping through at flood stage, you get the idea. Not how I thought this day would turn out...

After a few hundred yards, the river turned northwest and outward toward the open ocean through the Sunset Beach channel. Suddenly, I was in deep water, away from my whitewater pounding. The channel continued to run like a rapid river, parallel to shore, before it cranked a violent right turn and returned home to the sea that created it. I knew a simple fact: On a really big day, when I hit this river within the ocean, I had 150 yards to swim to the other side of the shore, or I would be carried into the Pacific too. And when I returned to Sunset, that same ocean would send more 20-foot waves—only without my board.

Which is exactly what happened. I had been too slow to punch through the inside river, and now rode like a human package on a conveyor belt to oblivion. I was returned to the giant waves with less than 30 minutes of daylight to again scratch my way to the beach before darkness engulfed any remaining chance I had. Fortunately, a couple of things played in my favor. I was still physically fresh, as I hadn't surfed earlier in the day. Also, as the river took me back out to the lineup, I was back in contact with other surfers.

Now panicking, I swam up to an Australian friend. "Can you help me get back to the beach?" I begged.

I will never forget exactly what he said to me: "Get ahold of yourself, mate!"

Wow. Really?

Fortunately, he coupled his brusque coldness with a set of instructions. "Swim back to the outside," he said. "When there is not a set, swim in and over (toward the east), then when the set comes, don't fight it. Ride it to the deep water and save your energy. Then, when you hit the deep water, swim through the rip with all you have and you will be fine."

I did what he said—and for the second time on the North Shore, dodged a near-death experience.

As for my Australian friend, I didn't know whether to curse him or thank him! Nonetheless, I shook all over from the terrifying hour of swimming for my life in some of the meanest waves I'd ever experienced.

You would think two terrifying incidents like those at Laniakea and Sunset Beach would be enough for me to swear off big waves forever. However great that bit of common sense is, it cuts across the grain of our mettle and character as surfers, especially a surfer trying to be the best in the world.

So once again, I found myself in a precarious moment in the sea. Only this was even worse. One beautiful sunny morning, I paddled out at what was then considered the biggest rideable wave in the world, Waimea Bay. Unfortunately, I hadn't watched the surf for very long before paddling out. After many seasons on the North Shore, I learned that if the surf is good and not that crowded, you need to get out there and get some waves before the word gets out and hordes of riders arrive from both town and country.

Off I went! My paddle out was fairly simple and I made it out the back to the main lineup with minimal effort.

Once in the lineup, I saw local legend James Jones, who I first heard about on *Wide World of Sports* and saw on the magazine cover around the time that I bought my first board at Offshore Surf Shop back home, now charging a 30-foot face. I thought to myself, *Whoa! I'm out at Waimea Bay with James Jones!*

Then my elation evaporated. Quickly.

The horizon started moving. Headed toward the dozen of us in the water, lumbering and lurching forward like the End of Time, was the largest wave I have seen in my life. As I looked toward the open ocean to the northeast, the entire horizon seemed to rise with skyscrapers. My first thought was that my eyes were playing tricks on me. Yet, as I looked, I knew what I was seeing: waves the size of four- and five-story buildings. Without saying a word, I broke as fast as I could toward the west, to the safety of the channel, and out to sea. Initially, I was the only person that made that move. Truly, it might have saved my life.

Within a minute, the rest of the boys saw why I high-tailed it: A giant set 10 to 15 feet larger than all of the previous sets that morning was taking dead aim at us. Waimea Bay had just jumped from 25 to 40-plus feet—in one set!

I paddled as fast and as hard as I could straight toward the neighboring island of Kauai. As the set approached, the wave faces feathered under the soft trade winds, creating an alluring beauty. These waves were close to 50 feet on their faces, blue, beautiful, mesmerizing giants lit by the sun. I was awestruck by the beauty and terror. It was the first and only time in my career that I can remember paddling over waves so big that I found myself stroking at least 30 feet down *the back of the waves*. My beautiful morning had been turned upside down and now, for the third time, I was in a life-threatening situation on the North Shore.

When the monster set had passed me and laid siege to Waimea Bay, turning it into a frothy washing machine of whitewater, I turned around to see I was the only surfer that had made it out and over. The set had completely closed out Waimea Bay.

What now? I was at least 200 yards past the normal take-off spot for Waimea. The waves were closing out the bay and I was all alone. I immediately grasped I was in a life-and-death situation.

It was then I learned a lot about myself. I did what many of us would do. I cried out to God! I recited the Lord's Prayer:

Our Father, who art in heaven,
Hallowed be thy name . . .

. . . and thought of all my shortcomings and asked for forgiveness and safe passage back to the shore. I even promised to serve the Lord if He spared my life!

I regrouped and figured I had two choices: paddle in during a lull, or paddle for four miles toward the west to Haleiwa Harbor and return to the beach that way. Since I didn't like the idea of going farther out to sea, I opted to paddle in during a lull. I looked toward the shore and the Kam Highway bending around the bay, now packed with cars and people watching this raw spectacle of nature at her most furious. I realized my life-and-death moment was a part of their show. I felt like a gladiator trying to fight his way out of the Colosseum to the cheers of the Roman crowd!

Now I had to finish the job and get out of that pit alive. My first attempt to get back to the beach failed and struck further fear in me. I paddled about 100 yards toward the normal take-off zone of the bay. I looked to the north-east—and saw another one of those giant sets. Terrified, I quickly turned around and headed out to the open ocean. I finally saw another surfer in the lineup, Tony Roy, a well-respected and fearless big-wave rider. He was known to surf alone on the giant waves of third reef Pipeline, the outermost reef, a forbidden reef. When I saw it was Tony, I started a clear and memorable self-conversation that went something like this: "I am out at giant Waimea Bay with Tony Roy!? Oh God, what have I done? I am going to die. No! Don't think like that. We will get out of this. Oh God, please help, it's me and Tony Roy!"

While fighting panic, another lull chilled out the frothy, foamy bay. I gave it all I had, paddling eastward toward the take-off zone and the point, reckoning it was my best chance to survive. I moved water with my arms like an Olympic swimmer till I reached the point of no return. Now fully committed, I had to charge straight toward the original take-off zone, and figure out my survival strategy, because there would be no turning back to the open ocean.

I could see in the distance another huge set approaching. Within two minutes, it would arrive and bombard me. *Paddle, paddle, paddle harder! To the beach!* I moved farther inside of the normal take-off zone ... and there it was, a gift from God. A 15-footer with a nice safe shoulder. A completely rideable wave for me. *This is it!* I thought. *My get-out-of-jail card! Go! Go! Go!*

I caught the wave, made a smooth drop down the face, and kept cutting back in the whitewater as if my life depended on it (because it kinda did). I looked over my shoulder to see the wave behind mine closing out the entire bay ... and Tony Roy rising *over* the set, left out by himself. I rode my wave all the way onto the sand.

Yet again, my life had been spared. I was safe! I was numb, beyond any feeling other than massive relief. Tony Roy also managed to get in a few minutes later.

As for my promise to serve God if He delivered me? I distinctly remember saying to Him, "Thanks, maybe tomorrow."

It remains my most terrifying moment in the ocean, worse than Laniakea, worse than Sunset Beach.

Laniakea, Sunset Beach and Waimea Bay were terrifying and truly life-threatening experiences. Over the past 40 years, surfers of various abilities have died while surfing these and other breaks on the North Shore and other huge-wave spots, some even elite pros. Something about which we were all reminded in the winter of 1995, when renowned Hawaii big-wave waterman Mark Foo died beneath the frigid waters of Maverick's in Northern California after wiping out on a 30-foot wave.

I might have met an early demise like Foo or the others through any of these experiences. However, by the grace of God, I did not. Little did I know at the time, while surviving these near-death events, that God held plans for my future that even these terrifying monster waves could not stop.

6

GETTING PAID TO SURF? REALLY?

Remember the schoolteacher who confidently told me I could never become a professional surfer because there would never be a pro tour?

Well, as they say, famous last words. By the time I began winning and then dominating WSA events, becoming California's top young amateur surfer in the process, a world tour was up and running—and I was preparing to be a part of it.

Led by Gerry Lopez, Michael Ho and Dane Kealoha in Hawaii, Michael Peterson, Peter Townend and Ian Cairns in Australia, and Shaun Tomson in South Africa, talented surfers from around the world began to establish themselves in a series of professional events that sprang up in the first half of the 1970s. The events were held primarily in Australia and Hawaii, along with the Gunston 500 in Tomson's native South Africa. For those who traveled to Australia for six weeks late each Australian summer (February to early April), or late each autumn in Hawaii, a couple of wins or high finishes meant some prize money.

In 1975, two men met with these trailblazers and took the sport another step forward. Make that a quantum leap forward. Visionaries Fred Hemmings and Randy Rarick, both from Hawaii, saw the potential for the growth of pro surfing. Hemmings, a natural organizer and politically savvy man, was a Hawaiian legend as a surfer from his exploits in the World Surfing Championships in the late 1960s, so the media knew him well. Rarick, who lived on the North Shore four doors from the back gate that led to the paddle-out position at Sunset Beach, was a young surfer who delighted at the idea of forming a true world tour and providing opportunities for international stars like Peterson, Cairns, PT, Wayne "Rabbit" Bartholomew, Tomson, and Hawaiians Lopez, Dane Kealoha, Reno Abellira and others.

Hemmings and Rarick proved a worthy duo. They pooled resources, found some sponsors, created an official points-ranking system and formed the International Professional Surfers World Surfing Tour (IPS). The circuit opened in early 1976 with the New Zealand Pro, offering a purse of $2,850. It wasn't much, but it was a start. Michael Peterson became the first-ever IPS event champion.

The tour continued onward, picking up events and surfers as it went along. A hearty 20 or so wave riders surfed all 12 events, while many others tried a few events here and there, among them Californians like Mike Purpus, Chris O'Rourke, Carlsbad local Randy Laine, and Dru Harrison. From New Zealand, the circuit proceeded to three events in Australia, two of which already existed—the Bells Classic and Surfabout—then to South Africa, Brazil, Florida (won by Greg Mungall, the first American to win an IPS event), and a four-contest grand finale in Hawaii. The two biggest Hawaiian events, the Duke Kahanamoku Surf Classic and Pipeline Masters, were appropriately won by two local superstars, James Jones and Rory Russell. After Aussie Ian Cairns won the season finale, the World Cup in Haleiwa, the final points were tallied. Surprisingly, though Cairns and Tomson each won twice, it was a diminutive Aussie who did not win an event, Peter Townend, who claimed the overall title.

In all, the 12 rated events offered a total of $73,500—about 10 percent of today's average $607,000 purse *per event* in the rebranded World Surfing League. As Townend later noted in the 1988 Association of Surfing Professionals Media Guide, "There wasn't a banquet that year. I didn't even get a trophy for winning the title! For photographs, Fred Hemmings removed a trophy from the Outrigger Canoe Club trophy case [in Waikiki], and we held it together."

But our sport had a world tour—and I was ready to jump on it. The tour's total prize money increased 30 percent in 1977 and another 30 percent in 1978, to $128,000. The sport was quickly becoming global, more surfers were taking their shots, and as it did so, an economy began to grow around it. The emerging surf industry was mostly built around clothing brands like Quiksilver, Billabong, Stubbies, and Lightning Bolt, which joined old favorites like Hang Ten and Ocean Pacific, with OP eyeing a much bigger investment. These were brands that everyday surfers wore.

As 1978 began to unfold, a few key elements coalesced to carry forward a new chapter in my life. The first dealt with high school. As already noted, I did not do well in school at all. That never changed from grade school to high school. A few years earlier, I had convinced my parents to let me transfer out of conventional public high school and attend what was then known as "continuation high school." In what was already a very difficult time for our family, my parents reluctantly consented. Their resistance was hardly a surprise, as they had recently begun the process of marital separation. Throughout this time, they were moving toward what would eventually become an amicable divorce, not such an easy thing to do at any time—but especially in the 1970s, with three kids in the middle. Plus, it was hard on all three kids, since we Burans were a tight crew who looked out for each other. Mom continued on with primary parenting duties, while Dad made sure we had whatever we needed. Thankfully, their divorce gave highest priority to their kids. I always advise people, if they must divorce, to be as amicable as possible and to keep attention to those kids above their own problems or issues. I speak not only from common sense as a minister, but as one who knows what it's like.

Throughout 1976 and 1977, I was a student at La Palma Continuation High School, attending class from 11:00 a.m. to 2:00 p.m. This fit perfectly with my desired surfing schedule, since morning dawn patrols and evening surf sessions are far better than midday surfs, when the onshore winds tended to blow shape and form off the waves.

As spring 1978 arrived, I began preparing myself to graduate after my junior year, as I had no use for a senior year and all its bells and whistles while attending a continuation school and itching to get onto the pro tour. I took the California Proficiency Exam in late May. My goal was absolute: pass the test and become a full-time pro surfer! Never mind that few, if any, surfers were making money at this time in pro surfing. The 1978 tour's prize pool of $128,000 sounds good at first glance, but that was spread over 11 tournaments with 8 to 16 surfers receiving checks after each event, depending on individual prize money distribution.

I was truly ready to wrap up my amateur surfing career. It was time. There was a clear distinction between being an amateur or professional athlete, and since I was now out of school, I needed to earn money doing what I loved doing. From 1966 to 1972, the World Amateur Surfing Championships had served as the *crème de la crème* of global competition, but once professional contests started popping up in 1973, the event went on hiatus. As fate would have it, the powers that be reinstated the Worlds in 1978, and I was invited to represent the USA in the event.

One of the greatest aspects of the 1978 World Amateur Surfing Championships was its location—South Africa. The home of another of my heroes, Shaun Tomson. Even better, the IPS Tour was stopping there at the same time. My plan snapped together faster than a hard cutback: If I made the finals of the World Amateur Championships, I would turn professional and enter my first pro contest later the next week. I put all of my concentration, focus, mind, heart, body and soul into lighting up the waves in my heats, as I'd done for two years in WSA events and US Nationals, to reach those finals.

Which is exactly what happened. I made the World Amateur Finals and completed my amateur career on a high note. Before heading up from East London to Durban for my first pro event, I also received the opportunity to surf Jeffreys Bay, one of the most revered surf spots in the world. It's like a golfer playing St. Andrew's, or a distance runner competing in the Boston Marathon. Moreover, as good fortune had it, the surf was pumping at six to eight feet, a perfect wave size for me. There I was at the age of 17, surfing one of the best waves in the world, on the other side of the planet, living my dream with all those great world tour pros out in the same lineup. I had the time of my life.

Now it was time to put on my game face for a whole new realm of competition, against guys older than me, sometimes up to a decade older. When I arrived in Durban for the Hang Ten Pro, the waves were smaller, but contestable, in the range of three to four feet. I surfed well in the early qualifying rounds and made it into the 32-man main event draw. A worthy accomplishment for a young rookie making his debut.

My reward for making the main event? A man-on-man heat with the current face of Australian surfing dominance, the world's top-rated surfer, Rabbit Bartholomew, who was on his way to winning three events and the 1978 world title. While most people didn't know me or give me any chance against Rabbit, I went to bed the night before quite confident I was going to beat him. I have never really understood why I always believe I can win, or achieve goals that seem greater than what is possible at first glance. However, throughout my entire life, I generally have believed I can—and usually do! And those times when I fail, I don't think I will, and typically shake it off and use it as motivation for future success. After all, what is true success but the learned lessons of the failures that preceded it, followed by the strength and determination those failures give you?

In addition, in a purely strategic sense, while amateur surfers throughout California and the US knew me and my style well, the top surfers in the world did not. They'd never seen me compete before. That is a huge advantage if you have the mindset to deal with the mental side of that as well.

The next morning, in beautiful, blue head-high surf conditions, I surfed the heat of my life. To the surprise of everyone in the surfing world, industry and media, but not myself, I surfed the heat of my life and clearly defeated Rabbit, winning my first-ever man-on-man pro surf heat. I won the next heat as well, before finally getting taken down. I finished ninth in the event, received a small paycheck, and officially realized the first part of my dream: to become a pro surfer!

When I made my professional debut, the internet was a top-secret communications platform developed by the US Department of Defense and a couple of computer scientists. It wouldn't become all the rage for another 20 years. We had no ESPN, and virtually no television media coverage outside Australia. Surf magazines were everything. It's where we studied pictures and stories on our heroes, were introduced to world-class waves being surfed for the first time (that we knew of), and it's where we saw the newest ads featuring our heroes representing all of the coolest surf brands.

Enter my good fortune again. It so happened that 1978 was the year that the two primary magazines, *Surfer* and *Surfing*, sensed the emerging growth of a surf industry that could financially support two monthly magazines. They also saw the increasing number of stars being born on the IPS tour. Both magazines took the bait and became bona fide monthlies, with their own editorial and photography staffs filled with hungry young scribes and shutterbugs, and a few veterans as well. Since there were no Californians in the IPS Top 16 at the time—or Top 30, for that matter—my upset victory over Rabbit drew instant international attention. Leading the way were the three established Australian surf magazines—and the two mags sitting in Orange County, California, *Surfer* and *Surfing*. The Southern California–based magazines needed to sell issues, and a 17-year-old Californian beating the number one in the world was newsworthy. Especially one who had the gift of gab, made for a great interview, and harbored no reservation about saying where he wanted to go—right toward the top, with a King of Pipeline crown on his head. It was perfect, perfect timing. I was the lead story in *Surfing* magazine, and the top Californian to receive coverage on a regular basis. People would read about me every month.

What a great way to begin my career.

Over the next few months, I competed in a few pro events throughout the United States, including the IPS Tour's Grog's Seaside Pro and Florida

Pro on the East Coast, with solid, if not spectacular results. By July, it was confirmed that I had indeed passed the California Proficiency Exam and had now officially moved on from high school. My "senior year" would be spent in some of the greatest waves in the world, competing against the best surfers on earth, living the life of a pro surfer pursuing my dream!

Late that summer, under the warm California sun, I found myself eagerly looking forward to the biggest pro surf contest held in California to date, the California Pro. It would be held at a surf break I was familiar with, the nearby North Jetty at Oceanside Harbor. The event was to be held in early September. Around the same time, to my surprise, I also received notice that I was invited to compete in the 1978 Pipeline Masters. My dream event! *How did that happen so fast?* I was so stoked! My confidence was at an all-time high and I entered the event in Oceanside with the expectation to win.

Alas, it seems, some dream-come-true stories are just too good to be true, carrying hidden within them a dark moment or period of time that tests you to the core. The fact it happened at home and affected me directly put the spotlight right on me.

The surf was fantastic for the Oceanside event, the waves were firing all week with a five-to-eight-foot swell and classic North Jetty conditions. Because of its prize purse, which exceeded $10,000, the event was filled with many of the top pro surfers in the world, although it carried no affiliation with the IPS World Tour points race for the 1978 World Champion. I'd spent the summer paying my dues as a fledgling pro in everyone else's waves, but now, the tables were turned: We were in my wheelhouse.

Not surprisingly to me, everything went my way that week and I won my first pro surfing event. The first prize was $3,000—more than the entire purse of the first-ever IPS event just two and a half years before!

I floated on a cloud from the time I received that check until I went to the bank—and the check bounced. All of the top finishers, including myself, were stunned to find out that the event promoter had taken most of the entry and sponsor money and gone into hiding! After collecting our entry fees and money from the sponsors, he conveniently failed to show up at the beach *the day before* the event began. After a series of frantic phone calls, the promoter appeared for the contest itself. A local reporter who wrote a preview story on the tournament ran back to his office and told his sports editor, "Something weird's going on with this surf contest and this organizer. Want me to stay on it?" Well, the reporter got his wish and covered the event and its disappointing aftermath.

Plus, my mom was having none of it! She began to do some personal research, informing the reporter all along the way, and she eventually found the promoter's hideout in nearby Laguna Beach. Mom showed up with the cops, who arrested him. When the promoter showed up in the North San Diego County municipal courthouse, he looked around and saw my mom, the reporter, and a few other faces he didn't want to see. He pled out and was found guilty of various charges, did a bit of time in jail and was forced to make restitution on all the bad checks.

To his credit, he did. Years later, in 1983, I received the final installment of my $3,000 first-place prize money. Thanks to my mom's efforts, justice had been served, even if it took five years to do so!

After I won the California Pro, my thoughts began to move toward Hawaii and competing in my first Pipeline Masters event. It would be my third year in a row surfing the infamous North Shore, but now, instead of just being there for a week or so, I would be there for the entire prime contest season of November and December. I would have to fight my fears and push my limits in daily life-threatening surfing circumstances to gain the respect of my IPS peers—and to reach my goal of becoming King of Pipeline.

Apart from the big and challenging waves, I would have to compete every time I was in the water with other top local and international surfers for every wave, even far outside the contest arena. The reason had nothing to do with good-natured competition. Quite the opposite. With my long blond hair, aggressive surfing style and go-for-it attitude, I was a despised *haole* from the mainland, and not only that, but a *haole* pushing the limits. The Hawaiians are a proud, strong culture, one very protective of their thousand-year-old heritage. They are also territorial, and do not take kindly to visitors in many surf spots. Even though I wanted to befriend everyone and just enjoy a good competitive surf with them, the idea of difference based on skin tone, cultural background and lifestyle—or any combination of the three—was something I found really repulsive, having already seen enough of it while a small child in Virginia. Now I represented everything wrong about the presence of *haoles* in Hawaii. To excel on the very waves on which Hawaiians made surfing a sport? The sport of kings? A core identification marker of their waterman culture?

To quote Apollo 13 astronaut James Lovell when he radioed to Mission Control on his ill-fated mission five years before, "Houston, we have a problem."

I was the problem.

Even worse, in recent months, I had become somewhat of a known personality in the sport. Many still and video cameras and eyes trained on me every time I pulled up at a beach, waxed up and went surfing. I was in the magazines, and the newspapers mentioned me more than once. It got so bad that one day, when I was hitchhiking on the island, a local woman pulled up alongside me, stopped her car, jumped out of it and yelled a no-nonsense expletive. Then jumped in her car and sped away.

Finally, my sanctuary arrived: the 1978 Pipeline Masters. The preliminary rounds began around the first week of December. From its first year in 1971, the Pipe Masters rose to the top as the most prestigious surfing contest in the world, given the sheer beauty, size and mortal danger of Banzai Pipeline. Unlike Sunset Beach, where set waves broke a quarter to a half mile offshore, Pipeline sets exploded onto first reef just 50 feet from the shoreline. Spectators could not only see us trying to slot ourselves in and make our way out, but they could *feel* it.

Now I was competing on surfing's biggest stage as the youngest in the event, still a couple months shy of 18. Although I was nervous, I was also excited and confident in the opportunity. This was my dream, the one I told my mom about five years before, the one I'd gone on and on sharing with anyone who would listen ever since—and I was sure my time had come.

The day before my first Pipe Masters event was quite memorable. The waves built and built to quite enormous size, about 15 to 20 feet. I'm not sure why, but that afternoon I was surfing Sunset Beach about a mile to the north of Pipeline. After that session, my roommate on the North Shore, fellow Carlsbad local and well-respected Pipeline surfer Billy Stang, rode up to me on his bike and engaged me in serious conversation. He had just come from Pipeline.

"The waves are pumping," he began. "I'm pretty certain they're going to call the contest on tomorrow."

Billy, who was a few years older than me and a mentor, then looked at me with a deadly serious expression. "You need to get down there right away and start practicing," Billy said.

Off we headed to Pipeline.

When we arrived, I saw the lineup—and almost froze with fear. I was terrified! It was the biggest Pipeline I had ever seen. Thoughts of my near death in Laniakea the previous year raced through me. *We are going to compete in THIS?*

I shook my head, swallowed my heart after it all but lodged in my throat, and tried to shake off my fear. When we paddled out, I started by sitting in the safe spot of the deep-water channel, watching the other surfers. I was nowhere near ready to ride one of these explosive cylinders that could literally swallow a Mack truck, let alone compete for a victory in them. I watched

Billy, who did not share my fear, calmly catch wave after wave, dropping into and spitting out of those huge tubes. I felt like I was catching a live surf movie, and I had the best seat in the house. It was amazing!

Eventually, I did catch a wave or so, but nothing of significance. I was too scared to swing my board around and roll the dice on any of the bombs, the bigger, scarier tubes that sounded more like explosions than waves when they broke onto the reef. It was all a very humbling experience, yet I had at least paddled out, seen the big waves up close, and most importantly, survived without having to swim for my life.

That night, sleep proved very elusive. I kept picturing those waves, me in those waves, me *having to ride those waves* if I wanted the respect of my peers, let alone a chance to win the event. Respect is earned in surfing not only through performance, but through the willingness to and guts to tackle whatever you find when you pull up to the beach. The bigger the wave, the greater the respect. Especially from the locals. All I could think about was how terrifying the next day could be!

When Billy and I got to Pipeline the next morning for the contest, the surf had settled down to a far tamer 10 to 15 feet. Unlike the previous day's more dangerous, unruly and bigger west-northwesterly swell, which even shaped the breaking waves differently and provided less chance for success—or escape—these waves marched in from a westerly direction, ideal for Pipeline. In addition, the wind blew in from the east, a gentle, steady trade wind. *Perfect again.* My fear and trepidation started to evaporate as I watched wave after flawless wave crackle across the reef, producing pristine barrels that spit out large plumes of whitewater spray.

The competition format for that day called for six heats with six surfers in each heat. Much like amateur competitions, the IPS tour ran on a 50 percent advancement rule until the finals. In these heats, the top three finishers would advance to the next round. The judges would count the top three waves of each rider for their total score, with each wave graded on a scale of 1 to 10. An important note on the criteria: We each had to catch a minimum of three waves. Even if we scored two perfect 10s, if we didn't have a third wave on our sheet, we were out.

To a bright-eyed 17-year-old from Carlsbad who'd had, oh, a thousand dreams with Pipeline in them, every heat looked like a final! I may have seemed calm on the outside, but on the inside, I was so nervous being in awe of all the prestigious names, ready to join them in tackling the big, perfect surf.

Wouldn't you know it? Once again, fortune found a seat on the plane and joined me in Hawaii, then popped up its head at the right time. Right off the bat, I caught a huge break in my first-round heat. My performance was okay, as I caught a few smaller waves and worked my way into a couple of decent tube rides. As a whole, there was nothing too risky or spectacular in my performance. I was pushing myself to new personal limits, since I'd never really ridden such a perfect day at Pipeline before, but was playing it safe at the same time.

However, the ocean was stingy and fickle in providing waves in my heat. Because a few of the more seasoned and renowned surfers who definitely should have beaten me struggled to find their necessary three good waves, I managed to uneventfully sneak past them to finish in an advancing third-place position. I did so by surfing smart and building my scoreline, a strategy I'd mastered from many WSA events held in lackluster surf.

What happened after that set into motion events that truly forever changed my life.

In the next round, among the five other surfers in my next heat, stood none other than two-time defending champion Rory Russell, one of the greatest Pipeline legends ever. As we paddled out, an event happened to me that triggered and motivated me to perform the best surfing of my entire life. I paddled over the shoulder of a wave, where I saw a well-known and world-famous surf photographer. He looked at me and said, "You made it out of your heat? I can't believe it!" Rather than a compliment, this was a cutting remark intended to intimidate and discourage me.

Well, that was all I needed to light my fire! Joey Buran was about to show the photographer, Rory Russell, and every soul on the beach that day that I was here to win and someday become King of the Pipeline. Nothing motivates me more than someone telling me I can't do something, that I did something he or she thought was impossible for me. As *Star Wars* filmmaker George Lucas, who loathes the word "impossible," angrily told his personal assistant in front of a friend of mine in 2005, "You know how we got to where we are today? Why we've made all these movies, and done all these special effects? Because people in the studios told me it was impossible."

Count me in as a member of that club.

When the heat started, Rory Russell caught a wave, wiped out—and lost his board. When you lose your board at Pipeline, and your leash snaps, you have to swim in above the dangerous reef, with set waves detonating on your head, and then paddle out again. It was a mistake fatal to his chances of three-peating.

After that, it all went surreal. I caught big set peaks along with midsized perfect barrels, stuffing my fear as deeply into the tubes as I inserted my body and board. I was in the zone, where time and space seem to stop and everything connects and it all feels like a blur. While I couldn't recount every move of every wave in my heat now, I do remember being spit out of the biggest tubes of my life and hearing the spectators on the beach, screaming and hooting, locals and seasoned surfers and visiting surfers and tourists alike!

Then, just like that, the heat was over.

Word buzzed up and down the beach, and spread from Honolulu up to and through the entire North Shore through the artery of Kam Highway: Joey Buran, the 17-year-old *haole*, had just electrified the crowd and judges with his performance in perfect 10-to-15-foot Pipeline in front of the entire surf world! In so doing, not only did I win my semifinal heat, which advanced me straight to the finals, but I also outsurfed the two-time defending Pipeline Masters Champion Rory Russell in the process.

When I returned to the beach, Billy Stang was so fired up for me. Billy kept saying over and over, that I had beaten Rory Russell and I was in the finals. He didn't seem to believe it either. What a great moment! It almost didn't seem real and yet, at the same time, it seemed as if I'd scripted it the night I told my mom I would win this event ... or that a power far greater than myself had scripted it for me.

Then the surf died. Fred Hemmings and Randy Rarick were not about to stage the made-for-TV finals of surfing's grandest event in small, junky surf. So we waited ... and waited ...

Two weeks later, we returned to Banzai Pipeline for the finals, and were greeted by extremely dangerous 8-to-10 feet conditions. While smaller than the waves in my epic semifinal performance, these were more terrifying because of the swell direction, and the wind. Just a slight shift from due west to west-northwest, or a change in the winds from perfect trades to imperfect westerlies or dreaded northerlies, alters the shape and power centers of Pipeline waves, and makes them much bumpier and challenging at the point of takeoff. A wipeout at Pipeline is not only a knock on the head from a powerful wave, but also a face-to-face encounter with the razor-sharp coral reef and its caves, a few feet beneath the surface.

Of all the big waves in the world, Pipeline truly is one of the greatest shape-shifters.

Unfortunately, I brought the wrong board to the beach. I could not repeat my semifinal magic, but still managed to catch a couple of decent rides, finishing in fifth place out of six surfers. The final also included my hero, Gerry Lopez, and was later featured on the legendary ABC's *Wide World of Sports*. It was during this heat that one of the announcers, legendary broadcaster Jim McKay, simply said, "There goes Joey Buran, the California Kid!"

That is how I came to be known as the "California Kid."

It was a mere formality, and more than a coincidence, that when *Surfer* magazine did a feature interview on me around the same time, they, too, used the same title, "Joey Buran: The California Kid." Although I did not emerge victorious in my debut performance at Pipeline, I was nonetheless triumphant in my own way—not to mention being able to say I took down Rory Russell during the height of his powers.

When I stepped off the plane upon my return to California, I had found my new identity and place in the universe. I was Joey Buran, the California Kid and not just a rookie pro surfer, but a professional who was respected the world over. Including by a few Hawaiians.

7

THE CALIFORNIA KID

When good fortune and great blessings descend upon us, the feeling is almost indescribable. We feel almost invincible, like we can achieve anything, that we can go out into the world and find what we need, when we need it—and then use it to build our lives, successes and even greater achievements.

It also helps to have an unquenchable energy, will and drive to succeed in our goal, to fill it with purpose and with the absolute feeling that *this is exactly where my life is supposed to be and what I'm supposed to be doing right now.* I thought this was really well described years later in an article in *Breakout* magazine, a hotbed of quality surf journalism throughout the 1980s, when Dave Hirschman wrote, "Unlike most people who experience the paralysis of ambivalence when their expectations collide with actual reality, [Buran] feels none, and pursues his goals and objectives with single-minded determination. His desire to succeed is unmitigated . . ."

Which is exactly how I felt after the North Shore season ended. I soaked in all the accolades, the pure stoke from my friends and my fellow competitors on the world tour, the media, and everyone with whom I talked in those days and weeks after my out-of-time, out-of-mind performance at Pipeline. And I talked to a lot of people. I was so full of energy and passion for my sport, for everything to do with surfing and our lifestyle, that on many occasions, I felt myself close to bursting. Though I'd achieved a lot in my amateur career, nothing in my 17 years to date—absolutely nothing—compared to this. Wasn't I supposed to be cracking the books and getting ready for my finals as a senior in high school?

No, I was doing exactly what I was doing, where God carried me, elevating to the highest heights of my sport. Getting a taste of glory before the real glory showed up in my life almost a decade later.

Then there was the timing of my takedown of Rory Russell and appearance in the Pipeline Masters Final. It was just such good timing that by the time Californian surfers finally decided contests were cool and the new generation wanted to compete, I was already way ahead of the game. Now was that time. Some really good surfers from California rose with me, and some great ones followed our lead all the way to taking over the world—yes, I'm thinking about you, Tom Curren—but when the surfing world woke up on January 1, 1979, Joey Buran was the top-ranked Californian surfer on the IPS World Surfing Tour. I had made that Pipeline Masters Final and was now known as the California Kid. I was living my dream and loving every minute of it!

As I mentioned earlier, there are surfers who have had memorable nicknames, ever since Duke Kahanamoku turned on the world to our sport, won an Olympic swimming gold medal and became globally known and beloved as simply the Duke. His legend and nickname are so endearing and enduring that you can pull up in Huntington Beach, or Malibu, Oahu, Kauai or a few other places, walk into a Duke's restaurant—and feast yourselves on walls of pictures of Hawaii's greatest ever waterman. When anyone in our sport hears of Duke, they immediately think of *the* Duke, although I worked for a while as a sponsored athlete for another, Duke Boyd, the founder of Hang Ten, the first surf apparel company to sell big-time coast-to-coast.

On our IPS tour and the Hawaiian stops, we had a few surfers with enough international profile among wave riders to need no more introduction than their nicknames; the most recognizable were Rabbit, MR, PT, Buttons, BK: Wayne Bartholomew, Mark Richards, Peter Townend, Montgomery Kaluhiokalani, and Barry Kanianupuni. Before then, there were Malibu legends like Da Cat (Miki Dora), Tubesteak (Terry Tracey) and the most famous of all, Gidget (Kathy Zuckerman).

Like the Duke, their nicknames seemed to call forth their personalities and exploits more than if we'd said their full names. In Kathy Zuckerman's case, her nickname, given to her by Tubesteak on the beach in Malibu (it means "girl midget," owing to her tiny build), led to a series of movies that earned millions at the box office in the early 1960s and made surfing a cultural phenomenon. Just as with global soccer superstar Pelé, the media clamped on to their nicknames, and the surfers obliged, creating logos and even alter egos to fill the seemingly larger shoes they now occupied. The most memorable is certainly Mark Richards's MR logo, a mash-up between his initials and the iconic Superman design. He measured up to that lofty ID with his four-straight world titles, that's for sure.

I was the newest to join this exclusive club. *The California Kid.* Like the others, someone else dropped that nickname on me, in my case the ABC's *Wide World of Sports* commentators. Shortly after the 1978 Pipeline Masters, *Surfer* magazine followed suit, featuring me in a full-length story with a cover blurb that simply said, "Joey Buran: The California Kid." Anointed. Branded. Legitimized as a rising star on the world tour. I couldn't get enough. I wore my nickname like my father, a proud Marine Corps officer, wore his dress blues, bars and medals, feeling great honor in representing my state, and loving every bit of the notoriety and attention it shined upon me. As I was quickly learning, notoriety and attention went a long way in the surfing world, especially for a 17-year-old building his career and his brand, long before that word became everyday speech for Generations Y and Z. From our local surf spots to the full community at large, we take great pride in honoring and celebrating those nicknamed surfers (and some without nicknames) who stand out over a period of time; we call them "local legends." That tight personality-based community aspect is something I love so much about our lifestyle.

But as 1979 dawned, it was rather new stuff. *The California Kid.* Right on! Time to make the most of it!

I walked into 1979 with an immediate goal, the same goal that would propel me for the next five years: to remain the top-ranked Californian on the world tour. I succeeded in meeting my goal, missing out only in 1979, which prevented a clean sweep. I posted a few good results, but I found out that being 1978's rookie sensation with the distinctive nickname and proud confidence came at a cost: The older, veteran surfers knew who I was, and knew how to surf against me. No longer could I surprise them. I needed to make adjustments to my strategy, my approach to waves, my game, but I didn't.

Appropriately, my disappointing sophomore year on tour happened in the 1979 Pipeline Masters, when I lost in the first round. However, because I had surfed nearly the entire 13-event IPS tour, I accumulated enough points to finish 28th in the year-end rankings. Our champion was the man with the Superman logo, Mark Richards, who broke out of the lead pack with four victories and began his four-year stranglehold on the world title.

It was my second year in a row as a Top 30 world tour surfer. I was still the lone Californian who traveled major parts of the circuit, though more than a half dozen others were starting to jump in and enter events. I could feel it in my bones: The Californians were coming. Unlike their elders, even their older brothers or sisters, the young surfers were aggressive, uncorking moves influenced heavily by pool and ramp skateboarding that the famed

Lords of Dogtown and surfer-skaters like Jay Adams and Tony Alva were throwing down. They also embraced competition, rather than blowing it off or ridiculing it like the soul surfers had done throughout the '70s.

When 1980 dawned, I knew I would experience a different result. I set my mind to it, determined not to have a repeat of the disappointment I felt. It became my breakout year and firmly established me as the US mainland's premier star. The new year and new season always started with the Katin Team Challenge event, a non-IPS sanctioned event which was held in Huntington Beach, California. While surfing for my main sponsor, Team O'Neill Wetsuits, I made the finals, finishing in third place. During that final, I pulled off a rare perfect score of 20.0 on one of my waves, which is just as uncommon in surfing as a perfect score in ice skating or gymnastics. It was my best result since the 1978 Pipeline Masters Final and sent me onto the IPS tour with a much-needed boost of confidence.

My big break came that summer. After losing early in both events in South Africa, our next stop on the tour was beautiful Arpoador Beach in Rio de Janeiro, Brazil, for the Waimea 5000. Because Brazil was far out of the way of our typical circuit, requiring a long flight for a single event with a middle-of-the-road purse of $20,000, many of the top Australians who dominated the ratings—MR, Rabbit, Jim Banks and Simon Anderson—opted to head back home after South Africa and skip the Brazilian event altogether. Yet for Hawaiians, Californians, and of course aspiring Brazilians, this was a great opportunity to steal a big result and not have to again run the gauntlet of the seemingly endless Australian juggernaut. Only a few Australians made it to Brazil, and those who did were led by defending event champion and world-title contender, Cheyne Horan. Like me, Cheyne was just 19. Unlike me, he was the number-2 surfer in the world, not fighting to rise above the Top 30.

For me, the event was to be a make-or-break moment for my career. Despite the fact I now received wetsuits and a small monthly check from O'Neill Wetsuits, and had a couple other sponsors, my mom had been my primary financial sponsor for much of my pro tour journey. A week before I landed in Brazil, she called me long-distance while I was still in South Africa and sadly informed me that there was no more money to support my dream. If I wanted to keep my pro dream alive, she said, I needed to do well in Brazil.

She had lent me $3,000 to go to South Africa and Brazil and now I needed to get the job done on Arpoador Beach, which interestingly sat in the shadow of the famous Christ the Redeemer statue and rock. It was the last time she gave me a loan for my pro surfing career.

Talk about pressure! The threat of my competition was not true pressure. This was. I easily could've buckled under the financial weight, as so many young surfers would do when pursuing their world tour dreams, and no one would've looked down on me for it. But I had thrived on peer pressure, people telling me I couldn't do something and the like for years, and while I won't say I *enjoyed* pressure, I seemed to always go within myself, marshal together all my inner strength and determination to prevail, and get the job done.

This was one of those times. Knowing that there was "no tomorrow," I surfed with passion, flair—and urgency! The great reality chasing me throughout the event was not Cheyne, or the others, but the raw realization I just had to find a way to win. As the event unfolded, I proceeded to blaze through three rounds of top Brazilians to reach my second-ever IPS World Tour semifinal, my first in almost two years, since the 1978 Pipeline Masters.

Then the biggest test of all came to visit, when I came up against the clear favorite to win the event, Cheyne Horan. The waves were quite small, one to three feet at best, but still contestable in the waist-high range. Cheyne was in peak form, but at the same time, I was surfing at a level my career had never previously seen. Plus, I was accustomed to the shape and size of this small surf, having thrashed around in it for many, many mornings in my home Carlsbad waters between swells. Furthermore, the large Brazilian crowd was really behind me, cheering me on.

The judging panel, made up of mostly Brazilians, would decide the outcome of this very close heat. We were still years away from live computer scoring, so we would surf, compete, ride into the beach, and look toward the judges' table or place on the scaffold, waiting for their subjective decisions to be announced. This system still exists in boxing, UFC and MMA sports. While I felt sure of my wins in previous heats, I did not feel the same confidence from the heat with Cheyne. I knew it was close.

A few tense minutes later, they announced the winner of our man-on-man semifinal: *Joey Buran*. I was so stoked! I knew I was one step from being able to afford competing on tour for the rest of the year, one step from setting my amazing mom financially free of my surfing burden. And I'd surfed the final with those outcomes in mind. My decisive win in the final against the talented young local Brazilian, Ismael Miranda, was a mere formality. I won the final convincingly and, in doing so, became the third US mainlander and first Californian surfer to ever win an IPS World Pro Tour surfing event.

When I returned home, the first thing I did was repay my mom the $3,000. It felt so good to turn her belief in me into a big result, and to settle the score in such a way that Dianne Buran could truly say, "My son is a responsible adult now." You can give me all the props and congratulations you want, but the most important voice in my life then was my mom—and I always wanted her to feel she'd made the right decisions in letting me bail public high school for continuation school, then surf halfway across the world when I was supposed to be getting ready for my senior year of high school finals.

My dramatic victory in Brazil ignited not only me, but my Californian peers. It proved that our mission to successfully contend on the international world surfing stage was far more than a future dream of a bunch of stargazing kids. It was a reality! The victory injected a huge boost into my career, moving me all the way to number 14 in the world, while at the same time becoming an even bigger hero in the California surf world.

With the newfound confidence from winning Brazil, my surfing improved. I backed up that big result with a quarterfinal appearance in Japan, then flew to Hawaii with an extra beat in my step and made the finals of the Pipeline Masters for the second time in three years. No longer was I just a one-hit wonder, at Pipeline or anywhere else. I was quickly becoming an established threat for any surfer against whom I paddled out in our man-on-man heats, a format I absolutely loved, far more than the six-man heats. While we still used six-man heats in Hawaii, it was man-on-man everywhere else in the world after we made the main event. *Mano a mano.* What could be better?

As I headed home from Hawaii, just in time for Christmas, I was filled with the joy and ecstasy that comes from accomplishing a really difficult goal. Not only had I become California's first winner on the world tour, but I also broke another barrier, by finishing 13th in the world, which placed me in the prestigious Top 16. One of the top 16 surfers in the world? The most elite competitive wave riders on the planet? Me? At 19 years of age? Unreal! Not only that, but a Top 16 ranking was strategically all important. We received advanced seeding at every event on the upcoming 1981 world tour. Now over were my three years of surfing the grueling qualifying trials at every event, where danger lurked in every heat and losers received no prize money; this world is filled with thousands of pro golfers and tennis players who know the pain. I was now officially one of the very best surfers in the world—and California's duly seeded top-flight surfer on the IPS World Surfing Tour!

The other thing that improved markedly was my surfing style, technique and collection of maneuvers. I was in another world from that herky-jerky, aggressive kid in Carlsbad; about the only thing in common was my pervasive love for tube riding. I was a standout in most surfing conditions at all contestable sizes, but being a goofy foot and excellent tube rider, I became a contest favorite in barrels that broke to the surfer's left and spectator's right, like the Banzai Pipeline.

That said, my real strength was my sheer determination and competitive tenacity. It poured through me in waves, no pun intended, always a part of how I approached surfing and my career. My outgoing personality added to it, which certainly benefited me with the ever-increasing media coverage, sponsorship opportunities, and maintaining my status as the California Kid.

What I was already learning is one of the qualities that separates those who try to excel, or want to excel, or nearly excel, from those who *do* excel at their skill, talent or chosen goal—determination and tenacity. What are you going to do when you climb 99 percent of that mountain and still have ahead of you the final hard push to the summit? Especially when others around you are trying to do the same? How are you going to get there when you're exhausted, perhaps even burned out from the effort, yet know that finishing that final 1 percent and attaining your achievement is something you've envisioned for years?

This is where champions, and the best of the best in every walk of life, the true greats, separate themselves from those who are excellent or good. Rather than thrash and struggle against their exhaustion to wrap up that final 1 percent, they call upon their inner spirit and strength to *double down and increase their energy*, or their focus—time and time again. It is one of the core truths of those who succeed most in life, or achieve their ultimate dreams, and I was blessed to possess the needed determination and tenacity, as well as the instinct to push that final 1 percent.

Even so, a whole new group of young amateur kids I had never really competed against were now on the rise in California. They were surfing in a new organization, the National Scholastic Surfing Association (NSSA). The NSSA featured a National Team headed by two great Australian coaches, legendary pro surfers Peter Townend, the first IPS World Tour champion, and Ian Cairns, one of the best big-wave surfers in the world. PT and Ian knew the formula for achieving greatness and thus were equally as successful as coaches. After calling it quits for their full professional competition careers and expatriating from Australia in late 1978, they began to shape the young Californians of the future, instilling in them the Australian aggrostyle of surfing and competing. On top of that, they brought along their marketing and branding prowess as members of the heralded Bronzed Aussies, the first group of surfers to chase sponsors inside and outside the sport. They were about to fundamentally change the fortunes of professional and amateur surfing in California and the world.

When these young California rippers saw me, their reaction was not one of "oh my gosh, it's Joey Buran," like my achievements were beyond reach. Not at all. Instead, they knew, some quietly and others more boisterously, that they could achieve the same results as me—and possibly more. By early 1981, numerous smaller pro surfing events began popping up all over California. Led by a revived, rapidly growing surf industry based out of Southern California, pro surfing in America began to rise and gain notoriety. As the new year unfolded, I found myself regularly up against what seemed like an unending group of very talented hot young California shredders. Their talent was matched by their confidence, I was the California Kid they'd read about in the mags . . . and they all wanted to beat me. At times, many did.

However, I reminded them that the old guy—all of 20 years old—still held the higher hand, winning the Stubbies California Surf Trials at Lower Trestles, a premier regional series that sent its top finishers to the IPS-sanctioned Stubbies Surf Classic in Australia. I didn't need the wildcard to Burleigh Heads, since I was already a Top 16 surfer, but I definitely needed the validation I was still the Californian to beat. It was a very satisfying victory, and a rare chance for my hometown peers and up-and-comers in the exploding Carlsbad surf scene to drive 20 miles up the coast and see me in prime competitive form.

That year on tour, I once again finished 13th, a very respectful placing but, for me, very disappointing. I pride myself on continual improvement, but I didn't improve at all. However, in the otherwise lackluster down year of results, I still managed to hold on to my spot in the Top 16, mainly from the strength of my second-place finish to Terry Richardson in the OM Bali Pro and another top-ten result at Banzai Pipeline, my favorite wave on earth. This came despite a disastrous wipeout in the semifinals of the Pipeline Masters. To add injury to insult that same month, I also made a mental gaffe by arriving late and missing my heat in the Sunset Beach World Team Challenge. Not smart.

And then it happened. The inevitable. A young and extremely gifted surfer, Tom Curren, surfaced from the quiet soul surfing haven of Santa Barbara with a perfect blend of grace, style, balance, and dynamic, explosive moves. He also came from surfing royalty: His father, Pat, was a trailblazer, an absolute surfing legend, and one of the first to surf Waimea Bay in the late 1950s. Tom blended this perfect style with a low-key demeanor and unbelievable competitive instincts, and an assassin's will to win you'd never guess existed in the quiet, shy teenager.

Now Tom was making his pro surfing arrival official.

In 1981, at the age of 16, the young NSSA amateur won the prestigious Katin Pro-Am contest to start the year. He did so against a field that included many top world tour pros, me among them. Yes, we had already started hearing about this rising megastar and tried not to think of his name and what his future held, but by January of 1982, he could not be ignored: Tom Curren, the future three-time world champion and iconic legend, had arrived. He was so unassuming on the beach, and yet so ruthless and artistic in the water. So stunning was his surfing that at the age of 16 everyone with a pair of eyes and any understanding of surfing ability knew his destiny would be winning world titles. The only questions: How soon? And how many before he called it quits?

Even so, I was still the California Kid, the current California surf hero, and to my credit, I believed I could hold him off. My determination, tenacity and desire to continue being the best carried a lot of energy and weight, and Curren and everyone else knew I was a very tough competitor and hard to beat in a contest. Plus, I had already beaten him in a regional Pro-Am final the year before.

However, I, too, saw the future. I was pretty much at my peak, atop my personal Mt. Everest, whereas he was sitting at Everest Base Camp, harnessing his forces to make what would become the biggest climb any pro surfer ever experienced to date.

And, like everyone else, I was vulnerable to basic human emotions. Like jealousy. I grew really jealous of Curren—jealous of his graceful communion with the wave, the ease with which he executed the most difficult moves, the sheer talent oozing from him, a style that was more the brushstrokes of a masterful artist than aggressive wave-smacking. Maybe most of all, I was jealous that the whole surfing world was already anointing him a future world tour champion. After I'd fought like a club-level boxer who made it big to bust down the doors for Californians on that same circuit, a *Rocky* story played out on the waves.

I'd been banging on that door and barging through it for four and a half years. This kid from Santa Barbara was just getting started. It didn't seem fair. Not at all. As Curren gained momentum and deserved accolades, plus growing media adoration for his modest demeanor and incredible blend of grace and aggression, I was in the midst of a horrible slump. Bad, bad timing.

I had other issues too. Physical issues. Shortly before leaving for Japan, I had my four wisdom teeth pulled, major dental surgery, which left me in plenty of pain and discomfort. Once I arrived in Japan, still hurting from that surgery, a huge swell hit Chiba. My first heat was against Mike Benavidez, a Los Angeles South Bay surfer and longtime personal rival. From 1978 through 1984, I was the top-ranked Californian on the world tour—except for 1979, when Benavidez finished higher than me. We'd been at it for a long time.

On this day, though, I didn't feel well, I struggled in the massive surf, and Benavidez clearly defeated me. What a disappointment. That should not have happened. Then the swell dropped, the surf cleaned up and pumped in one great high-performance wave after another, and Curren seized the day, beating everyone.

I felt sick to my stomach. I'd needed more than three years to capture my first world tour event. Curren did it on his second attempt. Despite being on tour for only the final third of the season, he managed to break the Top 20, finishing 19th. He made winning look so easy, while I struggled to advance through any heats—and entered the Pipeline Masters far from guaranteed of finishing the year in the all-important Top 16.

The way I was surfing, even I wasn't sure. My typical confidence and self-assurance fought hard against the doubters, both on the beach and within myself. "I crawled into this hideous shell," I told *Breakout* magazine. "Suddenly, I felt like I was nobody and Tommy Curren was everything. I felt like quitting surfing."

It would take a conversation with a missionary on a flight back from South Africa, and then an epic surf session with Curren in Mexico, to overcome the greatest of all challenges to my surfing career. My own self.

I did indeed hold on to that Top 16 seed, but after losing in the first round of the Pipeline Masters, my confidence receiving another hard jolt backward, it required a minor miracle. To stay in the Top 16, I would need to advance through at least one round in the season finale, the World Cup at Sunset Beach. The result seemed simple and obtainable enough, but there was a problem: I had never advanced through a heat in all my previous Sunset events. Not one. I knew the lineup of waves fairly well, but throughout my career, I had yet to taste any success at the notoriously tricky and scary wave. A sinking feeling came over me: *I'm not going to be able to do this. At least not without some help.*

I'd never asked for help as a pro, believing my skills, confidence and ability to drive myself to continually improve sufficient. But we all need to reach out at times in our lives, and I was smart enough to realize this was one of those times. And I did, making the very wise decision to ask 1976 World Champion Peter Townend to become my coach. PT was the man who turned all those young Californians on the NSSA National Team into clear and present dangers to me and the other tour veterans.

To my relief, he said, "Yes."

It is not an exaggeration to say he helped save my career. Advancing through that first heat at Sunset meant everything to my future as a Top 16 surfer and the highest-paid Californian in competition (with Curren right on my tail). PT's direction was the difference. I will never forget his instruction. He told me to ride a bigger board than normal, paddle out behind fellow competitor Dane Kealoha, already a living Hawaiian legend and master at Sunset Beach. "When he stops, paddle twenty feet farther out past him and wait for the next set of waves," PT said.

Then PT, a man with boundless confidence and bravado himself, declared confidently the first great wave of the heat would come right to me, as if summoned, and that I would catch and control it before anyone else. That would get me into perfect rhythm for the rest of the heat. "And you'll win the heat," he concluded.

I could scarcely believe it a little while later when I found myself dropping in on that first big wave of the heat, with Dane Kealoha looking at me from the side, an astonished expression on his face! I could imagine the questions racing through his mind: *What you even doing out here, Pipeline boy?! How you know where to take off?* It all went according to plan as I won one of the most important heats of my career and secured my spot in the Top 16 for the third-straight year.

After that heat, I knew my career was about to experience a full revival and that the legendary first World Pro Surfing Champion, Peter Townend, would be there by my side to help me revive it!

My career wasn't the only thing that would experience a sea of change involving PT. The entire sport was about to be revolutionized—and with it, an entire industry and lifestyle that would sweep not only the sports world, but also our culture.

8

THE WILD, WILD WEST

It's easy to view my surfing and ministerial careers, and my life, as a series of bridges.

As an aggressive, energized and occasionally obnoxious kid in Carlsbad, I bridged the gap between anticontest, antimaterialistic soul surfing and maneuver-driven, contest-oriented power surfing. Then I stretched out to become the connective competition tissue between California, and the US mainland, to the rest of the world tour. By 1981, when the new generation of hungry, eager and talented NSSA surfers started turning pro, I straddled two different eras—the old and the new. Funny to use the word "old" when I was 20, but a generation in competitive surfing amounts to four or five years. I also crossed over from one version of the world tour to another, from the IPS to the Association of Surfing Professionals (ASP). Along for the ride were this hot new crop of competitors, the media, and board shapers like Simon Anderson, whose three-fin thrusters poured pure fire on the face of what was possible on a wave and launched us into degrees of performance we'd never seen before, after they hit the market in 1980.

I wasn't alone. Surfing was about to become big business, with surfers the central attraction on stages much bigger, more lucrative and more widespread than anything the sport had ever seen in the thousand years since Polynesian kings and queens invented board riding in what is now Hawaii. Not only that, but suddenly, we competed for sizable endorsement contracts that gave more riders the freedom to compete worldwide, the media took high note, and the surf companies themselves blasted into an economic stratosphere.

The 1980s had arrived. And with it, the Wild, Wild West of sports marketing, with Southern California the epicenter in more ways than one. We surfers represented the coolness factor, and as the California Kid, I began to find a new role bringing the old ways into the new. More bridge building, for sure.

In just four short years, pro surfing had grown up and completely changed. In so doing, Ian Cairns convinced the clothing company Ocean Pacific to sponsor his new surf tour, the ASP. It was the end of the old IPS Tour and the counterculture rebels of the '70s. We early trailblazers who had traveled the world like a circus, with few rules in the water and even fewer on land, had run our course. Pro surfing had grown up and now, in the early '80s, it was about money and sponsors—and lots of them! The new tour featured a pair of huge changes that built on spectator interest—up-to-the-moment computer scoring updates and the innovative priority buoy. This buoy was a much-needed feature intended to keep surfers riding waves, instead of fighting the all-too-familiar paddle battles and hassling for position. The message of the new ASP was *lead, follow, or get out of the way!*

Ian pulled off the vision of his new tour after the incredibly successful 1982 inaugural OP Pro in Huntington Beach. Off the credibility of that event, he was able to attain the key sponsors he needed. With this new tour in front of us, and new young stars like Tom Curren rising throughout the world, the future was looking very bright for pro surfing. Which meant more and more competition-hungry kids would pile into contests, all chomping at the chance to take down the world greats, make their statements, grab new sponsors from equally innovative companies eager to spend endorsement dollars. In other words, they and their sponsors figured out how to brand themselves long before everyone on social media described themselves as a "brand."

Long before social media existed, for that matter.

The seeds for surfing's commercial explosion in the 1980s—and the larger explosion of sports marketing—started hitting the ground before the turn of the decade, thrown down by a few intrepid, innovative minds. The way any great endeavor begins.

Back in Australia, Ian and PT, along with Mark Warren and Greg Hodges, started it all in 1975 when they formed the Bronzed Aussies. It was a surf team built on a new, brazen concept: We're professional athletes, we're going to market ourselves like the country's athletes, we're going to advertise our sponsors on our boards and clothing like race-car drivers, and we're going to become media savvy. While winning events all over the world. The Bronzed Aussies caught the attention of the surfing world in a real love-hate way, flying right into the heart of the anticommercial soul surfer versus procommercial contest surfer battle. But it also gave surfwear, wetsuit and surfboard companies a physical, tangible way to promote their products, not only by sponsoring or cosponsoring events, but endorsing the four BAs. Who then became media spokesmen.

When Ian and PT called it quits as regular competitors in 1979 and moved to California, they saw unchartered territory in the surf sports marketing arena. I already knew both of them from competing against them, and I loved what they talked about. Bigger sponsorships? More surf companies involved? Convincing the media to cover surfing as a *sport* instead of countercultural lifestyle? *New events and possible tours?*

I watched them create minicircuits and stand-alone events, more than a little curious as to why two Aussies were doing this on California's shores instead of, say, in New South Wales or Queensland. They turned the NSSA from a cool school-based amateur organization, a new wrinkle to what the WSA and Eastern Surfing Associations offered, into a farm system for future professional surfing stars almost overnight. Not only did they teach techniques, maneuvers and contest strategies to these eager Gen X kids, but also how to do interviews, how to represent yourself as an athlete, and how to *represent your sponsors.*

At the time, few surfers held paying sponsorships. Or even good equipment deals. I'd kept my sponsorship with Natural Design Surfboards and Midget Smith since 1976, when he first lent me a board at the US Surfing Championships in Texas, and Mom and I drove up to his shop and he signed me. He had since become the Town and Country licensee on the US mainland, and I maintained a strong connection with him throughout my career. I did switch to Takayama Surfboards in 1979 to ride for my friend, the Hawaiian short- and then longboard legend Donald Takayama, but went back to Town and Country in 1980.

I also was sponsored by O'Neill Wetsuits, a foundational industry giant with one of the greatest slogans ever: "It's always summer on the inside." For Santa Cruz surfer Jack O'Neill and his buddies, that meant everything after spending their entire lives freezing in the Northern California waters to catch waves, then wrapping flannel shirts and blankets around themselves and stoking up huge bonfires just to get warm afterward. And I thought my Sand Crab days in Carlsbad were cold! In 1952, Jack invented the modern-day wetsuit, and now, O'Neill was considered the company with which you wanted to be associated in surfing. They cosponsored the Stubbies Surf Trials, a new series of regional events for surfers trying to kindle careers. They were on the cutting edge from technology to contests, and I wanted to be a part of their family. They signed me to a two-year deal that paid $100 per month—my first paid sponsorship. I was ecstatic! Not only did I represent them in contests, but I was featured in a lot of ads and became fully connected with the surfing world through Pat O'Neill, Jack's son and one of the great business titans of our sport.

When my O'Neill contract ran out in 1981, I'd reached two Pipeline Masters finals, won the Waimea 5000 and was about to win the Stubbies California Surf Trials, by now the hottest regional competition in the world. Body Glove Wetsuits, another family-owned business run by the Meistrells, came along and paid me $300 per month, then made me the star of the team! I also signed a clothing deal with Daystar Offshore, which felt like a perfect fit for two reasons: My hometown surf shop was Offshore Surf Shop (not affiliated), and my favorite contest was now named the Offshore Pipeline Masters.

At the time, my sponsorship portfolio was considered upper level among pro surfers anywhere: a few hundred bucks a month, products, and incentives for appearing prominently in surfing magazines. That would soon change.

During all of these changes, I started to recognize an entrepreneurial spirit within myself too. However, as a 20-year-old rising up the world tour ratings ladder with a compulsion to win the Pipeline Masters, plus my growing desire to serve and lead, I knew my time to join the business side of things was down the line.

Turns out I wasn't alone. Not by a long shot. Successful sports marketing and branding, and the benefits to teams, athletes, owners and companies, require a few key things to come together: Investment money. Related companies ready to push the sport through their products, advertisements and promotions. Athletes who endorse and fuel fandom and public attention through their presences and performances. And, importantly, their media savvy. Media willing to cover the companies, athletes and events in a supportive way.

But the catalyst of it all was location, location, location. The saloon doors of the Wild, Wild West began to swing wide open on the beaches of Southern California, where the eyes of the world turned from Hollywood to Malibu, Huntington Beach to San Diego, to see who was cool, what was hot, and how they could jump in. We had surfing, we had the radical new endurance sport of triathlon, we had the blazing-hot rec sports of skateboarding and bodyboarding, we had breakthrough athletes with strong media presences like myself, skateboarding greats Jay Adams and Tony Alva and *wunderkind*

Tony Hawk, and we had Julie Moss, a Carlsbad surfer who'd just stunned 40 million viewers on *Wide World of Sports* by crawling across the line to finish second in the Ironman Triathlon in Kona, Hawaii. Forget about the ski jumper crashing and burning on the launch on the *Wide World of Sports* open. Julie's was the true "agony of defeat," to use the back half of the show's motto.

Instead, it became the front half—"the thrill of victory." "When I recovered and flew home to Carlsbad, I had no idea what I'd done," Julie recounted in her 2018 memoir, *Crawl of Fame*. What she'd done was instantly turn triathlon and endurance sports into worldwide spectator *and* participatory sports. And, within a month, picked up a hefty endorsement contract from a Japanese company.

The fact Julie's rise to fame happened at the same time as surfing was on the rise was no coincidence. People were ready not only to watch sports, but participate in them. And what was more California lifestyle than surfing? Or a bigger test than triathlon or marathon running? Especially with surfers leading the way, as was the case with triathlon.

The surfing companies popped up—fast. Longtime owners of the clothing space, Hang Ten and Ocean Pacific, ramped it up in different ways. Hang Ten made a concerted effort to reconnect with a core surfing audience they'd largely lost when the label started selling en masse throughout the country—not cool to a core surfer. They desperately wanted to see their line hanging on surf shop racks again—the place a core surfer bought his or her clothes—so they devised a campaign with themed, crafty storytelling ads for *Surfer* and *Surfing* magazines, and little stories on their clothing hangtags. That was innovative. They dove into contest sponsorship as well with the Hang Ten Grand Prix Series, a precursor to the US Pro Tour—and then signed me for $2,000 a month, an unheard-of salary that made me the highest-paid pro surfer on the mainland. Hawaii's Buzzy Kerbox took it another way, riding his good looks and a strong IPS contest résumé into a modeling contract with Ralph Lauren that he still enjoys to this day.

OP took an even bigger leap to reclaim *its* rack and shelf space in a rapidly growing surf shop market, signing on as an NSSA sponsor, advertising heavily in the surf magazines, and then crushing it with perhaps the most important sports marketing coup in surfing history—signing Tom Curren to a reported long-term, *six-figure* contract in the summer of 1982, then hosting the inaugural OP Pro before 100,000 sun-soaked, surf-crazed fans at Huntington Beach Pier, in Surf City USA, the beating heart of the sport. I'd just made major news getting a five-figure annual contract from a single surfer, but in this round of the OP versus Hang Ten wars, the Coke and Pepsi of surfing in the 1970s and early 1980s, the California Kid versus the Heir Apparent, OP threw down the larger contract. While Cheyne Horan and Becky Benson were enjoying their hard-fought wins, and with OP's significant backing and blessing, Ian made his big move—and the IPS became the ASP World Tour, a circuit set up to grow professional surfing.

The Wild West really ramped up. Four established surf companies with Australian roots—Rip Curl, Quiksilver, Stubbies and Billabong—set up major operations in California. All of them sponsored events on the new ASP World Tour as well as the top surfers on it. They, along with OP and Body Glove, and a pair of core companies started by cousins Michael and Shaun Tomson, Gotcha and Instinct, formed a very strong industry to handle what happened next: a tidal wave of interest in the clothing, lifestyle, sport and even personalities that stretched from sea to shining sea, and all points in between. Within a couple of years, the surf industry jumped from the province of its hardcore customers to a multibillion-dollar presence in the economy, the biggest story of the decade in sports marketing.

I was right in the middle of all of this as a competitor, then a promoter, but always a media presence. I've always had the gift of gab, I'm curious and inquisitive to a fault, I love history, and I really wanted to see my sport portrayed as just that—a competitive sport.

Media buy-in was a huge part of the surf culture's economic explosion. And the way we were perceived by the general public as surfers. When I turned professional in 1978, we pored through *Surfer* and *Surfing* magazines, *Eastern Surf* in Florida and a few newspaper columnists who covered the sport; ABC was in its last year of covering the Pipeline Masters on *Wide World of Sports*. By 1983, the scene was totally different: *Surfer* and *Surfing* were joined by *Breakout* magazine in California, *U.S. Surf* on the East Coast and perhaps another dozen regional mags. No less than 15 newspaper sportswriters were writing surf columns; many of these guys covered all sports, not just surfing, an important point in how they portrayed us. Two of them went on to promote regional, national and ASP surfing tournaments, one in Hawaii and one in California, the Californian a member of my PSAA team in 1985. The surfing mags were joined by the illustrious *Sports Illustrated*, which covered the OP Pro, Stubbies Pro and Hawaiian events, and other mainstream magazines with huge national readerships.

But the biggest boost of all, and certainly my favorite, came from the interaction between music and video. MTV had just launched—and what could possibly be cooler than MTV videos of the breakthrough new-wave bands shot to surfing backdrops? MTV saw it that way too and started turning up on the beach. More and more videos featured surfing themes, backdrops or cultural references; these were to the early 1980s what hip-hop is to today.

Meanwhile, on the competitive front, a crew of young guys from southern Orange County showed up at the 1982 Stubbies California Surf Trials, calling themselves DynoComm Productions. Their ringleader, producer Alan Gibby, was an avid San Clemente and Dana Point surfer who wanted to see his sport brought back to TV. He convinced Stubbies executives Mike and Greg Bechelli, and contest director Jim Watson—yet *another* Carlsbad local; see a pattern forming?—to let them shoot the contest as both a video and sports show for film costs and clothing for Gibby's team. A week later, Gibby and company were on the beach at the OP Pro—and for the next 30 years, DynoComm-produced surf contest programming aired on ESPN, the BBC, Hawaiian television with distributed news clips fed to network news and sports magazine shows. DynoComm later did the same for skateboarding and snowboarding.

DynoComm's presence was followed by another media forerunner, Prime Ticket, best known for covering LA Lakers games during their showtime era of Magic Johnson, Kareem Abdul-Jabbar, James Worthy and Pat Riley. Don Meek, an executive at Prime Ticket, was very close with the Body Glove crew, as well as being a surfer, so he talked higher-ups into bringing the show onto the sand. They wasted little time hiring PT as a cohost and announcer for both surf programs and tournaments, an ingenious move. PT, who has no problem promoting his own brand, also happens to be one of the greatest promoters and positive forces on pro surfing the sport has ever seen, first in Australia, and for the last 45 years in the US.

The final piece of the media puzzle was the radio stations. We were richly blessed in the early 1980s to have a pair of stations, 91X in San Diego and KROQ in Los Angeles, that featured surf reports *and* DJs who surfed. Not to mention the music. Surf music originated in Southern California in the late 1950s and early 1960s, becoming immensely popular. It was still popular in a classic-rock sense in the early '80s, but my generation wanted something else—and we got it with new wave. New wave and surfing? A perfect fit. Contest promoters like Jim Watson figured that out too, and Watson quickly signed on 91X to be the official station of the Stubbies California Surf Trials. Which led OP to sign on KROQ for its massive tournament in Huntington Beach. My perceived place as a jack-of-all-trades came rising forth again; thanks to my stature in the sport, talking about it, knowing its history *and* making many of the headlines in the moment, *both* stations brought me on as a regular guest commentator, which led to paid jobs commentating at surf events in which I didn't compete.

I can tell you, when I turned pro, *none* of these opportunities existed for me. They were on the other side of the horizon. Now, just a few years later, I was an athlete sponsored by a clothing company, wetsuit company and board manufacturer, and was a paid commentator and a paid guest commentator with California's two hottest radio stations. And a four-time Top 16 world tour performer, still atop the ranks in California, though Curren and his peer group were catching up fast. Talk about being in the right place at the right time to learn about entrepreneurship!

Our sport had truly outgrown its old clothes. We entered our new phase on all cylinders, with everyone from athletes to sponsors to promoters to media members super stoked and constantly pushing the envelope. I knew, if I was going to be a part of this next chapter, I needed to find another gear, and up my game. I had to get better and that was what I fully intended to do.

Fortunately for me, time would prove that the best years of my career were still in front of me.

9

MOST IMPROVED

The excitement and anticipation surrounding the future of professional surfing were at an all-time high as 1983 began. There was more money and events involved than ever, and the anticontest vibe that lingered into the late '70s and early '80s completely dissipated. Big crowds, bright wetsuits and clothes, new-wave music, big hair, monthly global and regional surf magazines, and the action sports industry trade shows had all arrived. So had pro surfing. It was legit, and it was here to stay.

Australia continued to emphatically rule the sport of pro surfing, right up to the Australian who now operated the new ASP World Tour from his offices in Huntington Beach. Australia quite literally owned pro surfing. With the best surfers in their stead, the new ASP World Surf Tour made a bold and radical decision and restructured the tour so that it ended not with the epic big-wave events in Hawaii, but in Australia. Instead of closing out the year at Banzai Pipeline, it would now end at the famed Bells Beach break on Australia's southern coast, in Victoria.

My shoulders slumped when I heard the news; besides hoisting the Pipeline Masters trophy as the winner, I wanted to raise it as the winner of the last event on tour. That would not be happening.

Australia's beach culture is part of its national identity. It has been since 1915, when Duke Kahanamoku came to Oz and surfed with Isabel Letham and Tommy Walker, among others. Since the pro tour's formation, and even a few years before, the media covered Australian surfing tournaments like US media covers baseball and football. By 1983, surfing possessed innumerable veteran national stars like Rabbit Bartholomew, Mark Richards, and Cheyne Horan, and behind them many others who just kept on coming!

None broke out further or excelled more than Tom Carroll, an exceptional goofy foot who made it his mission to become the first goofy-foot world champion—and delivered. Twice. I'd thought about hitting that milestone many times in my five years on the tour, but it was Carroll and not Buran whose name went into the history books.

The performance dominance from "down under" was largely driven by another huge impact on the entire sport, Simon Anderson's three-fin thruster surfboard. He wasn't the first surfboard shaper to think of and try a three-finned surfboard; the Campbell brothers were turning out three- and even four-fin boards in California throughout the 1970s, and other prototypes pocketed the waters of Hawaii, Australia, the West Coast and South Africa. Simon, himself a great world tour competitor, was the one who perfected it. Then he started beating everyone in the world with it!

Not only would the 1983 tour end in Australia, but it would become a split-year tournament and *begin* in Australia as well. Ian Cairns made this decision for calendar restructuring purposes, but these events would not be part of the new season world tour rankings. They became known as the Australian Grand Slam of Surfing. There were some sound reasons for this decision, but in hindsight, this part of the ASP plan did not pan out well for the sport. As legendary as Bells was and still is, it simply could not match the intensity and drama of the Pipeline. Within a few short years, the tour would recalibrate, return to the calendar-year schedule and once again conclude at Pipeline. Though it all seemed strangely different from the traditional ending on the North Shore of Oahu with the Pipe Masters, there was still tremendous excitement for where these new elements were going to carry all of us in pro surfing's future.

I wanted to be a big part of it. That meant there was only one direction to go. Up. Especially after my very dissatisfying 1982 season. I now had a rival threatening my perch atop the competitive scene in California, and my stature among mainland surfers on the world tour. Even though I'd again finished in the Top 16, it also burned me up that people thought I was over the hill or didn't possess the old drive and determination to win. I was 22 years old. How can a 22-year-old be seen in this way?

Well, by looking at my inconsistent results. At a time in my career when I should have been driving toward my peak, I was stuck in neutral, more worried about Tom Curren than about my own game. Which, as any athlete knows, tends to seriously and negatively affect performance.

It was imperative I turned my act around and create success in 1983. Sure enough, when my mind again synced up with my capabilities, and my heart kicked in with the inner resolve to do whatever it took to succeed, things started happening.

In early January, while preparing for the Australian Grand Slam, I experienced the first and only true injury of my career. That winter was one of the best on record for large waves in California. In what is known as an El Niño condition, massive storms in the Northern Pacific Ocean sent us relentless northwest swells the size of two-story houses along the Southern California coast, mighty enough to cause serious damage to age-old piers in Oceanside, Ocean Beach, Redondo Beach, Huntington Beach and Malibu. Everyone who paddled out in the winter of 1982 to '83 has plenty of stories to tell their kids and grandkids today, I assure you. During one of these swells, I collided with another surfer at the famous Swami's Point in Encinitas. The pain ripped up and down my chest cavity, knocking the wind right out of me. When I bellied onto shore, got to a doctor and took X-rays, one of my fears was confirmed:

A cracked rib. For the first time in my entire career, I was out of the water for six weeks. That included the first event or two of the four-event Australian Grand Slam.

So much for stomping my comeback!

In the past—even as recently as the past year—I would've kicked and screamed to the high heavens about such a significant injury happening at such a crucial time in my career. Anger and frustration would have boiled through me. I might have blamed the surfers next to me at Swami's, plus God and country for hampering my serious attempt to regain my mojo, my competitive fire, my place in the world and national pecking order. When you put your whole life into one basket, as I did with surfing, and your basket is cracked, life can be a scary place.

Except I didn't. With my downtime came some serious self-reflection. As I rode out the clock on my recovery period (after all, there were no medical shortcuts to healing from cracked ribs, then or now), I committed to ride surfboards made exclusively by Oceanside local Mike Baron. We were already good friends and held a strong mutual respect. Beyond that, he was a fantastic surfboard maker and a pro surfer in California, so he knew what I needed. We began experimenting with the new design of four-fin surfboards, which turned out to be a success. A win. I also continued to work regularly with Peter Townend as my coach, at a time when very few surfers had coaches. Another win. My injury also caused me to prioritize my physical well-being for the first time. I began to seek guidance in health, nutrition and overall body care. Encinitas chiropractor Chris Miller gave me much more awareness of my diet, stretching and the physiology of my body. He made a big impact on my health, which I have prioritized since. Yet another win. These individuals became my new support team, which made me feel more professional as well. Surfing wasn't just an individual sport anymore. Not for me, anyway. Not for a lot of other serious competitors either. I now had a whole team of talented and dedicated people cheering me on and helping me to move forward in my career and reach my goals.

This was the full reset of my career I desperately needed. I just didn't expect it to happen out of the water. In retrospect, I can't help but think this was another path God presented me, since I never planned to work so closely with all three guys before the injury. But it's the path that turned my career around, and with it came a necessary life adjustment.

By this time, most people perceived Tom Curren as California's new top surfer. Tom was the talk of the surfing world—and rightfully so! While I was forced to sit and wait for my ribs to heal, Tom headed for Australia to compete in the Australian Grand Slam. Wouldn't you know it? He won the first event in Sydney. Then he finished third on the Gold Coast. For many, it seemed unbelievable he was really that good. In his first pro events in Australia, he made it clear he was not just an American honorable mention but a global phenom coming for it all, wins and world titles!

I was quite jealous of his success, but in this, I was not alone! My jealousy would soon eat me up—and lead to another breakthrough moment that propelled me forward.

But first, a word from my main sponsor, Hang Ten. They wanted to cut my salary in half, from $2,000 a month to $1,000 a month, just as other surf companies were paying top surfers *increasing* amounts of money. Their big investments in core surf shops through ads and sales pushes, with me the face of the campaign, hadn't worked out, they said. When your brand isn't in the core shops, you lose identity with the hardcore surf crowd—and they were pinning it on me in a soft-landing sort of way. They made it a point to add that my surfing seemed to be on the decline, and Tom Curren was on the rise.

Ouch!

"No," I told them. "I will not renegotiate." And I didn't, holding firm until walking away from Hang Ten shortly thereafter, one of their final core links to surfing gone after the brand had represented so much of California's surf identity in the 1960s and 1970s. If you were a junior high or high school kid in Carlsbad or any other coastal town in that era, and you weren't wearing Hang Ten shirts with their signature bare-feet logo, well, you didn't fit into the beach scene.

I eventually made it to Australia for the finale of the Australian Grand Prix, only to draw none other than Tom in my first event back from my injury. It took him little effort to soundly beat me and seal his place as the overall Grand Slam champion. He was 19. As always, I was confident I would win, but even I didn't need the new revolutionary live computer scoring to tell me Tom was beating me. And that was it, all the way to Australia to surf one heat and get beaten by my personal California rival, everyone's new favorite surfer on planet Earth. It was a humbling defeat for me, especially because he took me down in conditions that favored my surfing, the long lefts of Narrabeen Beach in Sydney.

My jealous streak over Tom's quick ascension to the top, aided by my mediocre 1982 season and rib injury, burned through me deeper and deeper. After I let it get to my head yet again on the South African leg of the ASP World Tour, I found myself sitting next to a missionary on the flight back to the US. I started telling him about my jealousy toward Tom.

The missionary promptly broke out a Bible and opened it up to some powerful scripture pertaining to jealousy. We read the passages together, I read them again when I got home, I soaked in reflection about how much my jealousy was hurting me—and then I got over it.

Despite now being in Curren's shadow, as the California summer arrived, my surfing looked fresh and strong! It felt that way too. Again I felt like that kid pulling off super-aggressive maneuvers and breaking down barriers, only these were barriers of limitation I'd started wrapping around myself, barriers formed by how deeply I took in others' expectations of me. When we do that, when we start bending to what others expect of us, we start to lose our authentic selves and the sharpness of our personal vision and purpose. In surfing, that translates to executing maneuvers you think the photographers want to see, the judges want to see. And it leads to a lot of pressure.

None of which I was feeling. Not like before. I was stoked to feel free again!

Many in the industry, media and water considered it too risky for me to be riding the new experimental four-fin board designs. Especially at the highest level of the sport. There we go with others' expectations again, but this time, despite the risk, I felt so good about my choice. The design was a good match for my hyperkinetic style of surfing. Using a video camera for the first time, I could watch my footage and make adjustments in my training. And so, for what seemed like the first time since maybe 1980, my surfing was truly progressing and improving. It was fresh and free. My personal life was in good order, and the fire again burned in my belly.

Time to prove to the world that I was still the California Kid and my best surfing was still in front of me. Despite not having any recent significant results in my career, I remained confident that somewhere in my future, I was still destined to win the Pipeline Masters.

In July, I had my first break. For two weekends in a row, with most of the world's top pros participating, I made back-to-back finals in California. After finishing second in the Manhattan Beach Hang Ten Pro, I followed it up by finishing second to Tom at the Ocean Beach, San Diego Hang Ten Pro. Rather than being bummed out by yet another man-on-man loss to Curren in that final, I took the positive view, greatly encouraged by reaching back-to-back finals since it had now been over two years since I made a pro final.

My next impactful moment happened south of the border, and had nothing to do with competition—but everything to do with Tom Curren. In fact, he was right there in Baja with me. I decided it was time to really get to know this quiet Santa Barbara kid phenom, to see how he ticked, to see what he was like when he wasn't crushing opponents in the water. It turns out he was harboring the same thoughts about me.

"It was sunny and a new south swell was hitting," I told *Breakout* magazine. "Tommy was on a full vertical assault, just crushing the lips. I had to surf above and beyond anything I've ever done backside just to keep up. I started pushing higher and higher for the lip and going out the back. Instead of snapping right when I got to the top of the lip, I was trying to go up and over it. He'd do the most outrageous bank and then I would equal it. The next wave he'd go beyond what I'd done. I saw waves he caught from the back, where his whole board was out of the back of the wave and he was throwing 12 feet of rooster tail and coming back down flawlessly."

It was the best backside surfing of my life. More importantly, Tom and I opened up to each other, talking about our lives, dreams and goals. To that, I also said in the article, "I sure hope we can keep that energy and pump each other like that for the rest of our careers, because if we do, the possibilities are frightening. It could end up what California's always wanted."

We kept up the energy. We pumped each other up. We propelled each other forward. And California experienced a summer surf season unlike any before, led by the surfers. After a good result in England, my focus and attention, as well as that of the entire world of surfing, was now set on Huntington Beach for the second annual OP Pro. The week before, one of the hungry up-and-comers from my home waters of Carlsbad and Oceanside, former bodyboarding champion Mike "Slambresi" Lambresi, made his switch to short boards complete by capturing the Stubbies California Surf Trials at Lower Trestles. With that, Slambresi served notice that he was determined for a piece of my California Kid pie, borne out a few years later when he won the US Pro Tour of Surfing overall title.

When we arrived in Huntington Beach, the scene was crazy, a surf scene gone mad in a great way. It was everything I could have ever imagined in an epic California event: Surf City USA, crowds topping 100,000, with sponsors on hand watching the action. There were also TV news crews, live radio reports from KROQ and others, a two-story scaffold for judges, commentators and officials, huge bleachers on the beach, and even some on the pier. It was unprecedented and indescribably amazing! Needless to say, we all wanted to perform and deliver in the clutch in front of those record crowds.

Over time, the OP Pro would give way to the US Open, which continues to be one of the most prestigious events in the world. For us, it was the world's top surfers, the typical '80s bikini contest, and the thousands of people screaming and cheering every cutback and shore-break barrel. As circumstances unfolded, the judges couldn't ignore the opinion of the crowd as they voiced their approval of the best rides. All of this worked to my advantage as I was cheered on by the hometown crowd and made my way through the draw to my first major world tour final since the 1981 OM Bali Pro. Could I finish the deal and walk away with a coveted ASP World Tour event title in my native California waters?

Sure—except wouldn't you know who was waiting for me in that final? Tom Curren! What a marquee showdown for the surfing world to digest and the California scene to celebrate: the California Kid versus the Future World Champ in the first all-Californian final in the seven-year history of the world tour. With thousands of spectators watching and waiting to see who was truly the top dog in California, we paddled out on that hot August afternoon to make surfing history. As we did so, I was certain that I was going to finally get Tom this time. And I had a good final, truly surfing well, strong enough to beat anyone else in the competition draw, even the mighty Aussies.

But not the already great Tom Curren.

How did he do it? Well, he pulled off an impossible reentry maneuver that put the crowd in an absolute frenzy. I simply had no way to respond to that defining moment. For the third time in six months, Tom Curren had defeated me man-on-man. He won the event, the top prize money, and a brand-new Dodge truck. What a difference from the couple thousand bucks and pats on the back I'd received in Brazil just three years before.

However, I didn't start kicking and screaming. I didn't let my jealous streak toward Curren impact my feelings or the strength of my own performance. That streak was gone. Truth be told, I was stoked to be in the

Huntington Beach Pier surf with him in an all-Californian final. My pride for my state, and how very far our community had come as an international juggernaut of high-performance surfers in just a few years, took away a lot of the sting of losing such a big event. Getting second didn't really bother me because of the respect I'd gained for Tom, the respect and the friendship. Of course I wanted to win, but it felt so great to be a part of the event, the crowd and all the energy on the beach. For that, I quietly thanked God.

Despite finishing second, I hit some major milestones. It was my third final of the year—a lifetime best. For the first time in my career, I was ranked firmly in the Top 10 in the world, holding down the number-8 ranking. Of course, Tom was right there in front of me at number 7.

As the Southern California coastline continued to buzz from a most incredible late summer, trouble brewed in Hawaii—and it erupted right over the other event that meant the most to me, namely the Pipeline Masters. As the new ASP World Tour continued to grow and thrive quicker than anyone thought conceivable, there was a lingering animosity from the old IPS tour directors, which was not only understandable but foreseeable. It wouldn't have mattered, except for one thing—those same IPS directors controlled the TV rights to the Hawaii events. Ian Cairns of the ASP and former IPS director Fred Hemmings, now lead producers of the Hawaiian events, could not find a middle-ground solution. Their inability to resolve it resulted in the Hawaiian events proceeding as scheduled, except the ASP World Tour prevented the Top 16 surfers from competing in those tournaments. *But these are the events we look forward to the most! The biggest waves, the most famous surf! And we can't surf?* We were told by the ASP that if we surfed the Hawaiian events, we would lose our world tour Top 16 seedings, which essentially would mean the end of our careers.

Well, I certainly was not going to risk that. It gave me great pain inside, but I bit the bullet and didn't surf the three events of what became known as the Triple Crown of Surfing.

When it was all said and done, three famed Top 16 Hawaiians broke the boycott, Dane Kealoha crossed the line and won the Pipeline Masters, then Michael Ho did the same and won the Duke Kahanamoku Classic at Sunset Beach. Joining them was Bobby Owens, the quiet but highly respected North Shore standout. Nobody knew what to expect of it, but in the end, they were all fined for breaking the boycott. Michael Ho promptly paid his fine, but Bobby Owens, who had intended to retire anyways, did not as a matter of personal principle. As for Dane, he refused to pay the fine and, in a turn of events that shocked us all, was stripped of his world tour seeding. The legendary surfer, still considered one of the greatest Hawaiian surfers of all time, ended his career in this manner. In future years, he would still compete in the Hawaiian events, but this was essentially the end of the road for the perennial world title contender.

As for me, it was yet another disappointment with Pipeline. The surf was marginal for the finals that year, but even so, it was surreal to watch Dane win it all while sitting on the beach, a few meters from those waves, with no chance to be in the mix. This was my 1983 Pipe Masters experience. While it was a bitter pill to swallow, I didn't allow it to dampen my enthusiasm or the momentum my career was enjoying.

It was now Christmas break, and the tour would be starting right back up in early January at one of the most unlikely places imaginable, Jensen Beach, in South Florida.

As 1984 began, all the world's best surfers descended on South Florida to the little town of Jensen Beach for the next major stop on the new tour and its final push toward Australia and the crowning of the 1983–84 World Surfing Championship. For the only time in my career, I was technically in the world title race! The world's best surfers had all arrived in Florida and we were all ready to go, except there was one major problem: The Atlantic Ocean had gone completely flat. Waves come to Florida in the summer and fall, primarily hurricane and tropical storm swells from the southeast. When winter weather arrives, the best one can hope for is a good wind swell or a major low spinning off the Carolinas that is about to reform as a Nor'easter and pummel New York and New England.

No such luck. Kirk Cottrell and his team at Island Water Sports, the biggest chain of surf shops on the East Coast, did their best to try and do something. They even drove large boats back and forth in the hope of generating rideable waves! Fortunately for all of us, just as the contest waiting period was winding down, a little wind swell snuck in, providing small but contestable two-to-three-foot waves. They held the entire main event in one day, 32 surfers in 31 heats—a first for all of us.

It worked out very well for me. In the early morning, I defeated future World Champion Derek Ho, then bumped off Florida legend Matt Kechele at noon, brought down Cheyne Horan in the afternoon and then Rabbit Bartholomew in the early evening. I was used to surfing in small, beach-break conditions in California, and putting in long hours doing so. My degree of fitness was strong—and it showed. I advanced to the final, where who awaited me but soon-to-be World Champion Tom Carroll? In the waning hours of daylight, I took him to the edge but lost a close final.

Still, my result brought with it huge implications. A week later, I followed up the Florida success by winning the Katin Team Challenge in Huntington Beach. While the Katin is not a world tour event, it is a California classic that draws the best surfers in the world. Winning the Katin had been a longtime career goal of mine. I was stoked! In the first two events of the new year, I was firing on all cylinders and only one man, Tom Carroll, had been able to beat me. My four-fin surfboards were working fantastically, as I was surfing by far the best in my career. My confidence was booming, limitless. I was truly at the peak of my career.

Next up? The trip to Australia for the final three events, to finish off this sizzling hot streak with strong showings in the same events I couldn't surf the year before due to the cracked rib. Also, I wanted to excel at a place where I had historically struggled to compete successfully. My previous poor results in Australia were not so much because I had not surfed well, but because there were just so many good Australians I had to compete against. It appeared as though there was one thing they all had in common: They wanted to beat the California Kid. So they surfed their best, in some cases their lifetime best.

After the first two events in Australia, I was still ranked in the Top 10 and coming off my best Australia result ever, a quarterfinal finish in Sydney, where, yet again, I lost to Tom Carroll. That mathematically eliminated me from world title contention. I still held two primary goals headed into the final event of the season at Bells Beach: to finish in the Top 10 globally, and finish as the top Californian on tour. If I could finish ahead of Tom Curren in the Rip Curl Pro at legendary Bells Beach and its powerful right-hand waves, I would control my destiny. I was presently ranked 7th, just in front of Tom, who was 8th.

Well, fate and destiny wanted in on this juicy scenario—and sure enough, Tom and I found ourselves paddling out against each other, this time in the Round of 16. As with all the other man-on-man meetings against Curren, I was certain I would beat him. I paddled out full of confidence into conditions that accentuated Tom's strengths and magnified my weaknesses. Even so, I was just so certain I would win! Alas, within ten minutes of the start, he posted two near-perfect scores, effectively ending the contest.

Even so, what I remember most about that heat is I kept trying to improve my scores, and never quit. With little chance of winning and changing the inevitable outcome, the pressure of holding my rating off and my own internal pressure released as well, my last two waves turned out to be the best two of the heat. But for the fourth time, I lost to Tom in a man-on-man heat.

Still, it did nothing to diminish the shining truth: I'd completed the best year of my career after beginning it with a cracked rib while trying to clear the bad taste of 1982 out of my mouth. In many ways, I felt like a phoenix, the mythical Greek bird that rises from the ashes. But I'd been giving more and more thanks to God, and let's face it: I didn't get to this point in my career on my own.

I arose the next morning, Easter Sunday, for a sunrise surf with my good friend from Oceanside, rising star Mike Lambresi, who would go to win three US Pro Tour titles. I was relaxed and enjoying the beautiful day; my 1983–84 season was now officially over. I was in a good mood knowing that the worst I could do on the rankings was 9th. After six years on the world tour, I had finally cracked the Top 10! Also, the night before, while looking at various year-end point scenarios, I had figured out a detail previously missed. Despite defeating me the day before, Tom Curren had not passed me on the year-end ratings. He would still need to advance one more heat to move past me into 7th place or better.

Tom paddled into Bells Beach surf a heavy favorite against Glen Winton, a stout, squat Australian with the mysterious nickname, "Mr. X." To everyone's shock and surprise, Winton did it! He beat Tom in that Easter Day quarterfinal! When I showed up later in the day to watch the event final, I was stunned to look at the large Bells Beach scoreboard and see that Winton had defeated Curren. Then I realized I had finished 7th in the world—one spot in front of Tom! Together, we became the first Californians ever to crack the world tour Top 10. That I was 7th and he was 8th made for a very enjoyable Easter Sunday evening!

Later that week in Sydney, at the ASP awards banquet, Tom Carroll was crowned as World Champion of Pro Surfing, officially ending the four-year reign of the great Mark Richards. At the same event, I was recognized as the Most Improved Surfer. In my rookie season on tour back in 1978, I had been recognized by the IPS World Tour as the Most Inspirational Surfer. Both of these honors touched me to my core, because they not only represented good performance, but continual improvement in both my surfing and my attitude toward competition and toward others.

However, the biggest smile belonged to me alone. Despite the meteoric rise of my rival Tom Curren, the California Kid was still the number-one-ranked Californian surfer on the world tour.

Buran family archives

Mom and Dad's wedding in Cleveland, Ohio. Both my Catholic mom and patriotic dad were from the Midwest and their life values reflected the character of the region. They were extremely hardworking and penny-wise with finances. Through them, God and country, faith and patriotism shaped my personal character, convictions and worldview.

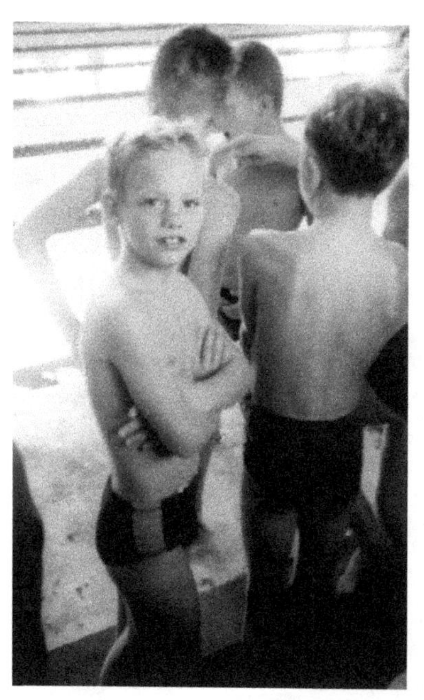

Buran family archives

Quantico, Virginia, and the Devil Dolphins Swim Team. Probably 1969, around age eight. I pretty much spent every day after school practicing for two hours in a 50-meter pool. My childhood swimming career instilled in me a sense of confidence from my successful results. No doubt my swimming background saved me on more than one harrowing occasion in the ocean.

My fifth-grade school photo, 1971, Charlottesville, Virginia. My dad was gone in Okinawa that entire school year. During this time, I had my first job, a paper route for the *Jefferson Journal*. Almost every Saturday I was at a swim meet with my mom, followed by Sundays with mandatory attendance at St. James Catholic Church with my brother and sister. I have always appreciated my Virginia heritage and memories.

Buran family archives

Buran family archives

Western Auto Baseball Team, 1973. That's me to the far left on my knees. Coach Max is in the back and the star pitcher, Bill Yehling, about whom I wrote, at Max's left. As a kid I enjoyed playing baseball and still occasionally watch it on TV. As a young player, it seemed that I was at best an average athlete, which makes my rise to the top of pro surfing seem even more improbable.

Buran family archives

Buran family photo, 1975. My dad, mother, brother Phil and sister Barbie. Phil was a mid-70s hippie, a straight-A student and a good surfer in his own right. Barbie also surfed, had reasonable success in competition and often tagged along with me and the Carlsbad boys on surf adventures. The board I'm holding was the first I received from my original sponsor, Midget Smith. By this time my bedroom walls were covered in surf photos and my surf dreams had no limits!

Photo courtesy Breakout *magazine*

With the Carlsbad crew at the California Pro, September 1978. To my left is good friend Billy Stang. Billy was highly respected for his ability to charge big waves, including those at Pipeline. For the next eight years he would be my Pipeline coach and mentor. He was the first to greet me on the beach after I won the 1984 Pipeline Masters, moments before he paddled out to pursue his own Pipeline dreams.

Photo courtesy Jeff Divine

1978 Pipeline Masters, the day I became the California Kid after legendary broadcaster Jim McCay gave me the title in front of the 30-million-strong ABC's *Wide World of Sports* national TV audience. It was a dream come true to be surfing in the final with my hero, the great Gerry Lopez. I paddled out, watched him drop into a wave—and hooted for him! I'm not sure how many other competitors did that while competing, but how could I not? He was my hero! To this day, I still consider it one of the top-five best experiences of my career.

Buran family archives

1979 in Japan with future two-time World Champion Tom Carroll. Tom and I always got along really well and enjoyed a good friendship with mutual respect. While my brashness and American patriotism rubbed a lot of Australians wrong, it never seemed to bother Tom. He just made sure he never lost to the California Kid, except at Pipeline, where he never beat me.

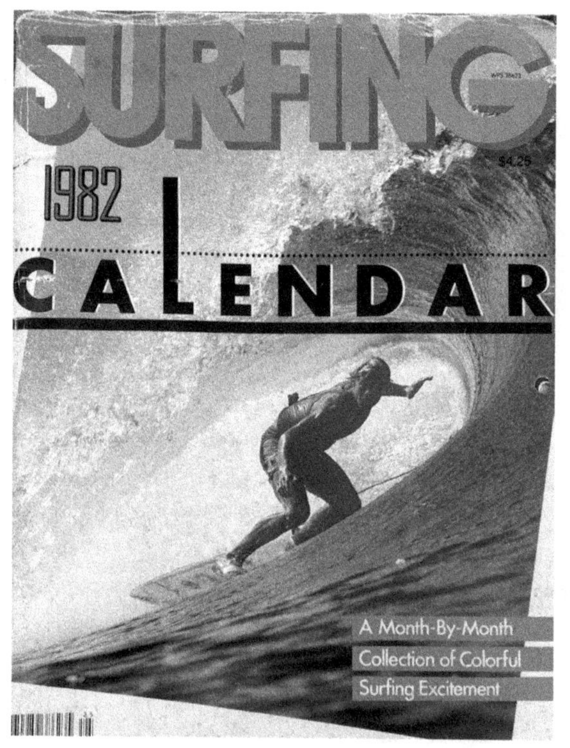

Photo courtesy Aaron Chang

1980 Pipeline Masters Final. The reigning world champion, Mark Richards, won this final in conditions that mostly favored the "backdoor" wave, which breaks to the surfer's right. I did better in this final than in 1978, but in a critical moment, I hesitated to take off on the best wave only to see MR catch it instead. I determined that I would never make this mistake again in any future Pipe Masters—and I didn't. A side note: Magazine cover shots were a big deal in the 1980s. I had five of them in my career. Stoked!

Photo courtesy Brian Beilmann

This disastrous wipeout with New Zealander Allen Byrne happened in the 1981 Pipeline Masters semifinals. The waves that day were terrifying and treacherous! It was also my first wave of the day. Not surprising, I never recovered, failing to qualify for the final. I woke up that morning sure that I would win, but my day turned into a nightmare and a loss that humbled me more than any other.

Buran family archives

1982 Body Glove ad. This ad boldly proclaimed I was California's #1 surfer. It would have been more believable had I not been mired in a career slump and Tom Curren not just won California's premier event at the time, the Katin Pro-Am. Even so, I was still Top 16 in the world, and a standout in the Pipeline lineup ... with the two best years of my career in front of me.

*Photo courtesy Allen Carasco/*Breakout *magazine*

Water-angle view at the legendary 1983 OP Pro in Huntington Beach, California. Despite losing to the great Tom Curren in the final, I went home that memorable Sunday afternoon firmly entrenched in the World Tour Top 10 for the first time in my career. The all-California men's final was a first-time feat, rarely equaled since. Over the next three years, from 1984 to 1986, between the two of us, we would both finish ranked Top 10 in the world, win the Pipeline Masters and a World Title. It was a golden age for California pro surfing.

*Photo courtesy Allen Carasco/*Breakout *magazine*

Yours truly, champion of the 1984 Katin Pro-Am. From 1977 to 1982, the Katin contest was the premier pro event in California. By 1983, the OP Pro eclipsed it. Even so, in 1984, all the top pros competed, and I fulfilled a career goal by taking out the win. I was joined in the final by my good friend and surfboard maker, Mike Baron from Oceanside (to my right). Mike's friendship and boards were a key factor in my career turnaround in 1983.

Photo courtesy Brian Beilmann

In the early '80s, Waimea Bay was the most revered big wave in the world. I was always terrified out there the few times I surfed. I only surfed it once after my near-death experience and that was for a contest. In the contest, I "chickened out" and pulled back from catching a 30-footer that would have advanced me to the next round. Without any remorse, I lost the heat, paddled in, went home ... and never surfed Waimea Bay again.

Photo courtesy Aaron Chang

Winning the Pipeline Masters, December 17, 1984. After falling on my first wave, I never fell again. It was my dream come true. In a defining line of surf history, I became the last surfer to win the Pipe Masters on a single-fin surfboard. In the 50 years of Pipeline Masters contests, Rob Machado and I are still the only Californians to ever win surfing's most prestigious event.

*Photo courtesy Allen Carasco/*Breakout *magazine*

In early 1985 David Barr won the first event on the PSAA US Pro Surfing Tour, the tour I had just established. In a win that surprised no one, my good friend dominated the event in his convincing win held at his home break, the Warm Water Jetty in Carlsbad. After completing his stellar pro career, he established himself as a very successful and well-respected surfboard shaper in our hometown of Carlsbad. He remains one of California's greatest pro surfers of all time.

Buran family archives

At the most critical juncture in my life, God brought into my world Brian Brodersen, a former surfing standout from Huntington Beach, not to surf with me, but to give me solid and healthy spiritual direction. At the time, Brian was serving as the senior pastor of Calvary Chapel in Vista, a large, prestigious ministry in the town where I was living. It was Brian who first recognized the call of God upon my life, inviting me to join the church staff in 1988.

My wedding day, March 12, 1988. The first time I ever saw Jennifer George, she walked into my college classroom and took my breath away. Three months after we met, I asked her to marry me. A couple months later, we were married and she became a pastor's wife. For over 35 years, we have shared our amazing journey of life, filling it with friendship, love and ongoing ventures of faith. And now, the life of an author!

Buran family archives

The Buran family, 1999. Upon returning to California after five years on the East Coast, we settled into Jennifer's original home in Cardiff. We lived there for almost four years before ending up in neighboring Orange County. By this time, our family was complete. Our four kids would grow up in Orange County, enjoying and thriving in the church and school at Calvary Chapel Costa Mesa.

Buran family archives

Buran family archives

El Pastor en el Tubo! It doesn't seem possible that after barely surfing for a decade while living in obscurity, I returned and won the 1998 ASP World Masters Surfing Championship. Reuniting with old world tour friends and rivals was a lifetime highlight. So was winning the contest—which qualified me to compete at Pipeline for the next three years! Unbelievable! Sometimes, you never know that what you let go of might just come back and be even better than you imagined.

Buran family archives

Early days with Worship Generation, hanging out backstage with Jeremy Camp. Jeremy played the music and I did the preaching. His story is well documented in the movie, *I Still Believe*. Apart from all the Dove music awards and Grammy nominations, Jeremy's love for people has always stood out. God loves people, Jeremy loves God and Jeremy loves people.

Buran family archives

How about a water baptism from a pastor in a wetsuit? Doing one of my greatest ministerial duties at Pirate's Cove in Newport Beach in 2002. As the Worship Generation ministry grew in influence, we held numerous beach baptisms at the famed location, on the other side of the jetty from world-renowned surf spot the Wedge. There is something so very special in faith, forgiveness and fresh starts. True to my waterman's ways, I have performed baptism in creeks, rivers, bays, lakes, pools and oceans. It never gets old!

Buran family archives

My wife, Jennifer, with our oldest daughter, Hannah, pictured here in the early 2000s. I have often thought that one of the few things more challenging than being a pastor, is being the pastor's wife. The expectations, humility, grace, conviction and courage required is known by only those who have experienced it. Hannah and Jennifer both know the experience and calling, one they have both embraced and then flourished in.

Photo courtesy Jacob Harman

My family in 2006. While Jennifer and I grew up in our beloved North San Diego County, it was God's plan for our kids to grow up in the fast-paced world of Orange County California. Thanks to their mother, they were all outstanding students, and they also participated in high school sports and grew up surrounded by loving family, friends—and, of course, the beach!

Buran family archives

People often ask me if any of my children surf or take after me in personality and pursuits. Of course, everyone has their own personality, interests and dreams, and so do my children. Having said that, yes, they all surf. Three of the four participated on their high school surf teams, but more importantly each grew up to pursue their dreams and find their own success along the way. Most people do say Leah (on the left) often reminds them of me . . . go figure!

Photo courtesy AJ Neste

2008 USA Junior Surf Team. This team included future World Tour standouts Kolohe Andino, Nat Young, Conner Coffin, Courtney Conlogue and Sage Erickson. Our girls alternate Kaleigh Gilchrist was a starter the following year in 2009 and then went onto water polo greatness, winning an NCAA title at USC and then two gold medals with the Women's USA Olympic Team.

Buran family archives

A candid moment during a youth conference in Santiago, Chile. From 2013 through 2016, I was very involved with the Chilean people, traveling there regularly. During that time, I served as the head coach for the Chilean National Surf Team while also being involved with some of the local churches. Chile is a beautiful country filled with amazing people. My time serving the people of Chile is one I hold very dear to my heart.

Buran family archives

In Costa Rica, serving as head coach for Team Chile at the 2016 ISA World Surfing Games. Pictured from left to right, Guillermo Satt, myself, team trainer Pancho Veliz and Manuel Selman. It was Selman who, five years later, would shock the pro surfing world by claiming the 20th and final qualifying spot for the Tokyo Olympics at the 2021 ISA World Surfing Games. Although I was no longer coaching at the time, watching his qualification brought me tears of joy. Such a great and proud moment for Chilean surfing!

Photo courtesy Ben Reed

On the podium with Team USA being recognized as World Champions at the 2017 ISA World Junior Surfing Championships in Japan. This win was the highlight and pinnacle of my surf coaching career. This team that became World Champions featured four alternates and had the least clarity of expectations for any team I'd ever coached. At the event, everything went our way as we fulfilled our fullest potential and pulled out the dramatic win. I wore my gold medal all the way home from Japan.

Photo courtesy Sean Evans

At the 2018 ISA World Junior Championships, Team USA won the prestigious Aloha Cup. This event is surfing's version of a relay race and is extremely challenging to win. This was the final jewel of my coaching career. I had suffered numerous defeats in this special event in prior years. In 2018 the event was held in Huntington Beach and our athletes, led by Jett Schilling and Cole Houshmand, knew exactly what to do. They crushed it, leading Team USA on to a convincing victory.

Buran family archives

My daughter Hannah with East Coast surfers Rachel Wilson and Sarah Abbott. This photo was taken in 2017, just after I had been invited back by USA Surfing CEO Greg Cruse to coach the Junior Surf Team for the second time. With years of experience teaching and leading church youth groups, Hannah and her husband, Nate, were a great fit to volunteer and help with the many practical needs of the USA Team. They were a blessing to all and a great example of servant hearts.

Photo courtesy John Jackson

A leadership dream team for USA Surfing in the summer of 2018. From 2017 to 2019 the USA Junior Surf Team won two ISA World Championships and finished runner-up in the other. USA Surfing's CEO and team manager Greg Cruse, second from the right, was the fearless and resourceful leader who made it all possible. Now retired, he has proven to be irreplaceable. To the far right is my assistant coach, Brandon Phillips. After I retired in 2018 he stayed on to win gold with the 2019 team. Far left, my son-in-law Nate Gallagher was a huge blessing to all of us, serving however needed and was a favorite with the athletes.

A special moment with all four of my kids, Hannah, Leah, Timothy and Luke. I value these moments beyond description and never take them for granted, especially since they have all now established their own lives and families. Jennifer and I long ago learned our children are a gift from the Lord and they belong to Him. In this truth we live in parental faith, purpose and peace.

Buran family archives

In Florida with a couple of my grandkids, Clementine and Wilkie. I'm convinced that one of the greatest joys we can experience in life is to become grandparents! Just when you accept the realities of getting old, you take a look at your grandchildren and think how blessed you are and how happy you are to be alive. Sharing life on the backend of your journey with your children's children is the best!

Buran family archives

Photo courtesy John Jackson

The Buran family in 2022. This photo was taken days before our oldest son Timmy's wedding. The Florida family was in town and our home was filled with laughter and dancing! My dad was able to enjoy us all as well. Needless to say, our family continues to grow since that beautiful late winter day in 1988 when Jennifer and I married and started our life journey together. I am a very blessed man. Always forward in faith, hope and love!

Buran family archives

People often ask me if I still surf. The answer is *yes!* I still enjoy being in the ocean, preferably in warm water and smaller, softer waves. In fact, what I enjoy most in surfing is teaching my grandchildren how to surf and sharing waves with them. On the occasions when the surf is really good at home in California, you can still find me out there in the lineup looking for some tube rides and a few radical turns. Even after 50 years, I'm still out there finding barrels and living the endless summer dream. Stoked!

10

THE GREATEST OF DAYS

It only took a year for the face and presence of the world tour to look and feel completely different, so great was the transformation brought on by ASP World Tour director Ian Cairns and this new generation of hungry, talented and competition-ready surfers.

It was a swift and decisive changing of the guard. Thankfully, I was young enough, hungry enough and ranked highly enough to not get swept aside like so many of my elder IPS peers. They either didn't like the new format, all of the additional events, the presence of more beach-breaks, loss of the Hawaiian events ... or simply aged out. It was out with the old and in with the new! The new guard was led by Martin Potter, Tom Curren, Mark Occhilupo, Derek Ho, Barton Lynch and Damien Hardman. They were all young and extremely talented, and they were quickly finding their traction into the world tour Top 10. All of these surfers would eventually become future world champions.

So I sensed, going into 1984, what my future held. I needed to pray that Ian and Fred would find common ground, so the Top 16 could surf the Hawaiian events, and I needed to win the Pipeline Masters very soon. Led by the two Toms, Curren and Carroll, the young bucks were rising fast, and in California, they had one target in mind above all others—me. David Barr, now a Top 30 surfer as well, and I were the remaining warriors of the IPS in the state, now seen as salty veterans playing a young man's game. I was determined to stay in the world tour Top 10 and hold these guys off.

By the summer, my feelings changed. Drastically. I had matured as a person and grown in my ability to understand my world. My assessment and conclusions of what my pro surfing future looked like were humbling—and, as history proved, accurate. I knew my days were numbered. Some of these well-schooled NSSA graduates and teenage overseas phenoms were already better than me, and some would soon surpass me. More to the point, after my fantastic season of the year before, I found my surfing ability leveling off again. For the first time since my career began, I found myself losing interest in remaining on tour.

It's like it all hit at once. I was tired of nonstop travel across six continents for seven years, accompanied by the stress of always being on the edge of a career disaster, which ages both your body and soul very quickly. I'd consolidated my sponsorships, dropping Hang Ten and riding exclusively for Mike Baron Surfboards and Body Glove. Without consciously intending to do so, I had begun to transition toward a growing interest in surf event promotion and organization. Still, though, I wanted to go out in the same flamethrowing way I leapt into pro surfing: repeat the Top 10, maybe remind Curren the old guy could fend him off once more in the ratings, and take a few more cracks at my ultimate career goal of winning the Pipeline Masters.

Wouldn't that be a great way to call it a day?

I was still the California Kid. Even though Tom Curren was now clearly recognized as the best surfer in California, I was okay admitting to myself Tom now prevailed.

The tour rolled through Europe and the East Coast as summer moved into fall. At the end of September, for the first time in my career, the world tour camped out in my backyard: Oceanside's North Jetty, one of my favorite spots for free surfing for years. It was also the site of my win in the infamous California Pro, after which the promoter split with all of our prize money. How much the sport had grown since then. Stubbies saw the writing on the sponsorship wall—"Go big or go home"—and discontinued its important regional surf trials series. In a hurried decision, they morphed the trials into an ASP World Tour event in Oceanside, to be held three weeks after the OP Pro.

I don't know how, but in eight weeks' time, Carlsbad local Jim Watson, Oceanside board shaper Gary Linden, local photographer and resident Offshore Surf Shop big brother Jerry Calkins, Stubbies' Mike and Greg Bechelli, the City of Oceanside, and my future memoir editor breathed this tournament into being. "Jimmy and I put in 18-hour days, then drove up to the North Jetty at midnight every night, ate the burritos we bought at a Mexican fast-food place, and visioned both the next day's workload and the tournament as a whole," my editor remembers. "We wanted the world to see Oceanside, the world tour surfers to see our focus was purely on them and their needs . . . and the locals to feel honored."

I knew all these guys well. They delivered. What an incredible feeling to come home as a top-ranked ASP surfer, and to do so in a world tour event. At one of my home breaks. Internationally, despite my success at the Tropix Grand Prix on the East Coast, I endured loss after loss to some of the younger surfers. It wore down my resolve. I began to consider my tour exit strategy. On paper, a win in Oceanside would be an awesome conclusion to my career in California, and then if I could triumph at Pipeline, I'd raise my arms after the ultimate storybook ending.

At the Stubbies Pro, part one didn't quite work out. I surfed quite well, but for the third event in a row, I was eliminated by the amazing 18-year-old Australian youngster, Mark Occhilupo. There would be no storybook ending for me in Oceanside.

Following the Stubbies Pro, I made the decision, publicly: I announced my official upcoming retirement from pro surfing. I would step aside in two months, after the next event, the 1984 Pipeline Masters. If the ASP chose to continue its Top 16 boycott of the Hawaiian Triple Crown, as the three events were now called, I wouldn't be governed by my spot in the ratings anymore. I was free to surf Pipeline.

Further, I told the media, I would also begin a whole new career as a new tour event director, establishing and running the Professional Surfing Association of America (PSAA). I had blazed a trail on the world tour for this next generation of American rippers, and now I was going to create an American surf tour on which they could hone their skills and eventually turn the tide on Australian world tour dominance. I figured that as a longtime pro surfer who studied how the contests came together, knew the industry a bit, knew how to obtain sponsors and certainly understood promotion and how to work with the media, I could follow a tried-and-true course walked by Fred Hemmings, Randy Rarick and Ian Cairns and switch from competing to running a pro tour.

There was only one thing left for me to do: win the 1984 Pipeline Masters, plain and simple. I had bet my entire surfing-career legacy on winning the Pipeline Masters, and now I had essentially given myself one last chance to do it. Yep, that's me, and by plopping that expectation onto my plate, I did not sleep particularly well in November and December of that year.

Planning out the PSAA Tour kept me busy and, thankfully, a bit distracted. It also gave me cause for much stress over an unknown future, which I feared might impact my chances to win Pipe. Plus, due to the boycott, I was unable to surf in the 1983 Pipeline Masters, after losing in the first round of the 1982 Pipe Masters and my disastrous loss in treacherous conditions in the 1981 semifinals. I hadn't been to the finals in four years. Yet, I willed myself over and over, Joey Buran, the kid from Tamarack Beach in Carlsbad, California, just had to somehow find a way, any way in our giant universe, to move heaven and earth to fulfill my dream.

There was no other alternative. I had to win. That was that.

In early December, I left for Hawaii with my childhood dream in my heart, and one chance left to get it done. It would require marshaling all my forces, the greatest day of my life and cumulative effort of everything I had ever done, reflecting the very best of who I was at the age of 24.

Which brings us to December 17, 1984. The Greatest of Days.

December 17, 1984, was my absolute destiny. In a universe with trillions of galaxies and all that makes the universe work, somehow, it had to work perfectly for me on that day. Every movement in the entire Pacific Ocean, the upper atmosphere, the direction of the swell, the cells in my body, the neurons in my brain, the data in my subconscious, the fiberglass and foam under my feet, the rain, the rainbows, and all the elements of my universe had to align with my board, my knowledge of the wave, and my desire to win. In some ways, it's a blur, yet in other ways, there are moments and pictures in my mind that are so clear I suppose I could never forget them.

Starting with a midnight dream the night before, a clear, a very clear, absolutely literal dream. A lucid dream. I dreamed I won the Pipe Masters. It was a scene I had never seen before, so it didn't come out of memory, but felt more like a projection backward from the future. The future of that very day. Not only had it been my "dream" to win the Pipeline Masters for the 11 years since I'd proclaimed my victory-to-be to my mother, but in the early hours of December 17, I believe God intentionally showed me what part of it would look like, so I would know it was from Him when I experienced it.

When I woke up, I did not consciously know this. I was very disappointed to rub my eyes open and realize it had only been a dream.

Yet, the dream had felt so real. Never before had I ever lived a dream with such clarity and detail. The most memorable part was paddling out while competing, looking at a giant barrel from the side view, and seeing young Hawaiian Pipeline favorite Derek Ho. He was coming right at me, locked in the sweetest spot deep inside a tube that could easily fit a semitruck—then at the very last second, the wave hit him on top of his head, resulting in a major wipeout and making the wave and its score inconsequential. It was at that moment in my dream I knew that I had won.

Contest organizers only invited 24 surfers to the event, the very best Pipeline surfers. The event was recognized by the new ASP World Tour, which ended the boycott and allowed Top 16–ranked surfers to compete. However, it would carry no points for the current world tour ranking system. In previous years that might have upset me, but I was retiring anyways, so it meant nothing to me. Ranked or unranked, it was the Pipeline Masters, the tournament surfers considered tougher and more prestigious than any other. I needed to win. That was all that mattered that day!

To prepare for my big day, I chose a different place to stay when I arrived in Hawaii. First, I showed up later than normal. Then, instead of staying in the condos at the Turtle Bay Hilton, 10 minutes northeast of Pipeline, I decided to encamp at a friend's house, even farther to the east, past Kahuku, about 20 minutes away.

So, early that morning, a few hours after the dream, I headed out to Pipeline to pursue my life dream. There was no doubt the contest would be on that day, as we all knew the swell would arrive early that morning. It had been a dismal December for waves, and the Pipeline Masters contest had already limped through its entire original waiting period without being held. Even the contest directors, for years notorious for driving sponsors, media and even competitors crazy for waiting interminably for "the perfect day," were eager to run it. This swell was their golden opportunity. The month had been so poor that there were no guarantees they'd see another good swell again in the calendar year.

I arrived at Pipeline in predawn darkness, turned on my Walkman cassette player, and blasted a Christian rock album by the well-known band Petra. I filled my mind with praise music (albeit rock) to start the day. On this day of all days, I was asking God for it all! I figured it was probably good luck or something like that to listen to rock music about God that morning, and so I did. I danced and hooted on the beach, feeling and hearing how big the surf was. It was for sure going to be big—and dangerous!

What made the waves extra dangerous? The mixture of swell directions, plain and simple. And the size. The Pipeline breaks best on a pure, 270-degree west swell. On a full north swell, it doesn't break properly and is rarely surfed; the wave looks like a merciless liquid guillotine. On this day, it was what we call a combination swell, incoming waves from both directions sometimes merging offshore and then driving into the reef. But a lot of very dangerous closeout waves sweep in from the north, and occasionally, a few perfect waves from the west. The most essential strategy on this kind of day is to dodge the scary north swell waves that close out and swallow riders and boards like tasty meals, causing dangerous wipeouts on a coral reef five feet below. Or less. And that reef has it all—mushroom-topped coral, jagged coral, tabletop coral, caves, fissures . . . a recipe for injury. Or death. And I've seen both at Pipeline.

The second strategy involves patience . . . lots of patience. Not always my strongest quality, but my years at Pipeline taught me that on this wave, in these conditions, patience was both a winning strategy and a survival tactic. My job, and that of the other 23 stars, was to patiently wait for, recognize, and catch the relatively "smaller" and "cleaner" west swell waves.

Which brings me to a huge key to my chances at victory: I was familiar and comfortable with these conditions. In competition surfing, wave selection is everything, as is knowledge of the local lineup. Most locals and top pros avoid these types of days at Pipeline because of the sheer danger. Yet for me, in my pursuit to become King of the Pipeline, I had surfed every possible day I could over the last seven seasons, including treacherous conditions, which involved swallowing fear and having faith in my ability to do it in my earlier years. And saying a prayer or two, for sure. Like a hitter knowing what pitch is coming, I instinctively knew which waves to avoid and which waves to catch. That degree of experience and trust in my instinctive judgment was going to be a huge factor on this day, the decisions of knowing which board to use, where to sit, where to drop in, which waves to take—and how deeply to burrow myself inside them—and not least of all, how to wipe out without losing my board or being injured.

By 7:30 a.m. most of the competitors had arrived and were on the beach, getting ready. Spectators began turning up as word was spreading via radio, morning TV news, weather forecasters and North Shore locals: Pipeline was big and dangerous, and the contest was on! The morning dawned clear and sunny, but off-and-on cloud cover would persist throughout the day, and by late afternoon, significant rain squalls would arrive.

I paddled out for a warm-up surf on my mid-range board, seven-foot-three in length. After paddling out, I realized my board was too short and I would need to ride my bigger seven-foot-ten board. In an unprecedented experience, I did not catch even one wave during my warm-up. I had seen the look of the ocean in the lineup, helpful information for sure, but not catching a warm-up wave was hardly a confidence booster! The waves were big, scary and incredibly dangerous. The mix of swells was still building, ensuring that the waves would continue to grow, to get bigger and meaner. It was obvious to everyone in the water and on the beach that this day was going to be filled with historical drama.

Finally, contest director Randy Rarick fired off the air horn, getting us started. Of the six opening-round heats in the 1984 Pipeline Masters, I drew heat five. My first good break. It gave me a chance to watch the heats and get a feel for what was going on in the ocean, how it was moving, how the surfers were positioning, where the waves with the biggest barrels with longest stand-up time and highest scoring potential were breaking. It was terrifying! Nobody stood out in the first four heats. The tone of the morning stopped on "safety first," as if it were a radio dial stuck on a station. The very best Pipeline surfers in the world were doing just that, surfing safely and conservatively, staying well within their perceived thresholds, never so much as edging up to them. There were some solid rides, a few crazy wipeouts, but no injuries.

Then it was time for heat five to paddle out.

I was grouped with the great Shaun Tomson, a former World and Pipeline Masters champion, local Pipeline standout Marvin Foster, like me a goofy foot, and John Damm, another Pipeline local known and respected for his bravado, particularly his ability to sit and wait for the very best and biggest barrels. His patience at the break was greater than mine, which I duly noted. My Pipeline strategy has always been about tempo and flow. Get busy, catch waves, build confidence and rhythm with the ocean, get in the flow, and then attack the bigger "bomb" sets. No one found anything unique or special to the strategy. But the big question was, could I execute the game plan?

Of my time spent in the water all day, ironically I remember the first 15 minutes the most. The paddle out was much more difficult and dangerous than normal. Timing was crucial for paddling out and when I did, there to my right was Marvin Foster. Paddling with the urgency of a drowning man trying to find his next breath, we both timed things right and made it to the safe area of the deep-water channel, just to the right side of the thunderous take-off zone. However, before we could even catch our breath, a gigantic set of 20-foot waves from the northwest came through, causing the huge waves to break on the outer second and third reefs of Pipeline. A quick reference: Most Pipe contests were and are held in good to great first-reef conditions. Some are blessed with even riskier second-reef waves, but the third reef is reserved for the biggest bombs, monsters and rogues the place can hold.

This particular second- and third-reef set created a massive wall of powerful whitewater that looked like an oncoming avalanche! In the rarest of events, it even rolled right through the deep water of the Pipeline channel. There was no alternative for Marvin and me but to throw our boards to the side, dive deep under the massive wall of whitewater, and hope our surf leashes wouldn't break. Talk about a wake-up call! For all the times we had surfed in the Pipeline lineup together, we had never experienced something like that, let alone in the Pipe Masters! The contest I felt destined to win, that I had to win. *I don't have time for my leash snapping and having to swim in! I don't have time for this! How could this already happen?*

Fortunately, both of our leashes held. The giant wall of whitewater snapped me out of my preheat nerves. I was no longer nervous about the contest and what it meant to me—but was positively terrified of the waves!

As soon as all four surfers were safely in position, our heat started. I looked around, and noticed we were more spread out than we might have been on a normal 10-to-15-foot day. The Pipeline take-off zone is normally tight and compact, with a radius of about 20 yards, but not on this day. The surf was so big that the mixed swells created an unfamiliar and unpredictable take-off zone, spreading us out about 75 yards in different locations. Since there was no man-on-man priority buoy in this format, the key to wave selection was to hold the "inside position" against the other competitors and establish the right of way. The risk in doing so was to find ourselves too far back to drop into and then speed out of the huge tubes within the waves. The other well-known strategy was to try and sit a little more inside and over from the deeper take-off zone and look for the shifting, cleaner inside 12-to-15-foot waves. That was my usual Pipeline strategy as a whole, as it also was for Marvin. True to form, Shaun and Damm opted to sit deeper and farther outside, while Marvin and I took our more comfortable inside positions.

My first wave that day remains one of my most memorable. A set wave swung toward me as if I summoned it, shifting away from Damm and Shaun. I charged for it and pulled into a giant barrel, big enough to drive a bus in! That's not hyperbole; that's a measurement. I got to work on my trusty seven-foot-ten single fin, a board I had ridden for a couple of previous winters and with which I was very comfortable. I knew the nuances of the board quite well and trusted it in these big and powerful waves. Quickly, I slotted myself inside the barrel. I found myself so deep that I rode atop what surfers call the foam ball, a compact ball of whitewater trapped by the waterfall-thick lip spilling over my head. My board passed the test, and my trusty single fin held on as I drove through the deep barrel, but before I could come out, the entire wave closed out and crashed on me. The ride was spectacular but the score insignificant, like a deep, potential touchdown pass on the first play of the game that barely slips off the wide receiver's fingertips.

Even so, when I popped up safely out the back side of the wave, I was pumped! My board had passed the test! And I knew how very deep I could go! Several times throughout the day, I would stand far back in the barrel, riding on top of the foam ball. Every time my board would provide the control and stability I needed to make it out of those giant tubes!

All the nervous energy of the last few months disappeared at that very moment. That giant barrel reminded me of what I loved to do more than anything—catch and score big tube rides at Pipeline! My switch was on, and it stayed on till I went to bed that night! It is worth noting, I made every other wave I caught for the rest of the day. Every one of them. I never fell or failed. I caught barrel after barrel until it became a blur. I was always in the right spot and, simply put, everything was going right for me! Compared to other sports, surfing is a lot like golf. A lot can go right, but a lot can go wrong, and it often does at the Pipeline. So to have everything going right was an indescribable feeling! I just *knew* these truths were going to happen as I paddled for my next wave.

I caught some great barrels and never looked back. I don't remember anything about the other surfers. It was my day and I was in the zone. Shaun finished second, which set us up to advance on to separate heats later that afternoon. I was so excited after my first-round win that I couldn't wait to get back out in the lineup and catch some more huge barrels! The field was pared down to the final 12 surfers; the top 2 from each of the three semifinal heats would advance to an extravaganza of a final: one hour and 6 surfers.

In the second round, the tone of the day had shifted. So had the weather. The summeresque morning had ceded to a more seasonal autumn pattern, with puffy tropical white and gray clouds coming and going throughout the day, carried by the typical 15-to-20-mile-per-hour trade winds that crawl over the hills to the east and keep the waves, for the most part, well groomed with their favorable side offshore direction. I took stock of both the shifting winds and the contest, which was certainly going my way. I was stunned as I watched many of the other competitors, the world's very best surfers, pursue the wrong waves, while I instinctively caught nothing but the right waves! It almost felt like I was cheating. It became clear that not only did I have the best wave selection of the day, but of equal importance, I was making the most of the opportunity those waves were giving me.

My next heat was a rematch with perennial Pipeline standout, Allan Byrne from New Zealand. Back in the 1981 Pipe Masters, I suffered a horrific wipeout in the semifinals due to interference from Allan. He blocked and then interfered with my ride after I had already established priority for the wave, which is illegal in competition surfing. This is to be avoided at all costs, because the penalty for interference is the loss of total points for one of your top-three-scoring waves. At Pipeline, an interference not only hinders the scoring potential for the primary rider but is also very dangerous for everyone involved. In our situation, his wipeout in front of me forced me into wiping out behind him. Although we both fell, I took the brunt of it and never fully recovered. I fought hard to recover from the wipeout, but it was not enough to advance to the final.

For some inexplicable reason, the IPS judges never called Allan for the interference. He was able to finish ahead of me and advance to the final. I never held it against him, as he intended no malice in that dangerous situation. Had he intentionally tried to stuff me in the pit of the wave, he would've suffered huge grief from all the surfers, likely made worse by the fact that he was not Hawaiian.

The impact to me lasted far longer than shaking off a wipeout. From that moment three years before, I had not advanced through a single round in the Pipeline Masters. It threw a lot of question marks around my dream of winning the event, for sure.

Now, three years later, I watched Allan paddle out next to me for our semifinal. I found myself fighting my emotions and the skeletons of that unforgettable event, so I could focus on the task at hand. Right next to him was my teenage nemesis, Mark Occhilupo, who had eliminated me in man-on-man events all season. The fourth and final competitor in this semifinal heat was someone I had never previously surfed against, unheralded Brian Buckley from Laguna Beach. Buckley was part of the "Pipeline Underground," a group of talented, but lesser-known Pipeline standouts. In reality, he wasn't just one of the underground, but considered by many to be the best Pipeline surfer in the world on a day-in, day-out basis. Like Jon Damm in my first-round heat, Brian was fearless and liked to sit way out the back, patiently wait for, and then charge the biggest waves of the day. Perhaps his greatest asset was his comfort level and experience in these unique and dangerous conditions. We held that in common. Simply put, Brian knew the Pipeline lineup as good or better than anyone in the world. On paper, this was an amazing heat and could have easily been the final.

Unlike my first round, I started slow. Early on I was a little bit out of rhythm and could not seem to get the best waves. Halfway through the 30-minute heat, I found myself in last place. Normally, I might tense up, feel the pressure of having to catch up, especially at beach-break contests where conditions were small and sporadic at best. Not at Pipeline. One thing that makes Pipeline different from a lot of other surf spots is that you can catch a wave and be back in the main lineup within two minutes. Every Pipeline Master competitor knew that, even if you were way behind, you could flip a heat with two great waves in less than five minutes.

Unless north and northwest swells influenced the lineup. Which is precisely how it was playing out in our semifinal—and every heat. For the most part, northwest swell sets presented unrideable waves, as literally tons of violent moving water created temporary strong riptides that destroyed the clarity of the take-off zone. Just one of those big sets would require at least five minutes for the lineup to calm and reset itself to provide the ideal conditions for the perfect barrels that formed from one of the smaller and cleaner westerly sets. This was a major factor. Very few surfers would choose to surf a day like this were it not for the fact it was the Pipeline Masters. You had to be elite, confident, knowledgeable and wise on this day. As well as able to gulp down your fear and trepidation and trust your instinct and skills implicitly. It was quite amazing no one was seriously hurt or injured.

Now, I would have to come from behind in these same conditions.

I snagged a clean inside wave, about ten feet in size, but to great fortune, it drew back into a beautiful, long and clean barrel. I slotted in and, after a few seconds, slingshotted out to the cheers of the crowd. I knew the score would have to be big. Equally important, that wave put me on the right cadence with the rhythm of the waves and the lineup. I needed three good waves in ten minutes and now I had the first one. To my continuing fortune, the lineup remained clean and settled. I would have to focus on perfect positioning to snatch the additional two waves from the other three competitors.

That's exactly what happened. I caught another good wave and posted another high score. I kicked out, paddled back into the lineup—and established the inside position. A must in any surf contest, but in this horse race, a particularly high-risk, high-reward post. A fantastic bomb set wave out of the west was headed right for me to my left side, the perfect wave to put this heat to rest. However, as it drew ever closer, my anticipation threatening to fly off the Richter scale, so did Buckley. He paddled hard and right at me from the east, trying to cop the inside position.

What ensued was a classic old-school, no-priority-rule paddle battle for inside positioning and the right of way to control and catch the wave. In this career-defining moment, there was just no way I was going to let Buckley steal my inside position. I paddled side by side with a great and capable peer breathing down my neck for a wave that could be a perfect 10—or result in a life-threatening injury. I knew that no matter what, I just had to catch this wave! In doing so, there would be a split second where I would have to redirect my position from paddling toward the west, and then quickly redirect by a 45-degree angle toward the east, facing the beach, to swing into take-off mode. In this moment of truth, I would have to turn my back to the 20-foot wave, while also blocking Buckley so that he could not slip through that narrow gap and steal inside position of first priority.

Calling upon the experience and courage of my entire Pipeline surfing career, at that very last second, I whipped around my seven-foot-ten single fin, held my inside position, blocked Buckley, paddled with full commitment as hard as I could to catch one of the greatest waves of my life. This intense and threatening action happened within just a few seconds.

As soon as I got to my feet, down the steep face of the wave I went. I had caught it at the last possible second, made the drop, hit my bottom turn, and pulled right into a giant spitting barrel. What a ride! As I exited, I blew a kiss to the sky. I was headed to my third and last Pipe Masters Final, but unlike the other two, after that wave, I felt unstoppable. It had to be my day!

The beach went crazy as I went on to win the heat. Occy finished second and was headed to the final with me. Byrne was out, as was Buckley. Occy and I delivered in the clutch and held off the two crafty Pipe specialists to secure our spot in the finals. Interestingly, we were the tour regulars too.

Years later, in their end-of-the-century issue, *Surfing* magazine rated the 1984 Pipe Masters as one of the top-five greatest surfing events in the history of the sport. While the waves and the intensity of that day still have rarely been matched over four decades, what made the day so incredible was the list of competitors for the final. For the first and only time of the day, six competitors paddled out as we switched to a six-man final. Today, a pro tour final will only have two surfers in the water competing against each other. This kind of Wild West six-man surfing brawl still exists at some big-wave events, but not at Pipe anymore.

Who were the five other competitors with me? We'll begin with the sixth-place finisher, Tom Carroll, on his way to a second-straight ASP World Tour title. His second Pipe Masters Final was to be, sadly, a disaster for him. A horrendous wipeout early on in the final knocked him silly and he never recovered. He was a nonfactor, which is crazy and hard to believe, but things like that can happen at Pipeline. I remember looking at him about halfway through the final and noticed he was out of position, looking dazed, out of his realm. The footage of his wipeout would go on to be seen by the entire surfing generation in the VHS tape of the contest that came out the following year. It was just the worst and I'm certain he was probably concussed from it. He finished last.

Over the next few years, Carroll would figure out what he did wrong, adjust like great champions do and win three Pipeline Masters to add to his two world titles, securing the biggest event notch to what many feel is the greatest career of all time for a goofy-foot surfer. When he won Pipe in 1987, he did so by dropping in and literally snapping his board into tube-riding position halfway down the face—a 90-degree torque of the legs. No bottom turn, no angled drop-in, no slowing down the board middrop, no wiggling into position, just straight down—and straight across. Those watching at the home of the original Pipe Master, Gerry Lopez, were beside themselves, gasping and hooting while trying to figure out how Carroll did it. Well, quite simply, he has the strongest calf muscles this side of Dane Kealoha, veritable tree trunks. He used his fitness and his physique to gain advantage and carve out superior position inside the barrel, then his supreme tube-riding skills swept aside the field.

Champions always find a way to gain an edge. Just as I was about to do.

In fifth place was the Hawaiian legend Derek Ho, the younger brother of the iconic Hawaiian hero Michael Ho. Derek had won the Duke that winter, and his Pipe Final was so close to greatness and victory. However, despite charging some huge barrels, he came up short. But, like Tom Carroll, Derek was just getting warmed up. He went on to win two Pipe Masters and become Hawaii's first professional world champion.

In fourth place was the 1978 World Champion, Rabbit Bartholomew, the man I beat in my professional debut when he was the top-rated surfer in the world. Rabbit was arguably the best backside tube rider at Pipeline since first riding the wave in 1973. On this day, in the twilight of his career, he charged monster sets and surfed with abandon. To this day, he remains one of the greatest surfers in the history of the sport and will forever be remembered by an entire generation for his big-wave bravado at Pipeline.

In third place was Max Medeiros. Unknown to most, he was the classic Outer Island Hawaiian ripper, one of those innumerable Hawaiians who would show up on the North Shore of Oahu every winter and surf with great skill in the Pipeline and Sunset Beach events. Max was a goofy foot from the beautiful island of Kauai, which contained its share of great big-wave breaks and secret spots and also was home to a young grommet, Andy Irons, who would battle Kelly Slater for world supremacy two decades later. Ahead of his time, Max rode shorter boards than most, was a fearless charger, and caught some great barrels, but came up a bit short of a win. To prove his third place in 1984 wasn't a fluke, he would do the same thing the following year, this time in the even bigger and more dangerous waves of the 1985 final won by Occhilupo.

Speaking of Occy, there was my young Aussie nemesis again, in a stare-down with me in another event. But not just any event. *My* event, during my final turn on its stage as a serious competitor. He was already a brilliant surfer and ruthless competitor, as well as an outstanding tube rider. As mentioned, Occy would win the next year, and then many years later, in 2000, go on to win a world title.

Add it up, and there were four future world champions and four future first-time Pipeline Masters champions in that final. How much more historic could it be?

As for the final, my rest time on the beach after the semifinal sped by pretty fast. I surfed in the third and final heat of the second round, so after winning that heat and returning to the beach, I had to quickly reboot for a long, grueling final with these five great surfers.

The first minutes featured really clean conditions. The sun was out, and the swell had peaked in size and was now cleaner, slightly smaller, and more organized. The wind had let up a bit and the crowd on the beach was fully into it as the six of us paddled out together. This was it! The one hour of my life toward which everything had been moving since my parents bought me that first surfboard at Offshore Surf Shop in Carlsbad for my 12th birthday in March of 1973.

In the final, the top four rides would count in each surfer's final score. The ocean was still filled with many dangerous closeout sets and the great waves were far and few in between, and hard to come by. Wave selection would still be the most critical element of this final. Getting four waves was far from guaranteed, let alone scoring well on all of them. Whichever surfer caught four clean waves, big or medium, got barreled and came back out would probably win. Yet that is exactly what happened to me. I caught four good waves. I don't remember any great ones or bad ones, just good rides.

A funny thing about the final that sealed and defined my career: I don't remember much about it. Instead of a movie reel playing in my mind, and despite the fact that I've watched the VHS tape numerous times, my memories roll through more like Polaroid snapshots. Also, it wasn't nearly as dramatic as my come-from-behind win in Round 2. I felt it proceeded more according to the script. Reverting back to a golf comparison, it was like, birdie, birdie, par, and now, a two-foot birdie putt for the win! Occy scored a great barrel in the final, probably the best wave of the final. Rabbit was surfing huge waves on the second reef, but no barrels. Tom Carroll caught nothing after his wipeout. I never saw Max.

As for Derek? This brings us back to my dream from 16 hours earlier.

Derek had been in form all day, looking like a potential winner. In his two future Pipeline Masters wins, he would reach the stature of Gerry Lopez, becoming one of the greatest of all Hawaiian surf legends. Like Gerry Lopez and Rory Russell, he would become recognized as a true King of the Pipeline. But not on this day. If even just for one day, Joey Buran, the

Sand Crab from Carlsbad, was going to be the King of the Pipeline. That's just the way it was meant to be.

The slight edge I held over Derek was my knowledge of these types of conditions. It's that simple. I recognized, caught and properly surfed the right waves. Not the biggest and most exciting waves, just four of the best waves. As already mentioned, but worth stating again, over the last seven years I'd forced myself to surf these kinds of dangerous days, without the usual hectic crowds that the better days drew in. Those sessions gave me a database of muscle memory for this kind of day. I understood and had the code for recognizing and catching the winning waves of the Pipe Masters on December 17, 1984. In essence, every big scary day I had surfed Pipeline in times past, I was winning the Pipe Masters. Now I was in the process of making it official. I won the Pipe Masters, over and over, winter after winter, on those big uncrowded scary days.

Then the dream flowed into my conscious experience in the water. It reappeared during the latter part of the final, after I had just completed a ride and was paddling back out to the lineup. What pops up but a huge, big, beautiful barrel with Derek Ho perfectly positioned inside it. *This is MY dream!* I could hear the beach screaming and cheering for Derek, but I knew right then he would not complete this incredible ride . . . and he did not. The thick and thunderous lip of the wave smacked down and detonated on his head, knocking him off his board at the very last second, turning what could have been a perfect score into a low-scoring, insignificant wipeout.

As I pushed through the wave, I popped out the other side and thought, *This is my dream, and I am winning the Pipeline Masters!* Bang, Bang, Bang! That's how it was! Yet again, God had just revealed Himself to me and, in so doing, confirmed to my heart that at that very moment, I would win.

There were still 15 minutes to go. When you're winning a final, 15 minutes feels like an eternity, one in which countless bad scenarios dart in and out of your mind. But wouldn't you know it? Yet another ally appeared on my side . . . the *weather.* A big rain squall swept in to close the deal for me. Just as it did, lo and behold, a single wave popped up from the west, a perfect eight-foot barrel, inside of the other competitors. This was the fourth wave I needed! I surfed it perfectly, slotting into the clean, deep barrel and popping out equally as clean. It was like a short touchdown that secures a football game in the last minute for an insurmountable two-possession lead. Nothing exciting, not a mic drop, but more like a layup in basketball, an artistic spin to finish the long program in figure skating, or a standard blocked shot by the goalie in hockey. That's what it was. An easy eight-foot barrel in the driving rain to lock it down, fulfill my dream, and make surfing history.

I was the 1984 Pipeline Masters Champion.

After that wave, the weather turned more violent. My wave was the final decent-scoring barrel of the final. As the latest rain squall receded, a big closeout set from the northwest plowed through with unrideable waves, followed by a huge riptide that tore up and destroyed the lineup. Then the horn sounded, signaling that the final was over after the final hour of a full day . . . a day that encompassed my entire young adult life.

I was exhausted beyond measure when I reached the beach. Here now was the moment of truth. Without the computer scoring that the ASP World Tour used, the handwritten results were not officially known by the beach crowd. It was like going back to the '70s and the old IPS tour! One thing we who surfed in that era all knew was that the tone and veracity of the beach crowd and how it cheered would generally tell you who won.

As I exited the water, the crowd swarmed me, screaming "Joey Buran! Joey Buran!" They cheered and congratulated me as if I had won. My friend and Carlsbad surfing mentor in my earliest years, Billy Stang, had been by my side throughout my entire Pipeline career. He came up to me, hugged me and said, "Joey! You just won the Pipe Masters!" That was it! That's all he said as he hugged me and the beach crowd swarmed me. Those words from Billy, himself a great Pipeline surfer, carried the weight of a library of books. They meant everything.

Within moments, all the finalists were on the podium and the results were announced, starting with sixth place and then up to first. Here is where it again grew interesting for me. I had been in "the zone" all day, feeling that aura of invincibility and supreme concentration all athletes who are great at their sports experience on particularly special days, that level of concentration and situational awareness often making the difference between winning and losing. As it definitely did at Pipeline. But now, I was decelerating, coming back down to earth. That shield and focus were giving way to the present reality. I regained awareness of my surroundings just as they announced Occy's name. Did he win? Did I miss my name being called second? *What?* I wasn't sure if they'd announced him the winner. Strange, right? I suppose it all just seemed too good to be true.

For a full second, I didn't comprehend the results. Then I turned to Tom Carroll, who was on my left. "You won, mate!" he said, grabbing me, with a big smile on his face.

That's when I knew! If Tom Carroll tells Joey Buran he won the Pipe Masters, then by the powers that be, JOEY BURAN is the PIPELINE MASTERS CHAMPION!

Within about 5 minutes, rain squall number two came in, this one a screamer, a 5-to-10-minute monsoonal downpour. The beach party was over. The trophy I was holding was a perpetual trophy, so one of the officials came over and took it from me. I held it for 10, maybe 15 minutes.

But it didn't matter. Now, I had to wait for my ride home, my dream fulfilled, knowing my second life would begin, a life beyond the dream.

11

A NEW TOUR, A NEW CAREER

I sat alone on the beach at Pipeline, mulling over an interesting question: *What will my life be like now?*

I'd just fulfilled my ultimate dream of winning the Pipeline Masters. In my 23 years, no other life dream or life goal had really crossed my mind. Winning Pipe occupied me for 12 years, driving everything I lived for as a surfer and a man; now, as suddenly as being shot out of a Pipeline cannon barrel, it was behind me. I knew I was about to launch the US Pro Tour, which I was calling the Professional Surfing Association of America (PSAA), but in the moment, it seemed like an abstraction.

After such an amazing mountaintop experience, what could I possibly live for and pursue at that level of intensity? What could move me with that much fire in my heart? To be honest, after winning the Pipeline Masters, I felt completely spent from life itself. The relentless pursuit of the dream, six years of daily pressure of being the California Kid since *Wide World of Sports* and then *Surfer* magazine labeled me such, and seven years of nonstop travel had all caught up to me.

Still, I went to bed on December 17 elated, fulfilled and exhausted. The next day, I would be headed home to a completely new life.

I arose early that next morning to surf Pipeline on the back end of the swell that delivered my victorious waves. As I paddled out into the lineup, it hit me deeply, far more deeply than words alone: *I am the new King of Pipeline.* It permeated my heart and camped in the front of the brain, like great actions, wins or life-changing moments happen and leave you with the feeling of *I can't believe this is really happening to me!* A few surfers in the lineup congratulated me, while a few commented they were surprised to see me out so early in the lineup the day after winning!

I caught a few good barrels, returned to the beach, drove to the east side of the island, packed my gear, and headed to Honolulu Airport for a midafternoon flight to the mainland. Not surprisingly, it was the most joyful plane ride of my career. I could scarcely believe I was leaving Hawaii as the 1984 Pipeline Masters Champion. While in flight, I felt like an eagle gliding six miles high, atop the world, at the peak of my career. What made it more satisfying was to go out on top, like the most fortunate sports champions do. While I would still compete part time at some ASP World Tour events in the following year, I would never again come close to the focus, passion and skill of that amazing day at the Pipeline on December 17, 1984.

By the time I got home to California, word had already spread through phone calls, the local newspapers and the *San Diego Union* that I had won the event. I arrived to a hero's welcome from family and friends who were genuinely very happy for me that I had fulfilled my life dream. What I didn't realize at the time, although Tom Curren had finally passed me on the ASP World Tour ratings to officially become California's top surfer, was that I was still very much beloved and respected as the California Kid. By winning pro surfing's most prestigious contest, especially in epic conditions, my victory was viewed by many Californian surfers as their victory as well. Not many athletes in any sport experience that feeling. I lived my dream and in doing so, defeated three Australian world champions and the revered mighty Hawaiian locals as well. I proved that if you live your life with heart, passion, determination, and big dreams, amazing things really could happen, not just for Joey Buran, but for anyone who dared to believe!

It was now time to pass the California surfing baton on to the next generation of pro surfers, led by the amazing Tom Curren and a fleet of hard-charging up-and-comers already hot on his tail. Two-time World Champion Tom Carroll and the mighty Australians were still the kings of pro surfing, but their future was being challenged by the young and talented future generation of California pros. During the next ten seasons, Curren would win three world titles, Brad Gerlach would finish second in 1991, and my Carlsbad partner-in-surfing David Barr would join many others in the Top 30. However, it wasn't until a generation later, in December of 2000, that the iconoclastic surfer-musician-artist Rob Machado, also from North San Diego County, became the only other Californian besides myself to win the Pipeline Masters.

Christmas fell just eight days after my Pipeline Masters victory. I felt so much joy and thanksgiving for the privilege of accomplishing my lifelong goal. I celebrated with my family, surfed with my friends, accepted the congratulations flowing from up and down the coast, and felt the love of so many who believed in me and, in so doing, strengthened my resolve to fly to Hawaii and finish my career as the most talked-about surfer in the world. The King of the Pipeline.

What is it about climbing summits? We rejoice over our climb, our reaching the goal after so much hard work and planning, and we look out to the amazing view. Then reality hits and we have to climb back down and get back to work.

So it was for me—and quickly at that. For the first time in my life, I was an entrepreneur, and not surprisingly, I had ambitious goals. Like most who achieved great success on a large scale or stage at a young age, I was incapable of thinking small. The bigger the objective, the better.

My vision for the PSAA was to run a professional surf tour that sanctioned American surfing events. However, since there were no such West Coast events available (the two held annually, the Stubbies Pro and OP Pro, were both ASP World Tour competitions), I simultaneously started Buran Promotions to organize events that could be sanctioned by the PSAA. My ultimate goal was to motivate and inspire other promoters to rise and produce events that the PSAA could sanction. I envisioned an American surf tour that could become like the PGA Golf Tour. I even believed the PSAA US Tour could ultimately be bigger and stronger than the actual ASP World Surf Tour, since Southern California's exploding surfing and beach lifestyle scene drove the economic engine of the rapidly growing surf industry.

I'd spent five years watching Ian Cairns and Peter Townend build their enterprise, Sports & Media Services, from scratch in Huntington Beach and, in so doing, reigniting amateur surfing in the US and firing up the American pro surfing scene with one-offs, a couple of series and the OP Pro. Long before I decided to create the PSAA, I studied the ways in which events handled sponsorship marketing, media and promotion, how they treated the surfers, and how the surfers represented their brands and represented themselves and their sponsors with the media. My on-the-job research intensified when the ASP World Tour formed and I watched how other countries, like Australia, regarded surfing as a national sport, on par with football and baseball in the US. My goal was to harness the momentum now rising with surfing, the rapid growth in media coverage and general fan interest.

I wanted my tour to help surfers start careers, build great domestic careers, and gain needed seasoning before taking on the ASP World Tour. Most of all, I wanted to help our sport achieve a high level of national prominence.

Naturally, before we even announced the first event of the fledgling PSAA Tour, I started hearing from naysayers about my capabilities in all of these responsibilities—entrepreneur, promoter and producer. I wasn't even out of the starting blocks yet, and the skeptics and doubters of my capability started talking. Hadn't they learned anything about my resolve and determination to succeed from the way I brushed aside all the doubters in my surfing career?

This excerpt from an article in *Breakout* magazine fittingly (and fitfully, if you ask me) captured the industry sentiment toward my chances of achieving success as a pro tour director and event producer:

> *The critics of the new organization are not misinformed. They know that there is precious little money in the American surfing industry to support professional contests. They are aware that Joey Buran has never owned a business before, and they understand that he has had no formal education since age sixteen.*
>
> *What they fail to realize, however, is that making this new organization succeed means everything to him and he will not give up until everyone who ever doubted him has been silenced. Just as his prior competitive success has been an affront to Talent, it is equally insulting to things like Formal Education and Economics.*

The magazine's innovative publisher, fellow Carlsbad local George Salvador, made a rare decision for publishers—quoting himself in this piece, just to further emphasize to the surfing world the qualities I would be transferring from the waves to Buran Promotions:

"This story is far more than a testament to hard work . . . it deals with something only a very few people will ever come to understand; it deals with the powers of a person's will to have something succeed," George said. "The patterns of the successes and the achievements can almost be eerie. The impossible always seems to occur, eventually, for these people. The defiance of odds is second nature. Against All Odds—that's the story of Joey Buran's life. He's a man with the will to succeed in surfing."

I started by literally putting my money where my mouth was. I sold almost all my possessions and poured nearly all of my savings into the preparation work. I had a couple of months to identify event sites, start securing the ever-elusive and difficult beach permits, build sponsorship packages for both individual event and overall tour sponsors, get buy-in from many of the same surf industry executives and decision-makers who privately questioned my abilities, get buy-in from the surfers, and spread the word about this new tour through the media and its four existing prongs in 1985—magazines, newspapers, TV and radio. Landing my old friends at 91X and KROQ as radio sponsors early on certainly helped.

I knew I couldn't do it alone. Through the many sales, motivational and business books I'd already pored through, my voracious love of reading hard at work, I started by surrounding myself with people who were smarter in their areas of expertise than I was. My mom was the real think tank behind the tour, along with head judge and good friend, Midget Smith. My mom always possessed great organizational skills, and so running the PSAA administratively utilized her strengths to the benefit of all. Besides that, she was not intimidated by anyone or anything. Midget was essentially easy-going, but also of strong spirit. He proved to be the perfect person to act as our first head judge. He helped me recruit and train judges, which even included my older brother, Phil!

The third huge component I saw at all successful sporting events, surfing and otherwise, was a jack-of-all-trades. In surfing events, that was the beach marshal. He needed to advise me on everything from building the scaffold to overall beach presentation, from security to taking care of the surfers, from how we announced events to how the sponsors and communities felt about them. I turned to the perfect guys for the job, longtime Carlsbad friends Greg Marshall and Anthony Mata. The PSAA Tour became a great springboard for Greg, who launched a full career in the surf industry as a vice president for Aloe Up Suncare Products, as well as a very good event producer, and announcer on the PSAA and ASP World Tours.

My media director turned out to be the same guy who'd scored a ton of coverage for the Stubbies Pro on the ASP World Tour, promoted several other events, written a long-running and influential newspaper surf column … and even reported on the California Pro fiasco in 1978! He also had experience building sponsorship packages and directly assisting event producers, so he handled all of the above and got me the materials I needed to sell sponsorships.

Then, for what often became the most crucial job at a specific event—securing a beach permit—I was blessed by the presence of Leonard Ortiz. Like the rest of us, he wanted to see surfing grow and surfers have a chance to make money as professional athletes, but often we ran into some unbelievable snags with city, county or state officials who, in some cases, were still stuck in the soul surfing era or were overly territorial. In other words, *not on my beach*. I still don't know how Leonard successfully helped us to secure most of the beach permits in the first year, including some beaches where that hard-core, menacing brand of localism prevailed, but he sure did.

Led by my mom and Midget, our skeletal team of extremely dedicated officials did what we had to do, together we got things done—and we always paid on time. All of us knew we would not be making a lot of money for the thousand-plus hours we poured into the new tour, but it really didn't matter—my team shared my vision, found out ways to help and support each other, and helped me grow my tour and surfing in this very important way. My naysayers could talk all they wanted, but when it came down to Rule Number 1 of Entrepreneurship—surround yourself with a great team—they could only nod their heads in admission.

And with that, begin to respect me as an entrepreneur the way they had as a surfer.

As the new year began, there was a lot of anticipation and excitement for the first event of my new tour. It was only fitting that the PSAA Tour would begin in my hometown of Carlsbad. Our premiere event was held at the local surf spot known as the Warm Water Jetty, so named because of the outflow of warm water from the adjacent electricity power plant that gave us all plenty of comfort on cold winter days. Not to mention excellent surf. The break was considered by most to be world class and elite—just what I wanted.

I also chose Carlsbad to salute our talented, fired-up surf community, filled with wave riders that drew the respect of visiting ASP World Tour surfers in previous years. Besides David Barr, our locals included Dave's younger brother, Paul, plus Phil Treibel, Witt Rowlett, Anthony Mata, and Scott Chandler. Coming from next door in Oceanside were future US champion Mike Lambresi, Chuy Reyna and Danny Smith, who I mentioned earlier, and from up the Del Mar and Encinitas coast came Lonny Brothers, Todd Martin and budding superstar Brad Gerlach—all of whom gave ASP surfers fits at one point or another. Or, in Gerlach's case, finished second in the world in 1991 and then retired to fulfill his greater dream: riding elephant-sized surf and living a purist surfing lifestyle without feeling a need to compete. We'd been one of the nesting grounds for pro surfers for years, so opening the US Pro Tour at home offered up a worthy tribute and celebration to Carlsbad.

Sure enough, the first PSAA event was blessed with solid three-to-five-foot waves in clean conditions, allowing for high-performance surfing to be displayed by the competitors. Fittingly, the opening event was won by local favorite and world tour veteran David Barr. It was a well-deserved victory for my longtime friend and rival, now at the peak of his career and getting his long-overdue attention with me transforming from competitor to producer.

After that first memorable event, everything became somewhat of a blended blur, in which time seemed to speed past faster than I could keep up. As with my professional surfing career, I sank myself ever more deeply into the PSAA. Nothing else mattered but the success of each event, elevating the careers of these hungry surfers, and proving myself as a respected entrepreneur in the industry. I ran a total of 17 events up and down the coast of Southern California, from San Diego to legendary First Point in Malibu, scene of the first explosion of surfing in the late 1950s and 1960s, and the setting for the movies that followed. Our events featured waves both good and bad, sunshine and rain, fog and lightning, late entries and bounced entry checks, ecstatic winners and disgruntled losers, difficult beach permitting processes, and hard-to-obtain sponsors! Our core administrative team grew more and more tired, but as I pushed and forced myself to work harder, so did they, at times mindless of everything else.

One of the highlights of that first year was when we pulled off a seemingly impossible feat. I was determined to run an event in Northern California. Risky business, for sure, as anticontest and localism sentiments were still very strong in the northern regions of the state. After consideration, we committed to run an event in Santa Cruz at its world-famous surf spot, Steamer Lane. As the event date drew near, I began to have second thoughts and reservations about this bold new adventure.

Already anxious when I arrived in Santa Cruz, I was stunned to find out at the last minute that the city had rejected our event insurance upon final review of the permit. It was too late for me to notify the competitors, many of whom had already arrived in town and were training at the event venue. I was in a jam and felt like my entire reputation was on the line with this unfavorable turn of events. I had no idea what to do.

To this day, I still cannot recall the exact details of how it all worked out other than the fact that a local church, Lighthouse Christian Fellowship, came to my rescue. Somehow, that church and its leadership were able to put us on their insurance policy, then utilize their good reputation to get their insurance approved by the local city officials for our event. The final approval came late on Friday afternoon, less than 18 hours before we sent the first competitors into Steamer's booming late autumn waves. In less than a few hours, they had miraculously secured our permit. The following day, we caught another huge break when we gained the favor and cooperation of the infamous locals for our event. We were ready for takeoff.

Why did the Lighthouse Church step forward? Why did the hardcore locals, guys who would just as soon paddle you onto the rocks or break your board, turn into gracious hosts for the weekend? Had they read the *Breakout* article with Tom Curren and me the year before where we professed faith in God? I never asked, so I never knew. Also, incredibly, a friend told me while polishing up this memoir that Merritt Taylor, a Santa Cruz surfer, one of several who attended Lighthouse Church and was involved as a leader and historian in the local surf scene, had been a *reference librarian in Carlsbad City Library in the mid-1970s!* My mom and I happened to check out books from the library at that time. Hmmm . . .

Yet again, God had intervened in my life and bailed me out of a jam! And this time, one that directly impacted the lives of a hundred surfers who believed in our tour, not just for my own personal benefit.

As things turned out, the surf was fantastic. Much to the relief of all of us running the event, and to the delight of the spirited local spectator turnout lining the cliffs above Steamer Lane, Santa Cruz ripper and all-around good guy Anthony Ruffo was surfing on fire and dominated the event. It was a crazy and unforgettable scene as hundreds of locals cheered on Ruffo from the cliff above. I remember my mom saying to me something like, "God help us all if he doesn't win this event!" Our entire crew was just so relieved that Ruffo won, and did so without controversy. Ruffo clearly outfoxed and outsurfed the other competitors by working Steamer Lane's tricky lineup like the expert he was. His local knowledge clearly paid off.

The locals were all stoked, and thanked us for coming up to do the event. Then their other priorities took over, and they headed down the road somewhere to throw Ruffo a huge party! I perhaps have never felt more relieved than when I got behind the wheel and drove the eight hours home later that night!

Slowly but surely, we began gaining the begrudging respect of the industry naysayers, more fans started turning up at the beach, and the quality of competition kept improving—not only from occasional drop-in entries from big names of the present and past, but from the sharpening skills of over a hundred dedicated surfers being given a chance to surf regular competitions as professional athletes. They honed, they refined, they tried out and executed new maneuvers, and to the surprise of many but not our PSAA team, many rose to become major players on the global stage. Like the PSAA Tour itself, all they needed was a chance. When we gave it to them, they seized it.

Also, as the year drew to a close, we achieved many goals, and grew very close to locking down one central goal: to make the PSAA not a steppingstone to greener pastures, per se, but a tour that could stand on its own. Noted *Breakout* magazine:

> *Each of the organizations [IPS and ASP] has sought to create more opportunity for professional surfers, but the manner in which Joey Buran's PSAA is going about it is different from the others. While his predecessors have sought to gear their organizations toward international surfing competitions, the PSAA is the first to focus strictly on the American market.*
>
> *That difference in scope is what separates the PSAA from the other organizations and, possibly, what makes its potential for growth so much greater than the others. Some feel that Australia has reached its peak as far as corporate sponsorship for surfing is concerned, and all recognize that the largest commercial markets for surf-related products are here in America ... Whether or not America, the land of financial opportunity, is ready to wholeheartedly embrace professional surfing is the big unanswered question.*

After completing 17 events in that calendar year, John Parmenter, from the central coast town of Cayucos, won the inaugural PSAA title. He was the first professional United States Surfing Champion. John was a classic character with a huge personality, which worked out well for the tour. He was a popular champion, a fabulous media interview and a great example for other aspiring American pros who would follow his path. The best part? John was a huge fan of the popular '80s TV show *A-Team*, and specifically the famous tough-talking, physically menacing but kindhearted Mr. T, who coined the famous phrase "I pity the fool!" John used this term frequently to intimidate his fellow competitors—and it worked! That, and the fact that his nickname was "Bamm-Bamm," a nod to the *Flintstones* cartoon, rounded everything out perfectly: "Ladies and gentlemen, meet PSAA Champion Bamm-Bamm."

John's first words when claiming his final check and trophy? "I pity the fools!" It was so '80s and a great storyline.

Our new tour was up and running. We ended the year beeping strongly on everyone's radar in the industry. We even somehow operated at a profit that first year, a rarity for any fledgling sports tour, and good news for my aspiring venture.

However, a couple of underlying concerns were looming on the horizon as I looked toward 1986 and the upcoming second season of the PSAA.

I hadn't counted the physical and mental cost of what this new adventure would require of me. As the first season played out, and we set up and tore down in community after community, I began to harbor doubts regarding my retirement from full competition and what I was doing in its place. Not only was I no longer center stage, but I was required to serve and exalt and promote the feats of others in my new position. The stresses of running a tour were very different from any I had previously experienced in my life. At times, I felt ill equipped and overwhelmed by what I was doing. I held a huge vision, and I could see where I felt we should be and where I wanted to go, but now that we truly were growing into a tour with potential national clout—which meant bigger sponsors, corporate sponsors, business on a new level for me—I lost confidence in my degree of professional insight and my skill set to get us there.

In short, I had serious doubts about whether I wanted to run the tour a second year. If I moved ahead, could I even pull it off without suffering losses—or, worse, having this vision and tour grind to a halt midseason and perhaps set competitive surfing back on the mainland?

These doubts percolated from little nagging thoughts into looming storm clouds by the time I was approached by Robbie Meistrell, the boss at Body Glove Wetsuits, my major sponsor for the past five years. He watched the first year of the PSAA and saw the larger potential of the tour and its future. More importantly, he possessed the stronger business skills and knowledge on how to scale up the tour to another level, having just scaled up Body Glove to become a major player in wetsuits and apparel sales as surfwear and the ocean and beach culture became the newest fashion and lifestyle rage in America.

Robbie made an offer to acquire the PSAA Tour from me. Upon buying it, he intended to relocate the tour's operational offices to Body Glove's corporate offices in Hermosa Beach. He wouldn't pay a cent for the tour, but he would guarantee me a good paycheck for the upcoming second year to continue as the director and oversee the PSAA. With Robbie's support for the tour and his confidence in me to take it forward, and with the blessings of my dedicated staff, I eagerly made the move in January 1986 to Los Angeles's South Bay region for the next chapter of my life.

It didn't take long to experience a whole new world in the South Bay. First, now I was working *for* a company, rather than being the head of one. However, Body Glove was a great company and about the most comfortable fit I could hope for, in making that transition from employer to high-level employee. Family owned and operated by the legendary Meistrell family, it was a tight-knit group and had always treated and paid me well.

As a pro surfer, I signed on with Body Glove in early 1981. It was a big change and decision to leave the prestigious Team O'Neill. O'Neill, like Body Glove, was also family owned and, in the late 1970s and '80s, the leader in the surf industry. Riding for Pat and Jack O'Neill had been a huge opportunity for me, but in 1981, my contract was up. Body Glove offered me triple the amount of money as O'Neill, and they were also committed to building their brand around me in their future advertising campaigns. It was an easy business decision.

Body Glove also had achieved iconic status thanks to its founders, twin brothers Bill and Bob Meistrell, and now Robbie's leadership. The brothers had been extremely successful with wetsuits, initially and primarily for diving, including outfitting Lloyd Bridges and his young sons Beau and Jeff for episodes of the hit late 1950s/early 1960s show *Sea Hunt*. When I first signed, though, their surfing suits were not yet up to the same standard I had enjoyed at O'Neill, but by early 1983, Body Glove had tremendously improved their suits.

A huge factor in the turnaround and rise of Body Glove to prominence was Robbie Meistrell. Robbie had elevated from being in charge of a very successful local dive shop to directing the entire Body Glove company. An assertive and competitive man, Robbie was on it, improving the suits even more and adding key team riders, quick to see a direct benefit to Body Glove's exposure and sales from the success of his athletes on the PSAA Tour. He was very motivated to see the tour thrive and reach a new level.

I wasn't about to sell my tour to someone who saw it just as a business decision, something to give his company a better look. I needed more commitment and personal buy-in than that, and Robbie did a great job of convincing me to turn the tour over to him. The fact that I was willing to move to LA, a stark contrast to my life in San Diego County, is indicative of how encouraging and persuasive he was with vision and getting things done.

Robbie was a great boss, but I, on the other hand, was anything but a great employee. Now comforted by a guaranteed paycheck, I lost the urgency and sense of personal mission in how I went after sponsors and approached the job as a whole. I'd hoped the move to LA would revive my fire and vision for the PSAA, while revitalizing me as a whole after the enormous effort we'd just put out to run the 1985 tour, but alas, it did not. Without my usual high degree of personal motivation and vision, I did not approach my new position and opportunity at Body Glove nearly as seriously as I should have, and came up way short of my stated goals for the 1986 PSAA season.

My underwhelming performance had consequences. It was a disastrous scenario for Robbie and Body Glove. My inability to sell the PSAA brand and bring in sponsors, while also growing the tour in event and overall tour size, put the financial commitment squarely upon Body Glove. That proved to be my undoing—and, ultimately, the grounds for my dismissal as tour director.

The bad news fell on my good friend of five years, Robbie Meistrell, to deliver. He needed to intervene and find a gracious way to remove and replace me, which he accomplished with a great deal of class and respect I appreciate to this day. He gave me a face-saving soft landing, retaining me on the payroll as a pro surfer while bringing on one of his close friends to assume the PSAA director's mantle. As the season played out, there were fewer events in that second year, but they were better run and featured more prize money.

Upon completion of the 1986 season at San Francisco's Ocean Beach, a challenging big-wave spot in a great city with a surprisingly large, gritty cold-water surfing community, I was completely out of the leadership of the tour. However, thanks to Robbie and his team, my larger vision would play out, as the tour continued to rise and improve to greater success. By the time the late '80s rolled around, the PSAA became known as the Fosters Tour (ironically, the Australian beer brand) and later, the Bud Tour (as in Budweiser beer).

The Bud Tour became legendary in US surf history for its successful run of events from the late '80s to the late '90s. Robbie also pulled off a huge coup in 1990, producing something neither the IPS nor ASP world tours had ever done—a $100,000 event, the Body Glove Surf Bout. In one fell swoop, he served notice: This national tour would play on the same field as the world tour, and because of it, drive the economics of pro surfing forward to benefit competitors and industry alike.

During those ten years, the tour produced numerous events up and down the coast of California and helped birth many great surfing careers, including those who were to become known as the "Momentum Generation." The Bud Tour was dominated by future American greats Kelly Slater, Rob Machado and Taylor Knox, all three of whom would become Top 5 world tour surfers. Slater marched on to become the greatest pro surfer of all time, winning 11 world titles and 8 Pipeline Masters—including his final Pipe win when he was a few days shy of *turning 50!*

My original vision of starting the PSAA, giving mainland surfers a viable way to make a living as professional athletes, and then standing as a successful tour with its own big purses, champions, stars, and well-sponsored events and athletes, had come to pass. By the time it did, I was far removed from the sport of surfing. In fact, I was nowhere near an ocean.

Rather, I was living in and pastoring a church in Burlington, Vermont.

12

RISE UP!

Goals. Purpose. Optimism. Positivity. Drive. Faith. Sunny Disposition. If someone pulled these seven words from a hat when asked to describe me, they would be on the money, or close to it. The same could certainly be said for the first quarter century of my life, much of it tied to my ascension in professional surfing and to my mantle as King of the Pipeline.

So why did I go into the winter of 1986 feeling so awful? Why did I wake up every morning not to typically bright Californian or tropical Hawaiian sunshine, but to dark clouds that loomed and billowed like a cold, biting Pacific Northwest winter storm? Why did I feel like the thickest and blackest of those clouds consumed my thoughts, feelings and worldview?

What was happening to me? How did I fall into this place? How did Joey Buran, the California Kid with the radiant smile and unbridled optimism strong enough to inspire a generation of surfers to rise up and take on the world, begin the second quarter century of his life falling into a pit of depression and despair? A pit into which I plunged deeper every day, as the dark cloud grew to the thickness of quicksand rapidly engulfing me.

How did I roll from the mountaintop of that glorious day when I was crowned King of Pipeline to such deep depression, such hopeless despair? How did I get here? How could I get out?

This was not like dropping into an impossible tube on a sinister northwest swell day at Pipeline, taking my punishment when the cavernous tube crashed on my head, shaking it off and paddling back out for another wave. This felt like a wave that closed out on me and stayed shut down, with me helplessly flailing about, unable to escape, unable to see the light of day on the other side of the frothing whitewater.

I no longer felt like the King of Pipeline, or the king of anything else. Actually, quite the opposite: I felt like I had completely failed myself. Along with the people counting on me to represent the Professional Surfers Association of America Tour that I'd created—Robbie Meistrell, Body Glove, and the staff and competing surfers.

For the first time in my life, I felt like a loser. My gut tightened, my eyes fell to the ground, and that cloud cut off more and more light as it sucked the life out of me . . . my will to get up and rise above it and succeed again. Adding to my emotional and mental vulnerability was that I continued to live by myself in my apartment in Carson, a tough town with a dark, menacing edge and history to it, and a lot of houses with bars on the front windows to protect the owners.

This situation was completely out of my normal range of life. Everything had been turned upside down. For my entire ascension as a surfer, from a wannabe in sixth grade in 1973 to becoming California's best-known surfer in the world and winning the Pipeline Masters in 1984, my life had been one of confidence, clear goals, meaningful objectives, and absolute purpose. Yet now, after letting go of my dream and vision for the PSAA, I had no new dreams and goals to be moving toward. The first chapter of my life after my pro surfing career had ended in failure, as far as I was concerned. How could I possibly redeem it?

I had no idea.

What about returning to the ASP World Tour? Well, I couldn't go back on tour, as I would be facing the new generation that had become significantly better than me. Surfers like Tom Carroll, Tom Curren, Damien Hardman, Mark Occhilupo, Jeff Booth, Mike Parsons, Derek Ho and a number of others. Plus, Carroll and Curren had become world champions. Although I was just 26, I was beyond my prime; the tour belonged to the younger kids, the go-go-go generation for whom a 24-event circuit in breaks of all kinds seemed the perfect format. California was exploding as a surfing lifestyle epicenter, where fashion and waves and music and contests intermingled into a multibillion-dollar industry, and these kids were the faces of it. I was from the past, a forerunner and trailblazer with name recognition, but still a surfer of the past.

What a crippling realization.

I fell deeper into the pit and saw nothing but darkness in the cloud. Despite my nominal Christian faith and belief in God, I just felt like it was game over for my life. When I looked at my life every morning, I saw nothing. When I peered into the future, I saw nothing. No matter how hard I tried to scratch myself out of my despondency, the way I scratched and clawed to get over Waimea Bay monster waves before they crushed me, I couldn't move forward. My arms felt like lead. I'd lost the ability to scratch forward.

My despair came to a head in the early autumn of 1986, shortly after I left the PSAA Tour. I sat in Carson, home alone as usual. One black thought piled onto another. Then another. Then a decision. A dark resolution numbed my heart, my vision, my desire to move on. I decided to drink a large amount of alcohol and take a full bottle of Tylenol.

A suicide attempt.

The lowest point of my life.

Instead of dying, though, I fell asleep. A few hours later, in the middle of the night, I felt someone pushing me to wake up. Or something. At about 4:00 a.m., I woke up with a definitive thought searing through my brain: "I want to live." The first positive thought I'd held in quite a while.

I wanted to live. I really did.

I jumped out of bed and, despite being woozy from the Tylenol, hurriedly drove myself to the UCLA Medical Center in nearby Torrance. Upon entering the emergency room, I declared to them why I was there. The medical staff got right to work on me. Three things happened that remain with me to this day. First, doctors didn't have to pump my stomach. Miraculously, my body seemed to be unaffected by the large dose of Tylenol I took. Then they put me in a straitjacket. It was such a humiliating experience to go through! To this day, I shudder at the thought of this painful memory.

My final recollection involved my parents. Although my mom and dad had been divorced for many years, they drove the 80 miles from North San Diego County together to be with me at the hospital. When I was released, my father followed me to my dreary, depressing apartment in Carson, where we gathered all my necessities and left. I never spent another night there. I stayed at my dad's house in Vista, a few miles from the Carlsbad and Oceanside waves I'd surfed while enjoying the world's happiest teenage years.

I lived with him for the next year.

While working on this book, over the holidays some 37 years later, my wife and I received a call from the assisted living facility where Dad lived. They were raising the rates by 40 percent—an incredible jump, even in Southern California. My dad loved the place, and so did we. He could enjoy one of the most active lifestyles you'll find in a 93-year-old man, hang out with his friends, and know his food would be good, his needs met, and his comforts guaranteed. But now, we had to move him. As a retired US Marine Corps lieutenant colonel, a healthy pension took care of all his expenses throughout his residency, but this price jump flew right past what he could afford.

Jennifer and I swung into action. Amongst his kids, I decided to take responsibility for seeing to his living comforts. Jennifer decided alongside me. It's what you do for your parents, especially when he's the only one living, and most especially when he gave me shelter and a place to start over during my darkest hour. We spent several intense weeks checking out facilities that matched his needs and wishes, and his budget—not easy to find luxury assisted living in Southern California, not with health-care costs spiraling out of control. After finding one, we took him to see the place while talking with the staff and filling out initial paperwork.

Then Dad spotted someone he knew. A lady friend, from the facility in which he had been living. It was a comforting thing, for me as well as him, to know he had a friend and familiar face to help him adjust to his new home.

Jennifer and I looked at each other, smiles stretching across our tired faces. *Perfect.* God worked this out for us. Just as He did when Dad took me in after my suicide attempt.

Only I needed to realize it.

It was time to inch ahead with my life, to somehow dissipate the cloud that was suffocating my will to live. The way forward began by attending a mental health counseling session at San Diego County's Mental Health offices in nearby Escondido. At my first session, the counselor said I was filled with guilt and needed to forgive myself for the failures and shortcomings that I had confided to her.

When I left her office that day, I knew I would never go back. For me, it wasn't an issue about forgiving myself, but rather seeking God's forgiveness for my failures. I was thinking a lot about God again; a near-death experience can do that for you, no matter the type of experience. Since I was raised Catholic, it would stand to reason that I would know the way forward—through confession and forgiveness for the past. But, in my mind and heart, there was one key thought holding me back. Even if the way forward was to confess and turn from my actions, the real issue was, would I be sincere in doing so? Why would I seek forgiveness if I had no sincere intentions to truly change my behavior?

While I did end up praying for forgiveness from the past and strength for my future, I was not very confident in my ability to walk a straight and narrow path. I'd lived a fast surfer's lifestyle, and it would take more than prayers for me to lead a new life. It would take more commitment than I'd ever put into anything before.

Over the next few months, I spent my time healing and regrouping. While no longer participating in contests, I was still a professional surfer contractually, sponsored by Body Glove. I still received moderate income from them. Since I was no longer running the PSAA, the thought occurred to me to return to competition, surf in the PSAA, and pick up some badly needed prize money. I knew it would be a long road back, with no idea of the final destination, but many retired athletes in many sports had come out of their retirements to enjoy success, brief as it might be. I was only three years removed from being ranked seventh in the world. Like so many others faced with similar situations, I just fell back on what I knew I could do, the skill set and field of play with which I was most familiar.

Even as I got back in the water and practiced hard, getting my body back in shape and sharpening my contest maneuvers, I knew there had to be a bigger picture for my life and a new plan. Little did I suspect that plan would be a move toward pastoral ministry!

By early January 1987, I was again moving in a good direction. The sincerity of my faith and prayers seemed to be holding up. My younger sister, Barbie, a popular Carlsbad beach girl who had grown into a very smart young woman with a golden heart, the type of friend who welcomed anyone with a smile, suggested that I listen to a Christian radio station called KWVE. She also recommended buying a Bible with helpful study notes, which I did. Barbie and I were really tight as kids and into our early adult years, before I ran into the personal difficulty from which I was emerging. Soon, sadly, her own trials and tribulations would occur . . . though I'll spare you the suspense and tell you it turned out very well for her, and she is happy and well supported and surrounded by family today.

Barbie's suggestions harkened me back to those early Sunday school classes with our *Good News for Modern Man* bibles in Virginia, and how much I enjoyed them. Reading passages, taking notes, studying their meaning, absorbing them into my everyday life—my style of learning. This was perfect. I also enrolled in the local community college and, for the first time since I got my GED in the spring of 1978, returned to school and formal education. Over the next year and a half, I took several classes that would later benefit me in my ministry calling. They included public speaking, writing, and small business management. I was definitely moving forward in a positive direction, even if I wasn't quite sure of my new destination.

As the spring of 1987 unfolded, events and decisions kept nudging me into my growing faith in God. While I had visited a few different churches at different times over the last few years, I had never made any kind of serious commitment toward getting involved exclusively with one church family. I was very independent, fiercely so, especially concerning personal religion and faith. I didn't want to be held accountable to anyone about my business, nor was I interested in carrying or sharing in other people's affairs. I'd done that for two years with the PSAA, focusing on the pro surfers instead of myself, and I felt strongly I needed to keep the focus on myself as I continued to put quality time between myself and the darkest day of my life. I knew I should become more committed to going to church. For years I had heard about the Calvary Chapel churches. They were known for having lots of young people with contemporary music—something that most churches had never had before.

However, I wasn't quite there yet. My perspective was "to each his own"—

Until a fateful evening.

A few of my Christian surfing friends attended the Calvary Chapel in nearby Encinitas, just south of my hometown. I was a bit nervous to attend church, but Barbie was a regular attendee and agreed to meet me in the parking lot just before the Sunday evening service. That evening, I waited nervously in my car for her, but by the time the service was set to begin, she still had not arrived. Unbeknownst to me, she had sustained a fender-bender accident on the way down. She couldn't call, this being years before cell phones hit the scene, and she never made it to the service.

I sat alone in my car, waiting and waiting, slowly realizing that, for whatever reason, Barbie wouldn't be meeting me. Finally, I came to a simple conclusion, in retrospect a life-altering realization: *If I don't go into this church service on my own right now, I may never go.*

And so, with nerves rushing through my body as they did before major pro tour heats, I got out of the car and walked right through those church front doors. Since I was a well-known personality on the coast, a number of people recognized me right away. I said hello to a few as I headed into the main sanctuary. Once inside, who do I see near the front? None other than one of my former PSAA judges, Mickey Yarbrough. I'd grown up surfing with three of the four Yarbrough brothers—Mickey, Willie and Danny, a surfer on the PSAA circuit himself. Mickey recognized me and then called out for me to join him in the front—and that was that! I liked the style of the service, hung around talking with people afterward, and drove home full of encouragement and hope. I not only survived going to church on my own, but I also enjoyed it very much.

As spring turned to summer, I tried to go to church twice a week. I became a regular listener of the KWVE Christian radio station broadcasting out of San Clemente. Through radio, I began to become familiar with different Bible teachers, while at the same time reading my Bible daily and sincerely trying to move forward and make good decisions in my life. Because of my Catholic background, I had always believed in God, but even with the sacrament of confirmation under my belt, I had never really understood the idea of a personal decision of faith. I thought it went something like this: Go to church, do good, or at least more good than bad, and then hopefully you will head into heaven when life is said and done. The more I heard the Bible taught, though, the more I realized the key to me living a faithful, godly life was to hold an ever-growing faith in God for who He is and what He has done.

To this point in my life, I had always emphasized my own achievements, plus any good works that I could do to earn God's favor (and hopefully avoid His wrath). I kept hearing phrases like "Christianity is a relationship, not a religion" and "It's not our ability, but rather our *availability* that matters to God." These and other phrases tugged at my heart and drew me closer to God and wanting to serve Him.

One day, while reading through the Gospel of John, a certain Bible verse jumped out at me: "It is finished," spoken by Jesus on the cross. It caused me to ask, "What is *finished*?" Suddenly, it became very clear—it was the way to heaven. For the first time in my entire life, I truly understood that Jesus had died to save me. I realized that I needed to sincerely believe in and receive Him into my life! In times past I had heard this before, but somehow, while in my room at my dad's house reading that passage, it all became so clear to me! At the same time, I had another thought. I wasn't quite sure what to think, but I was sure what to do: whatever God was calling me to do.

After this epiphany, I got the idea that I should put together a surfing slideshow and make myself available for guest speaking at churches. A few invitations came my way and by the end of the summer, I began going out and speaking at various churches. It was a fairly simple ministry. I would present the slideshow, discuss my surfing career, share a little bit about my faith, and then eventually encourage those in attendance to personally trust in God. I was hardly an evangelist or anything like that, but I was willing to go out and share my faith, quite surprised that it seemed like God was using me! Even with the feelings of success and positive response surrounding these events, I was always nervous about them, as I felt like it was such a big responsibility.

One of my favorite slideshow presentations happened with a group in the North San Diego County town of Fallbrook. One of my longtime friends, *Breakout* magazine photo editor Allen Carrasco, personally assembled a carousel deck of shots he'd taken of me from the beach and water, some of which had been published in *Breakout.* Some I'd never seen before. I was so grateful and inspired that I treated the crowd to an evening of surf stories to go along with my larger experience and messages of faith. Already, my old life and my new were starting to blend in the best possible way. It would not be the last time, for sure.

At the same time, I was making progress in my return to competitive surfing. Once I got past the personal awkwardness of competing on the tour I had created, I began to post some decent results and to move up the tour rankings. A personal highlight came during the summer, when I surfed in the trials of the ASP World Tour's Stubbies Pro, which had moved from Oceanside Harbor a mile south to Oceanside Pier to accommodate the thousands of spectators. I looked around at the scene on the north side of the pier, amazed at how much this event, and surfing, had grown in just a few short years. The promoters even made it a point to direct some of the media toward me, you know, the California Kid coming back to his home surf for one more contest run. This gesture really touched me.

Unfortunately, I was still a bit rusty on the international stage, having not surfed an ASP World Tour event in three years. Rising stars Sunny Garcia and Richie Collins easily defeated me in our qualifying heat, but that's not what I remember most. After the event, local longboarder Paul Moretti came up to me, accompanied by a man I'd never met before. While catching up, I rattled off a New Testament verse attributed to John: "A man can receive nothing unless it comes from above."

The man with Paul? Brian Brodersen, who I would meet again shortly afterward.

When the 1987 PSAA season wrapped up in July, I managed to make finals in the last two events, which elevated me to the year-end Top 10 rankings. It was a far cry from being Top 10 in the world, but still, I was heading in the right direction with what was left of my surfing career. Overshadowing these encouraging results, though, was the great reality that I still had no idea what I wanted to do next in my life.

A very important event happened in the latter part of summer. I paddled out to surf at one of my local spots, Carlsbad State Beach, and saw only one other surfer in the water. This was unusual, as there were typically at least ten or more surfers in the lineup on any given day at that time of the morning. Even more surprising was that the surf was good, with clean three-to-five-foot waves . . . but no one else was out.

After I caught and rode a few waves, the other surfer in the lineup and I began to start up a conversation. Sure enough, it was Brian Brodersen and he was the pastor of the Calvary Chapel in Vista, where my dad lived, just inland from Carlsbad.

"I heard you attend Calvary Chapel North Coast down in Encinitas," Brian said.

"Yes I do, I enjoy it!"

"I go to Calvary Chapel Vista."

"Oh wow! I've listened to your pastor on KWVE! I like his teachings!"

He smiled as the sun beat on his wet face. "I am that pastor."

I will never forget that conversation.

Brian encouraged me to stop by the church later that day, which I did. From that time on, we connected and became great friends. Brian's strong faith inspired me, and he was someone I could relate to. Originally from Huntington Beach, he was a talented surfer in his own right. We had many mutual friends in Huntington Beach, and since he was about three years older than me, he became like my big brother in the faith. We established a strong friendship, so it was only natural that I began attending the Calvary Chapel in Vista as my home church. Now fully committed to a new church family, I was able to make a lot of friends and, like my time at the former church in Encinitas, I enjoyed it!

As September rolled around, I continued to surf and train regularly as I prepared for the new PSAA season. I had made it my goal to win the tour I had started! I was hoping to become the 1988 PSAA Champion. At the same time, in addition to emerging ministries and ongoing surfing, I was also carrying a full load of college classes. After a year of community college, I had begun to become comfortable and enjoy being back in school, and the classes I took encouraged and motivated me. I was happy and enjoying that season in my life.

Then things took a turn. A big, wonderful turn. A girl in my group communications class caught my attention. As time went on, I found myself very much attracted to Jennifer George, who lived 20 minutes down the coast in Cardiff. Jennifer didn't speak much in class, but she did listen. On one particular night, after I shared my faith in the classroom setting, she approached me during break time with some very sincere questions. In front of a group of other students, she asked me, "What do you think the world is coming to?"

I responded, "Jesus is coming back."

After the other students took off, she asked me a second question, "Why do you think that?"

I shared with her all that I knew about the topic. She didn't blink. After that, she had still more questions!

From that night onward, we became friends and I always looked forward to seeing her. Within a week or so of that initial conversation with Jennifer, in another turn of events I had not anticipated, Brian Brodersen asked me to consider becoming a pastor at Calvary Chapel Vista. I was quick to adamantly reply, "NO!" The way I saw it, I had failed at least once in just about everything in life, and I had no intention of failing God as a pastor, which I knew would be inevitable if I took the position.

In late October, I headed north to San Francisco to begin the new PSAA season. Heading into the event, I did not have a lot of confidence, as I was fighting a nagging back injury that had not fully healed. To make things worse, the surf was big, a solid 10 to 15 feet. Just seeing the surf made my back ache a little more. With no deep-water channel for safely paddling out, the surf presented extremely challenging conditions for all of the competitors.

On Halloween afternoon, my back couldn't support me properly on one of those large Ocean Beach waves and I took a serious beating, thus being eliminated in my first heat. Afterward, I was understandably disheartened and discouraged. Yet, I needed to stay positive and shift gears for my second task of that day.

Earlier in the month, I had committed to speak that night at a church in nearby Pacifica to share the story of how I came to faith. What I most remember about that night is that I shifted from being discouraged by my contest result to being encouraged as I shared my faith with the small audience. It struck me that these people had been interested enough to come to hear my story on Halloween night! There was a film crew there, working on a new Christian surf movie, which was to be called *SON Riders.* I don't think anyone at the time could have foreseen the far-reaching impact the movie would eventually have, an impact that continues to this day. *SON Riders* would be seen by thousands of people worldwide through video distribution. It is still the most-viewed video on my YouTube channel.

I shared that night about not the glory and majesty of winning the Pipeline Masters and fulfilling the goal of my surfing career—but the emptiness of it. My talk resonated powerfully with many in the surf industry and surrounding culture. My story of the pouring rain, the reclaimed trophy, and the loneliness and emptiness that followed, ended up in the movie. It literally became world famous. Like the Pipeline Masters video from four years earlier, *SON Riders* had a far-reaching global influence. Put together, the Pipeline Masters and *SON Riders* videos produced a powerful one-two effect. The story of "dreams come true" gave way to the story "dreams are empty, vain, and insecure without the Lord."

The next day, November 1, I drove back to Southern California. During that drive, I listened to some teaching cassette tapes by evangelist Greg Laurie. One of the tapes was called *Forgiven and Used*, about the Apostle Peter's restoration into ministry after he denied Christ. While listening to this message, I realized that if I became a pastor, I could fail God and that it would never surprise Him, though it could surprise me. Then, in a very clear and profound thought, I realized that "failure is inevitable, growth is optional!"

Somehow, that thought set me free from my fears of future pastoral ministry failure.

Shortly after returning home, I called Brian and informed him that I was now willing and excited at the thought of becoming a pastor and dedicating my life to serving God. I was both excited and nervous as I realized that, for the first time in years, my life now had a clear and absolute purpose. It had taken a while, three years to be exact, but I was certain I had found my true life destiny. God was calling me to become a pastor, and this new journey would begin with the arrival of 1988.

13

DIVINE APPOINTMENTS

I've always been a believer. There never was a time in my life when I didn't believe in the existence of God. I didn't believe because someone told me that it was required to be a good Catholic. It's always been more than that.

Still, in my journey of faith from childhood to young adulthood, the journey preceding my walk as a pastor, many things about God seemed mysterious to me. For example, I can remember, while we lived in Quantico, passing through a period where I constantly thought, *If God made everything, who made God?* Pretty heady stuff for a seven-year-old, right? Even then, I learned there are many things about God and the universe that were beyond my grasp. They still are. In my childhood faith, I was certain God was real, I was accountable for my actions and maybe someday I would try my best to obey Him.

This remains the premise of the child*like* faith I hold today.

As I shared earlier, I really liked attending Sunday school classes, and I continued going to Sunday Mass after we moved to Carlsbad. However, when adolescence and surfing became one within me and I neared my 14th birthday, Mom released me from my family obligations of attending church or catechism classes. I'd received the first three sacraments of the religion—baptism, First Communion and confirmation—and she figured it was up to me from this point forward.

Not surprisingly, with my newfound self-determined freedom, I chose waves over catechism and surfing over Mass. There were a few exceptions, but not many. My future was surfing. My world and my dreams revolved around surfing. My faith, and my total being? Everything was about surfing!

In my mind, religion and surfing had nothing to do with each other. God was church, surfing was the ocean, and they had no connection to each other.

Well, that's what I thought until that first big surfing trip of my young career in South Padre Island, Texas.

I'd received an invitation to the USA Surfing Championships. I was so excited to be in Texas with all of the top surfers in America. After arriving, I immediately recognized some of my heroes surfing in the water and walking around the hotel lobby. It felt like a dream come true to not only see them, but to be among them. At our official opening ceremony for the event, I was there front and center! We converged in Texas from different regional surfing associations—I represented the Western Surfing Association—so we were introduced by region, which made it feel really special. To be welcomed by name, as an equal with some of my heroes? Like any other 14-year-old, I was stoked beyond belief.

Later, the emcee mentioned that Gulf Coast surf star Yancy Spencer, from Pensacola, Florida, would be giving a special talk when the opening ceremony concluded. Well, I certainly knew who Yancy Spencer was. He was in the surf magazines, the type of surf hero I wanted to become, so of course I stayed and listened to whatever he had to say. I expected surf stories, tales of some of the biggest surf he'd ridden, the most prestigious contests he'd won, some of his favorite surf breaks and countries in which he might have ridden waves ...

Not quite. In fact, not at all what I expected. I don't remember anything from his talk other than he spoke generally about surfing and then switched gears to sharing about Jesus! It remains as amazing to me today in my recollections as it was then. I can still see him, picture the room and replay the scene.

After Yancy was done sharing, a definitive thought entered my mind and world for the very first time: *Jesus and surfing were not opposing forces matched against each other, but could coexist together.* That was it, that simple thought. I didn't go forward to an invitation, I didn't say a prayer or hear an audible voice from heaven, but I simply realized that night that Jesus and surfing could go together in my life. For a fleeting moment, it also crossed my mind that God was revealing Himself to me.

What a night.

And what a contest. Between making it to nationals as a 14-year-old and Yancy's message, this fired-up Californian enjoyed a great week at the event, making the finals in my division and flying home quite proud of my fourth-place USA Surfing Championship trophy.

Yancy's talk, the effect it had on me and my performance, was my introduction to the relationship between God and surfing. The second profound appointment came four years later, in early December of 1979. Instead of surfing the smallish waves of Texas, I was now riding the thunder swells of Oahu's North Shore.

A beautifully warm and sunny day welcomed my second Pipeline Masters, and first as a returning finalist. I was an unknown the previous year; now, I could consider myself a prime contender, one of the hunted among other competitors. The ocean texture was clean and glassy, with waves in the five-to-seven-foot range. I was nervous, excited and ready to win. I was brimming with confidence, certain that I was going to build off my fifth-place finish as a 17-year-old to win the event.

While contemplating the conditions and heat strategy, I was approached by one of the well-known surfing locals of the North Shore, Adam 12. Yep, that was his name, just like the popular early 1970s cop show. Adam 12 was a well-respected big-wave charger at Pipeline, and was also well liked by most for his friendly and positive disposition. I wouldn't say we were close, but we were respectful of each other in the lineup, and in Hawaii, that means a lot! So, when he approached me, I said hello and genuinely welcomed his presence. We talked about the contest and the conditions ...

... and then, out of nowhere, he started talking about Jesus!

First, he asked me if I knew Jesus. "Of course I do!" I replied. "Don't all Catholics know Jesus? Yes, I know Jesus. I'm a *Roman* Catholic!" I emphasized the word *Roman,* because I always thought it meant something more than just Catholic, but Catholic with a special upgrade. Rome was where the religion took root, where the Vatican was located, where the Pope presided over his global flock. Classic, right?

Adam 12 considered my answer for a second, then smiled and asked, "Have you ever asked Jesus into your heart?" He said it as if it didn't matter whether I was a Roman Catholic, Irish Catholic, German Catholic, Carlsbad Catholic or any other form of Catholic.

I'm like, "What?"

He followed up. "Jesus is for you and wants you to ask him into your heart."

I could see great value in that. Including an immediate benefit. "Well then, will He help me win the Pipeline Masters?" Doesn't hurt to ask, right?

Adam 12 smiled, not at all thrown off by my question. "Maybe ..."

Was this dude for real? He kind of had it all. He was a happy guy, most everyone liked him, he was a well-respected Pipeline Underground surfer, and he was competing. "Would you like to ask Him into your heart right now?" he added.

Well, I thought, *it's good odds, it can't hurt.*

"Yes!" I replied.

So right then and there, and thanks to Adam 12, I asked Jesus into my heart with the obvious motive that He would now be on my side and help me win the Pipeline Masters.

Convinced that God was now firmly supporting me, I paddled out with great confidence for my first-round heat—and was promptly and unceremoniously eliminated. I looked around. Did Jesus fall off my board? How come He didn't keep my feet on it? Or send me the waves I needed? Or draw up the most perfect tube of the contest for me to ride?

After my heat, I rode prone into shore, thinking, *Well, that didn't work!* Then I laughed at myself.

Even funnier is, I don't remember anything about my heat, who was in it, the waves I caught or what I did on them. Or, considering my result, didn't do on them. Yet, to this day, I remember almost everything about my conversation with Adam 12. The key thought was, *God is personal and wants a relationship with me.*

It would be years before I sincerely acted upon it.

Far more impactful than these two events came another moment that took place during a 17-hour flight to Australia while sitting next to California surfing legend Chris O'Rourke. Of all the conversations I've ever had in my life, this is still one of the most memorable and lasting for its deep, direct and permanent effect on my entire existence. In early 1978, I might have been on the rise, but Chris was without question the best surfer in California, and my biggest career inspiration other than Gerry Lopez. A few years older than me and a naturally gifted athlete, Chris performed moves on a single-fin surfboard that were years ahead of the sport. He surfed with a refined, polished style, fluid connection in his turns, plenty of radical surfing and, above all else in my book, he was a great competitor. During the mid-1970s, when locals were rejecting contests for their "commercialism" in a fierce display of surfer territorialism, Chris was both a serious, protective local at the notorious Windansea in La Jolla and winning regional events all over California. He was everything I wanted to be, an intense, blazing fire who burned for our sport.

Sadly and tragically, some flames go out before others.

I was just 16 and still an amateur when I heard the news that Chris, the Californian who was leading us all to the promised land of pro surfing, had Hodgkin's disease. Cancer. This news came out right before my pro career began, while I was also watching the cancer battle my best friend David Barr's mother was waging. That, too, was affecting me.

The timing of my rise and the sudden halt of Chris's career under the dark cloud of cancer were, and still are, inseparably linked. I can remember exactly what I thought when I heard the news: *It's a bad break for him, but a good one for me.* Looking back, it was an incredibly selfish thing to think, yet in the unfiltered rawness of my 16-year-old mind, it was my reality, absolutely true. Over the next three years, while Chris fought for his life, sometimes inspiring everyone by surfing at Windansea after a grueling chemo treatment, I fought for my pro surfing dream. In 1978, Chris ranked as the clear number-one surfer in California, while I was the clear number two. Three years later, in 1981, I was at the zenith of being the California Kid as Chris was dying.

Which brings us back to that flight to Australia.

It was early March 1981 when I arrived at LAX and checked in for my flight. I was headed to Australia for the opening leg of the 1981 season. It would be my first year of competing in every event on the IPS World Tour. After the success of my 1980 season, I was a seeded surfer in the coveted Top 16, the first to ever represent California. If Chris had been dealt a luckier hand, he likely would have carried that distinction, not me. But I was the clear and absolute star of California surfing.

While checking in, I realized some other California pro surfers were going to be on the same flight. As I looked around, I saw Chris O'Rourke. I hardly recognized him. He was pale and gaunt. I could scarcely believe it was him.

What is he doing here? I thought. Then I remembered: His sponsor, Stubbies Clothing, had decided to fly him down to their event, the Stubbies Surf Classic at Burleigh Heads, as a show of support and respect. He and event director Bill Bolman, one of the loudest, funniest and most signature Australian personalities ever, were also very close friends. Back in 1978, at the first Stubbies event, Chris shocked the surf world with his standout surfing. A year later, when Bolman and mainland Stubbies officials Mike and Greg Bechelli decided to launch a series of surf trials in California, Hawaii and Florida, Chris convinced them to hold the event at Black's Beach, which never hosted tournaments. Then, despite being weakened by his aggressive disease and chemotherapy treatments, he delivered a moment for the ages by surfing in the event—the last time he ever wore a contest singlet.

Now, two years later, Stubbies was bringing him back, not as a world tour Top 16 star, but as a cancer survivor, a symbol of inspiration. By this time, his surf dreams had long since been crushed. All of his goals were centered on his faith, family, and health, on growing his relationship with Jesus for what awaited him. I remember feeling great empathy for Chris as I looked at him in the airport.

After boarding the flight, I arrived at my assigned seat—and next to me was none other than Chris O'Rourke. The first California Kid and his heir apparent, numbers one and two in 1977, when our fortunes broke off in far different ways—mine to fight for victories as a pro, and Chris to fight for his life. How this came about, I'll never know. Well, I do know: It was God's plan. It just was meant to be. In a 747 filled to capacity, it would be me and Chris O'Rourke side by side for 17 hours. Chris would step into eternity in less than two months; I would live my dreams, win the Pipeline Masters, later make the International Surfing Hall of Fame, and proceed through a rich, full life for the next 40-plus years. And counting.

Yet on this day, the greatest contrast between Chris O'Rourke and myself was the strength of his faith in God, and my resistance to such a thing.

In the days before inflight entertainment consoles populated passenger jets, people talked on planes. That's what Chris and I began to do. Talk. We talked about pro surfing and the news, stuff like that. And then suddenly, Chris began to talk about life and death, dreams and tragedy, love and forgiveness, and most of all, his deep faith in God. Time stood still. In that moment, in that context, I was in eternity with Chris O'Rourke.

On our flight, Chris shared two things with me I never forgot. First, he disclosed to me that while people publicly thought his cancer was in remission, he was in fact dying. This made sense, since that was how he looked to me. In that private moment, he let me in on his great secret: He would die soon. The second thing he shared is that he was ready to die and go to glory, but I was not. He said he was ready, but Joey Buran was not. I didn't know what to make of such a stark statement, other than one thing: He was right.

Suddenly, I felt such conviction from his piercing words, and the massive discomfort I felt from his comment, that I was determined to get away from him and find another seat elsewhere on the plane. I got up and began looking around for any available seats, but there was not even one available alternative seat. This flight was jam-packed. I had no choice but to go back and sit next to Chris for the entire flight and listen to him talk about human failure, Jesus, God's forgiveness, and the hope of heaven.

So it was, by God's decree, I sat next to a dying man who talked about Jesus, on a 17-hour flight, with no choice in the matter. At one point in the flight, Chris asked me to put skin lotion on his back because his skin was so dry and damaged from the chemotherapy. It was so humbling to put that lotion on him and then rub it into his dying skin. At that moment, God made me touch death, but not just the death of any man. The death of my hero and rival, Chris O'Rourke.

A couple of days after we arrived in Australia, Chris collapsed on the judge's tower. Sadly, his time at the Stubbies Surf Classic, his beloved sport, and the ocean whose waves he rode so masterfully and beautifully ended. He was flown home to the US where he eventually passed away several weeks later—but not before spending his final day in the ICU at Scripps Hospital in San Diego, imparting his goodbye message for a newspaper column written by a friend of mine. As you might expect, it concerned fighting cancer to the very end, love of surfing, love of life, love of friends and family, love of his Windansea crew but most of all, love of God.

From that time on, I knew God cared for me and was interested in my life. I never doubted it again. I knew after my flight with Chris O'Rourke, that the God of a trillion galaxies and a planet with eight billion people knew everything about Joey Buran and cared very much about him. I was 100 percent certain that God had made me sit next to Chris on that flight. I knew and believed it was much more than a coincidence. God, through his faithful servant Chris O'Rourke, had revealed himself clearly and undeniably to me. After that event, there was no doubt, in the recesses of my heart, that I knew God was coming for me.

In the fullness of time, he did.

14

HEADING EAST: VENTURE OF FAITH

My life was about to take another huge leap forward—in a way that began with an event connected to surfing, and then centered on my new ministry. And on love.

As 1987 drew to a close, Calvary Chapel Vista committed to doing an outreach event targeting the youth and local beach culture. We showed surf videos and I shared my testimony of personal faith. I invited a lot of people to this event, including some of my college classmates and old friends from Carlsbad. My life had changed dramatically in just one year, and this was a chance for my hometown peer group to hear my story of faith and personal transformation. Among those who attended was Jennifer George, my college classmate.

After I shared a brief message, Brian Brodersen got up, clearly explained the Gospel of Jesus, and gave a formal invitation for those who would like to accept Him. When Brian was done, about a dozen people responded favorably and publicly to his invitation, including Jennifer. It seemed she'd already begun to develop a personal faith before that night, but this was the moment she chose to make a public confession.

The rest was a whirlwind, with my heart and Jennifer's whipping up the wind. While we previously enjoyed a couple of friendship dates, I now found myself falling head over heels in love with her. Before the year was done, I asked her to marry me.

"Yes," she said, her voice as solid and sure as the look in her eyes and smiling face.

Three months later, we were married on a beautiful late winter day in March 1988. I had already begun to serve as an intern pastor at Calvary Chapel Vista, so by agreeing to marry me, she also was saying yes to becoming a pastor's wife. Which carries some added responsibility. After our wedding, we jetted off to Colorado for our one-week honeymoon on the ski slopes, and then returned back home to Vista and launched full speed ahead into our new life of marriage and ministry.

What a huge difference one year can make! I never saw it coming when 1987 began, but I'd righted myself from personal disaster, committed myself more to serving God, worked hard at strengthening my faith and trusted that life was going to take a turn for the better. "Faith is the evidence of things unseen," as the scripture says.

I just didn't realize it would be such a big turn. After my single season in the US Pro Tour Top 10, I was no longer a pro surfer. Months after nervously entering the Calvary Chapel in Encinitas and seeing my friend Mick Yarbrough's welcoming face, I was now a pastor! I was no longer single but now married! Ministry and marriage had come in the same season, an incredible meshing of spirit and love, and Jennifer and I were in it together.

As we became more involved in the church, we also began to visit other churches to show the recently completed *SON Riders* movie and share our stories and ministry with attendees. We didn't limit ourselves to the growing number of Calvary Chapels in the area; we visited many different churches with their distinct denominational dispositions. It was an interesting time, truly a learning and growing experience for both of us. During our church tour, we received another tremendous blessing: Jennifer became pregnant with our first child. We carried the *SON Riders* tour through spring into summer, and through summer into autumn, then she began to show and understandably slow down. I also began to shift gears away from guest speaking at other churches and to focus on our life and church family in our home Vista church.

My first official ministry at Vista was the young adult group. It seemed a perfect fit, since I had spent my life in the youthful surf culture and talked to countless young surfers and spectators while being one of the world's top performers. However, it took a while for me to make that fit perfect. As I assumed leadership of this ministry, I found myself struggling with trying to figure out how pastoral ministry worked. I brought natural leadership gifts of vision and communication into the work, but I had not yet developed the character necessities of humility and listening to and serving others. I'd never had to; I was always the subject of attention, whether signing autographs, giving interviews, or hearing the hoots and cheers of fans when I tucked myself deep into tubes or cranked off body-bending maneuvers. Despite my sincerity in wanting to serve as a pastor, I was immature and woefully lacking in so many important areas needed for a successful ministry. As the holiday season arrived, I held serious doubts about being able to continue in pastoral ministry.

This was problematic—about the only problem I encountered during one of the most remarkable and beneficial years of my life. I was happily married and had clearly moved on from my professional surfing career. Maybe it was time to "get a real job," to focus on a more lucrative career, perhaps in the surf industry. It seemed like the logical place to work. Thus, as Jennifer approached her delivery date, I quietly considered and contemplated a face-saving transition out of pastoral ministry and into some other sort of new career calling. I was strong and sincere in my faith, but insecure and uncertain about pastoral ministry. I wasn't sure what I wanted to do or *could* do for a career. But I was fairly certain that I did not want to be a pastor anymore.

Then an unwanted challenge hit us. During the Christmas season, a particularly serious flu bug struck Jennifer and me, making us both extremely sick. As the new year approached, Jennifer, still recovering from being ill, grew concerned that the baby had begun to slow down its movement in her womb. Several women we knew assured her that this was natural in the third trimester of pregnancy, especially as far along as she was, but she was not convinced. For our peace of mind, we eventually drove to our scheduled delivery hospital down in San Diego so that the doctor could check Jennifer out. After running some tests, the doctor on call told Jennifer that she and the baby were fine and sent us home.

She remained unconvinced. This wasn't like her. She couldn't shake her concern. A few days later, on December 31, she shared with me that she had not felt the baby move that entire day. Back to the hospital we went, closing out an otherwise amazing 1988 in the emergency room.

A nurse examined Jennifer. A look of deep concern stretched across her face. Where was the baby's heartbeat? She couldn't find one. Without a word to us, she left the room and searched out a doctor. A minute later, the doctor came in and put his fetal stethoscope to Jennifer's stomach. Nothing.

He looked at both of us, calm as the sea on a windless day. "Your baby has died in the womb," he said simply.

The moment he said those words, I looked at the clock on the wall. Ten minutes after midnight. It was now the new year. *Wow. So this is how our 1989 will be defined,* I thought, my heart falling into that state between numbness and despair as I projected strength for my wife. I couldn't even imagine how she felt.

The doctor snapped us out of our stunned silence. He turned to me. "Jennifer is now at risk," he said. I caught the look in his eye and knew instantly what he implied, and then said: "She's in danger now. We have to get the baby out." He and a team of nurses immediately induced Jennifer into a long, unnatural forced labor. It took more than 40 painful hours before our firstborn child would be delivered.

Our lifeless child.

Jennifer's dad, Bill, came by the hospital to encourage and comfort us during 40 of the most grueling, tragic and sad hours imaginable. Despite feeling helpless, I determined the one thing I could do was read words of strength and comfort to Jennifer from the Bible. I stood by her side and read from the Old Testament book of Psalms.

Finally, after two long and difficult nights, wrung out by absolute physical and emotional exhaustion, Jennifer delivered our beloved firstborn son, Jesse, in the late afternoon on January 2. After his delivery, I held his lifeless body in my arms, said the Lord's Prayer and committed him to God. Jennifer was completely exhausted and numb; she never held our baby.

A day later, we left the hospital without our son, empty-handed, filled with so much sorrow that words cannot adequately describe it. The experience can only be understood by those who have gone through something similar. Jennifer and I couldn't speak one word to each other on the drive from downtown San Diego to our home in Vista. Our ride was one of shared silence and sorrow, with no words available to be spoken. Or necessary.

A day later, I took down and packed up the baby room we had so lovingly prepared in previous months for Jesse's arrival. I carefully boxed every item, feeling like I also was packing up a part of my crushed spirit in each box, then drove it to my mom's house up the street, where I quietly unloaded it into my former bedroom closet. Around the same time, Brian Brodersen expressed to me that he thought it best that his father-in-law, the legendary Pastor Chuck Smith, come down from Costa Mesa to perform Jesse's memorial service.

Brian made a great suggestion. As was the case so often with Pastor Chuck, his sincere words of truth brought great strength and comfort to Jennifer, me, and so many others on that difficult day. Later in the week, Jennifer and I scattered Jesse's remains in the Pacific Ocean just north of the Army and Navy Academy in my original hometown of Carlsbad. We were alone, the setting desolate, our state of devastation a sense of slowly dying, far worse than anything I'd ever felt. Or ever hoped to feel again.

Our shared sorrow under these heartbreaking circumstances forever brought us together, forged our bond in the raw, molten emptiness of losing Jesse, and established our strong friendship that would last over the next 35 years . . . and counting.

About a month later, we decided to move on from our cute honeymoon bungalow. We'd spent almost nine months as three spirits living in God's sweetest love, one of us inside Jennifer's womb. But Jesse was gone. It was too painful to stay there without our son. As our lives inched forward from our heartache and grief, we grew closer in our relationship as we chose to grieve together. We found healing and solace as we focused on the ministry and whatever calling God had in store for us next. Amid this heartache, one thing became very clear to me: It was too early for me to give up on my pastoral ministry commitments. I decided that at least for the foreseeable future, I should continue going forward in service as a pastor at Calvary Chapel Vista.

Within a few months, Brian entrusted another ministry to me, a drug and alcohol recovery group. As I got into the work, and watched the spirits of our group members shift from downtrodden to hopeful and then optimistic, their eyes growing clearer and their health better, I realized this was a ministry in which I could be successful. For the next two years, I ran this ministry with as much dedication and purpose as I poured into my surfing career. And then some. I found great joy in serving these men and women, some just teenagers, who viewed me as a catalyst to helping them get their lives back on track. *The glory goes to God, and I am here for you in service to Him*, I thought more than once. A lot of wonderful things happened in this season of our lives, and I was eventually very encouraged to continue forward in pastoral service.

Then joy really did descend upon us. Hannah Joy, our first daughter. Jennifer brought her into the world just as 1990 got started. Our loss of Jesse only intensified our desire to be good parents. I could see right away that Jennifer was a fantastic mother, even as we were learning how to become parents and adjusting to the changes in our marriage as a husband and wife with a little one! Every one of her cries, coos and laughs filled us with the deepest joy. There is no way words can describe the feeling. Truly, through Hannah, God had turned our sorrow into joy.

During our time serving in the ministry at Calvary Chapel Vista, God provided an opportunity to visit the East Coast of the US and show the *SON Riders* movie in both Virginia and North Carolina. It was a return to the state where I once was winning swim meets as a small kid; how much life had changed in the nearly 20 years that followed! While on the East Coast, we met and worked with a woman whose son was a Calvary Chapel pastor. One day, in a passing conversation, she shared with me her dream to see the formation of a Calvary Chapel church in the Virginia Beach area.

After we returned home, before we could unpack our bags, I prayed for this request. When I did, a very clear thought entered my mind, and then blossomed into form: I would be the guy to start that church! So, after three years at Calvary Chapel Vista and with our daughter Hannah approaching her first birthday, we loaded up the car and headed to Virginia Beach to start a Calvary Chapel.

On a scouting trip a few weeks prior, I secured a meeting place for the church, and met some people who were interested in being a part of our ministry. Some even looked for potential places for us to live—as we were driving across the country to start the church! With opportunity in ministry comes a season of personal growth, as I would learn many ministry lessons through trial and error. In Virginia Beach, I performed all the ceremonies, tasks and duties for which a lead pastor is responsible, including weddings, memorials, child dedications, baptisms, outreach events, and of course weekly church services. At times I felt very inadequate as a pastor and in fulfilling the responsibilities required of me. It wasn't so much the actual tasks that needed to be done, but more the commitment of leading and working with other people as a ministry servant leader. I had so many lessons to learn, and often, I learned them through mistakes and failures.

In spite of my lack of patience and the feeling I lacked enough life experience, the church grew and eventually found its niche in the historically transient region. Jennifer and I enjoyed our lives in Virginia. Virginia Beach is a beautiful city with a spread-out population of over a half million people. When combined with the surrounding cities, including neighboring Norfolk, it made up a metropolitan area of over a million. The region hosted a constant flux of year-round tourists and a very large military presence, bringing thousands of people in and out of the community every month.

During this time, with the help of our parents, we purchased our first home and went on to live in the area for about four years. We also welcomed the blessed arrival of our second daughter, Leah, who was born in 1992, and then of our son, Timothy, born two years later. We were a growing family and fully committed to one another while also setting our hearts on enjoying and fulfilling the ministry entrusted to us in Virginia.

Shortly after Timmy was born in late 1994, our family of five took a vacation north to the New England area. While in Vermont, I experienced the most unusual of thoughts. The idea entered my mind that we should leave Virginia and move to Burlington, Vermont, to start another church. Of course, Jennifer thought I was crazy, as did just about everyone else I knew. The California Kid living in Virginia Beach was one thing, but living in the landlocked state of Vermont? A place far from beaches, sand and surf? How could that possibly be?

Well, with God, anything is possible. Through prayer, we put forth a "test" or sign from God to make sure such a move received His fullest confirmation.

The first sign concerned the housing market. Interest rates were spiking above 9 percent, glutting the Virginia Beach housing market with houses for sale. It was a buyer's market. Our test with the Lord would be simple. Against all odds, if we listed and sold our house in Virginia Beach at full price by the end of springtime, we would receive it as a sign from God that we were truly called to move to Vermont.

Well, that is exactly what happened. We didn't even need to wait until the end of spring; our house sold right away at full price. In early April we said goodbye to Virginia Beach and drove through the night to Burlington to begin our newest adventure in faith.

Vermont is both gorgeous and unique. The people, culture, and climate have no equal. Located on beautiful Lake Champlain, Burlington is the largest city in Vermont; when we arrived, it had about 100,000 people. It is the home of the University of Vermont, a popular college town and the hub of the state. In contrast to the beauty of our autumn visit six months prior, though, when fall colors lit the trees afire in reds, oranges and yellows against sheer blue sky, the weather on the first day we awoke in our new state was composed of two primary colors, brown and gray. The dark gray sky was accompanied by cold temperatures and barren trees. The early spring green we had left behind the night before in Virginia was weeks away from migrating this far north.

Quickly, we learned the true seasons of Vermont from the locals. It went something like this: winter (long, very long), mud (in substitution of spring), summer (short to nonexistent), and autumn (short and beautiful). We also learned the locals didn't always take kindly to out-of-state transplants moving into their town or state. Ahhh, locals of a different type. Our arrival and purpose was met with skepticism and raised eyebrows, but I was not to be discouraged. I was confident we could make a great impact for good on the people of Vermont and we could do so quickly.

Our new life revolved around the hotel industry. On a previous ministry trip to the area, I looked for a viable meeting place for the church. During that search, it became apparent that the best venue available to us would be the meeting rooms at the local Econo Lodge motel. Its facility was affordable and clean, but quite the contrast to the many historical and traditional church buildings scattered throughout Burlington. Upon our permanent arrival in April, I felt certain I would have to find some kind of a part-time job to provide for my family while living in Burlington. While I was confident that we could be successful in establishing a lasting and fruitful church in the city, I was also realistic in my assessment that the new church would not be financially able to support me as a full-time pastor. As I applied for local jobs during that first week, it was another hotel, the Sheraton, that followed up on my job application and called me in for an interview.

My interview was classic. The restaurant manager interviewing me wanted to know why I had moved to Burlington. He said he had never met a pro surfer and wanted to know more about how anyone could even be a pro surfer and why they would move to Burlington. I responded by telling him some surf stories that made him laugh. "The real reason I'm here is to start a church," I finally added.

He laughed again—and hired me on the spot. Never mind my starting pay was the state minimum wage.

I received my green uniform and Sheraton name tag, undertook two days of orientation, and showed up to work in the room service department for about five dollars an hour. It was a match made in heaven. Joey Buran, the former pro surfer who stayed in hotels and motels in five different continents while being the US mainland's highest-paid surfer, was now 34 years old and working for minimum wage in a landlocked state, in a city on a huge lake with no waves. Thus began an important season in which I needed to become literally the servant of all, something I'd never experienced as a pro surfer or a minister. Among other things, the maids were Eastern European women who spent much of their time telling me what to do—in no uncertain terms. Even the dishwashers talked down to me when I brought in dirty dishes. *How did I end up being this guy?* I asked myself, more than once.

One day, as I was called to pick up some dirty dishes from the Presidential Suite, I thought, *Dude, I am Joey Buran, the Pipe Masters champion! Who do you think you are? Don't treat me like that!* I grabbed the dishes, putting them on the cart and thinking, *Wow, my whole career, I was always served by others. And God has brought me to this place of no ocean, no waves and no surfing, to teach me to be the lowest person, the servant of all.*

It was a very difficult lesson, but the lesson where I learned to serve others in my ministry.

From the first day, we welcomed familiar company after I persuaded some close and like-minded friends from Virginia Beach to make the move with us. Among these three families were our good friends the O'Connors. Jim O'Connor had faithfully served in ministry at the church. He was originally from upstate New York, hardworking, and a man of sincere faith. Accompanied by his wife, Pam, and the first of their four children, Sarah, they sold their house in Virginia, left behind his secure job, and made the move up with us at the same time.

Those first few months were trying and stretching for all the families. While Jennifer and I awaited a small financial gift of support, it was hardly enough for the financial realities that hit all of us in that first month. Jennifer and I were as prudent as we could be, managing ourselves and our young family while covering the rent. Jim, who had previously been an office warehouse manager in Virginia, secured jobs at the local McDonald's and Papa John's Pizza. Years later, I found out that the O'Connors lived on pancakes for the first week in Vermont. One of the reasons I knew nothing about this was that both Jim and I were heavily influenced by the ministry philosophies of renowned British philanthropist and evangelist George Muller of Bristol. As he fed and cared for thousands of orphans daily, his most basic belief was that Christians should take their financial needs only to God in prayer. That way, when the needs were met, personal faith would be strengthened and God alone would get the glory. This became a basic foundation of my ministry philosophy in the early '90s, one that has remained with Jim and me since.

We persevered in faith through these personal financial challenges while the church began to make favorable progress. We also learned that there were people in the Burlington region familiar with the ministry of Calvary Chapel churches. Eventually, some of them made it out to the Econo Lodge and became a part of the church family. Beyond that, we even realized some success in drawing out a few of the locals to our weekly services. As we passed through the first year, our personal finances stabilized and regular congregants began to establish a solid foundation for our church. We were so encouraged that we had every intention to stay indefinitely in the region to continue advancing the church.

As time went on, God began steering us in another direction. Westward. Toward our home state. Due to the higher cost of living in Vermont and how difficult it was to make ends meet on my minimum-wage income, we were certain by May of 1996 that we needed to overcome my reluctance to consider moving back to California.

Life experiences like our time in Vermont are important for molding and shaping personal character. I moved to Vermont hoping that I could do something great and profound for God. I dreamed of establishing a large church that would raise people in ministry to be sent all over New England to start more churches. In my mind, I determined with some certainty that I was destined to be a real Paul the Apostle kind of guy! In Vermont, what I found instead of outward ministry greatness was a minimum-wage job, pastoring a small church, making it all work on shoestring finances, and learning the value of serving others unconditionally to the glory of God.

My ministry highlight in that unique season was sharing my testimony and faith with a downcast coworker who then asked Christ into his life. In ministering to him, I remember thinking to myself, *I gave up a house in Virginia, secure income and a year of my life so this dishwasher could receive Christ?* Yep, that is exactly what happened—and with it, a life lesson worth a year of anyone's life. Thus, in the land of endless winter, God showed me how far He will go for one person and how much He loves us all.

With these life lessons behind me and substantial financial needs in front of us, we headed out on Memorial Day weekend for our long journey home to California during a late spring snowstorm, accompanied by a 20-foot Ryder truck fully loaded with our possessions. After five years of pastoral ministry on the East Coast, it was now time to return. I reflected throughout the drive on who I was in my journey of life, the lessons I had learned, and what would be coming up next in my ministry calling.

I tried to look into the future, only to see a lot of unknowns. However, I was certain of one thing in my near future: As soon as we spotted the Pacific Ocean, I was going to go surfing!

15

EL PASTOR EN EL TUBO

Sometimes, we do not know or cannot figure out why we felt led to make big changes or moves in our lives. Which was how I felt as we entered California. Though finances were tight in Vermont, our church was beginning to build momentum, and I felt more and more in the groove as a pastor who understood my many responsibilities and how to grow even further. Plus, I resisted the thought of returning to California. I had mixed reviews, thinking of my troubles after my world tour surfing career and losing our first child, but also the phenomenal blessing of marrying Jennifer, starting a family and becoming a minister. Also, we'd grown used to a slower lifestyle and fewer people, feeling Vermont would be a great place to raise our kids.

Then things happen—like they did on our first day back. And no, much as I fantasized stopping the car, grabbing a board and paddling out, it didn't involve surfing. Far, far from it.

A few hours after arriving in California, Jennifer's mother, Pat, suddenly collapsed right in front of us. We called 9-1-1 and then quietly looked on as Pat was taken away in an ambulance to the nearby hospital emergency room. After a few days of extensive tests, we learned the shocking news that Pat was sick with stage 3 lymphoma. We were completely stunned. Cancer is one of those diagnoses that levels everyone and turns worlds upside down, because you know that life will change for the person suffering from it, and those closest to that person. Plus, it brings along a set of questions that feel and look more menacing than a Waimea monster set that blackens the horizon—and more deadly serious: Can she survive this? How long will she live for? What will the treatments be like? How will she handle it? What will her life be like going forward? Who in the family can help her get through the upcoming difficult days, nights, weeks and months? Or years?

The last questions were the easiest to answer. We decided on the spot to stay at the house in Cardiff with Pat indefinitely. It was Jennifer's childhood home, and we would stay there to provide her mother with comfort, encouragement, support and whatever practical help was necessary. Needless to say, it was a very emotional and trying time for everyone in the family.

Shortly thereafter, Jennifer became pregnant with our final child, our youngest son, Luke. As she progressed through the first two trimesters of her pregnancy, she selflessly ministered to the needs of her mother, who was persevering through a season of aggressive chemotherapy. In December, Pat was able to take a break from her cancer treatment to enjoy the Christmas season in a house filled with the joy and laughter of her three grandchildren.

However, the chemo did not do the job. Just a few months after this special time, Pat passed away in early spring, and fittingly enough, her memorial was held on Good Friday. Apart from the passing of our first child, it was the hardest season of life I have ever personally been through. The sun punched through our profound grief and sadness, though, when Luke was born, bringing with him some much-needed joy to help lift our spirits. It had been a very trying and sorrowful first year back in California, but now with Luke's birth, it was time to turn the corner and begin to move forward into the next chapter of our lives.

What a powerful new chapter! During this new season, our faith was strengthened, our joy restored and our grief dissipated over time, but one thing remained as empty and dry as a desert lake—our bank account. I tried hard to use my gift of conversation, knack for inspiring others and ever-growing love of God and His message to make a living as a guest-speaking pastor. For some side income, I also jumped back in the water in a different way, taking on a little bit of surf coaching while trying to stay in the moment and seek what God was lining up next for me.

One thing was certain: After starting and pastoring two churches in four years, in two different states, I did not feel led at that time to do either, so I just tried to stay positive and take things one day at a time. I kept myself plenty busy and filled with purpose being a husband, dad, guest-speaking pastor, and surf coach. Not to mention a lot of variety in my everyday life.

Then along came a stretch of events I will never forget. They happened in quick succession and left me in a different place than where I started. It began with buying gas with pennies. Yes, pennies—in California, by far the country's most expensive state to buy gas (besides Hawaii). In the summer of 1997, I learned that if you are stretched financially, you might find yourself raiding the coin jar to buy gas. If it comes down to pennies, well then, let it be pennies. And that's what I did. *How humbling*, I thought to myself. Then a question popped up: *How many other people have had to do the same thing?* I was trying to live by faith and keep my ministry first on my priority list, but in doing so, I found myself increasingly frustrated and leaning toward states of bitterness and resentment over my circumstances.

Not where I wanted to be.

Well, within a day or so of using pennies for my gas purchase, I received a call from some people with whom I was familiar in the surf industry, but did not know too well personally. They tracked me down and told me that God had put it in their heart that they were to give me some money in support of my guest-speaking ministry. Really? Out of the blue? Just like that? But I remembered that when you put in the work, have faith in the evidence of things unseen, and stay open to *whatever happens next,* well, random people come into your life and tell you God moved them to work with you.

I drove out to their place of business, quite stoked. Then I became more stoked when I received words of encouragement and a support check in an envelope. The only thing I'd done for these people was agree to a meeting; I hadn't lifted a finger yet. I was so very grateful for the gift and I headed home with the check, not knowing the amount. I figured maybe $300, something to help us out ... even though I secretly hoped it was for $500. I drove and glanced at the envelope, drove and glanced, drove and glanced ...

My curiosity won the moment. About halfway home I decided to pull off to the side of the road. *The envelope, please ...*

I pulled out the check—and it took my breath away. I read it once, then again: $7,000. Seven grand! I took a deep breath, put the check back in the envelope, and drove home both happy and grateful, knowing our family of six had just been handed the very thing we needed at that moment.

But the day wasn't done. I mean, how much more manna could possibly rain down? My good friend, former pro surfer Sean Mattison, called and offered me a job at a local surf shop. I was ecstatic! In a matter of a few hours, my family had been relieved of financial distress, and I had a very cool job. When Jennifer and I woke up that morning, I was still grinding mentally over having to pay pennies for gas, wondering what I was going to do to support us. By the time we fell asleep that night, we'd found a whole new level of direction and stability.

Over the next few years, I enjoyed working retail at the Surf Ride Boardshop in nearby Oceanside. My personality is a good fit for retail: I love storytelling, I know the equipment and am not only a former world tour pro surfer but a pretty informed historian on the sport. How could working in a surf shop and chatting it up with surfers all day not be anything but enjoyable? Half the time, it didn't feel like work at all. It also often allowed me to run into former high school friends and acquaintances.

Eventually, I began to work with Surf Ride's promotional surf team, which folded right into my love of working with young people and proved to be an even better fit for me. I began to train our group of about 20 locals for regional surfing events. In a short time, they got better—and then they began to win! Every time one of the athletes won a tournament, or his or her division in that tournament, the thrill of victory poured through me again. It's such a wonderful feeling, knowing that on that day, you were better than everyone else in the water. Now these young surfers were experiencing it, and like a good minister, I was on it with life lessons, explaining how these wins were metaphors for winning in life, no matter whether the future lies in surfing, business, or being a plumber or carpenter.

The Surf Ride crew also served as the seed of a coaching journey that, 20 years later, would lead to the highest of heights in amateur surfing: the USA Olympic Surfing program! With my Surf Ride team, I developed three pillars of success that I emphasized, over and over. I call them the Three D's: Desire, Dedication and Determination. I was still using them with my athletes in the Olympic program, some of whom are now the world's greatest pro surfers. They have stood the test of time. It was a humble beginning to surf coaching, working with the surf shop team, but by the time my journey was complete, I was able to experience the joy of winning a world championship while also meeting some of the greatest Team USA Olympic coaches of this generation.

Since I was regularly at the beach again, I was surfing again. And, since I'm a hands-on coach, I realized that if I wanted to coach well and teach these kids winning maneuvers, I needed to surf well and execute the same maneuvers. I got right to it and began to prioritize my own personal surfing skills. As I felt the old moves, timing, wave selection, and quickness return to my legs and confidence to my mind, I began to wonder just how good I could surf while in my late 30s. For me, that didn't mean being the best in the water for my peer group. It meant being the best in the world.

The timing couldn't be better. The ASP World Surfing Tour had decided to present and produce a world championship event for surfers over the age of 35. It made perfect promotional and marketing sense: Even though we were older, we were the first professional surf stars, spending years on magazine covers and victory stands while the kids and young adults I coached were little grommets just learning about the sport. We were the icons, the living legends who gave way to the superstars of the Momentum

Generation of the 1990s. People like Mark Richards, Cheyne Horan, Tom Carroll, Rabbit Bartholomew, Shaun Tomson, Simon Anderson, and even further back to Peter Townend and Ian Cairns. I, too, was in that mix, no longer the California Kid in age but certainly in past reputation. We might be over 35, a couple of us over 40, a few pounds added here and there, but we still paddled out every day, we still ripped, and we still loved the thrill of the hunt, of competition.

Then came the big announcement, in early summer: The 1998 ASP World Masters Championship would be held in Puerto Escondido, Mexico, at the world-renowned Mexican Pipeline!

Once I heard the event venue was Puerto, my confidence surged. *Are you kidding me? At precisely my type of wave?* I knew I just had to go and win that event! Another wild little tidbit I later found out was that Bill Missett, the editor for my hometown paper which covered my early career extensively, was on the beach to watch us. After retiring, he moved to Puerto and was bodysurfing these same body-crunching barrels daily. His reporters had given me more coverage than any other newspaper during my career.

Because the event was to be held at such a challenging and dangerous wave, very similar to the Banzai Pipeline, I committed myself to undertaking some serious training before the event. After a ten-year hiatus from professional surfing, I fully intended to show up focused and well prepared to contend for that ASP Masters World Title. A friend from the local church knew someone at a renowned boxing gym in San Diego, and they allowed me to train there. Professional surfers had begun training like other pro athletes in the mid-1980s, leaving behind a whole host of stereotypes. By the late 1990s, you stood little chance of winning an ASP World Title of any kind without being a finely honed and tuned athlete. So it didn't seem strange at all to the boxers or trainers that a surfer would train with them.

Only these weren't just local or regional qualifiers getting themselves in shape to begin their careers. Instead, I found myself surrounded by some of the most serious athletes in the world. *Perfect.* Ever since David Barr and I had pushed each other to become the best young surfers in Carlsbad, then San Diego County, then California, I loved the added drive of training with others. I dropped excess weight, toned muscle, and built up my cardio. Then, when not working at the surf shop or training at the gym, I was in the water, pushing myself to get better in every aspect of my surfing.

There was, however, a potential snag in my comeback plans. Before the ASP had announced the location and dates, I had committed to officiating a wedding ceremony on the same weekend the event was scheduled to begin. Of course, there was no way I would try and cancel the wedding ceremony.

In the pecking order of important events in one's life, marrying your partner AND moving forward in God stood atop my list. Only one thing to do: see through my prior commitment and then head down to Mexico the second holding day of the event and hope everything I couldn't control would work out in my favor. Such as, the event being postponed on the first day because of inadequate surf. Like the Hawaiian competitions, organizers of the ASP World Tour Masters Championship were looking for the best waves within a period of days, not running the competition to a fixed calendar.

With this in mind, I followed through and performed the wedding, which was held on a Saturday evening. Early the next morning, I jumped on the 2,225-mile flight south, hoping that somehow, some way, Lord willing, the event would not begin until after my arrival ten hours later.

The Lord was willing. Sure enough, once I finally reached the airport in Mexico, I received two bits of great news. Earlier that day, officials called the event "ON"—not good at all. The first heat of competitors was literally on the beach in contest jerseys, about to paddle out, when an unfavorable wind hit them as they entered the water. The relentless onshore gust ruined the waves, forcing event directors to call off the event. The irony of this postponement served as the second piece of news: The moment my taxi pulled into the hotel later that afternoon, the wind switched to a perfect offshore direction. As I unloaded all my gear in the hotel parking lot, I saw a number of my former world tour rivals and friends excitedly running past me with their big-wave boards. "The surf is firing!" "It's over ten feet!"

Oh man! My heart began to race, my excitement over surfing these kinds of waves for the first time in over ten years racing through me to the point of shaking.

I unpacked my boards as fast as I could, grabbed my biggest board, and waxed it up. Then I ran across the street to the beach . . . and could not believe my eyes. Perfect 10-to-15-foot waves folded into triangles at their peak, then unleashed giant barrels, just like the real Pipeline in Hawaii. I had often heard of the comparisons between the two breaks, not quite sure if I believed that anything could be so close to Pipeline, but now I was looking at it with my own eyes!

I got out to the lineup as fast as I could. The water was filled with legends from my past. It was like the starting lineup cards of a baseball Hall of Fame game. As I greeted a few, my smile big and my excitement genuine at seeing them again, I noticed they all looked serious and tentative about the surf. Which caused me to feel the same way . . . *just how big was it? Could I handle it? Sure, when I was 24—but at 37?*

After about ten minutes of vacillating between being stoked to be there and pretty tentative about the size and power before us, a perfect 15-footer came right at me. This was it! The moment of truth! This was my wave and I was going for it.

I dropped in with perfect timing, made my left turn at the bottom, and stood straight up inside my first cavernous barrel in over a decade while it seemed like the entire Pacific Ocean pitched over my head. The lip of the wave was nearly as thick as a waterfall. I was so deep inside that very first wave, so far from the shoulder and my release to open sky—and then *whoosh!* It spit me right out as if I had been fired out of a cannon. It was an incredible barrel, one of the best I'd ever ridden, and the whole beach and lineup went crazy. That was it, the first wave of my comeback to the center stage of the surfing world after ten years of obscurity. *Welcome back, Joey. Welcome back to center stage.*

As I paddled out, I realized two things: First, this was my week. Second, I was going to win.

A few years later, when speaking with one of my peers who watched me surf that wave, he told me that when I rode it perfectly, he knew that it was a foregone conclusion that I was going to win. The best part? "I knew you were going to win, not because you were the California Kid or a Pipeline Master, but because I knew God was on the side of Pastor Joey!"

We both laughed. All I could say afterward was, "Who can even understand such things?"

I had an incredible week. Time and again, often in dramatic fashion, I defeated all my old rivals in surf conditions that never fell below ten feet. The night before the final day of the event, I received a faxed drawing from my oldest daughter, Hannah, that showed me on the podium as the event champion, telling people about my faith in Jesus. That's kinda how it went, as everything again swung completely my way on that final day and I gave God the glory for the win.

For the victory, I received the first-prize check for $7,000, this one well earned by surfing at my highest level in 15-foot barrels. I was once again a professional surfer and a champion. A *world* champion. I flew home basking in the afterglow of a big win, bought Jennifer a new kitchen floor, and spent $500 on the kids at Toys "R" Us. Hard to believe this was the same year that began with buying gas with pennies . . . God was so richly blessing us.

A few months after we competitors said our goodbyes, promised to keep in touch and left Puerto Escondido for our home countries, I received a copy of a Spanish surf magazine with a full-page water shot from the contest. The caption said it all: "El Pastor Buran en el Tubo!" I laughed out loud and thought, *Now I have a new nickname.* In my quarter century in the water, I'd gone from Sand Crab to Da Crab to California Kid, King of Pipeline, and now Pastor in the Tube, to fully complete the journey.

I was back in the surfing spotlight. The only question now was, "What next?"

Within a month, my face and photos filled the pages of *Surfer* and *Surfing* magazines once again. After ten silent years of ministry in Vista, Virginia and Vermont, years spent as far removed from surfing as a one-time Top 10 world tour surfer could get, it all seemed almost unbelievable. Then something that defied belief even more happened: Since I had won in waves of consequence similar to Pipeline itself, I was extended an invitation to the Pipeline Masters Trials. To many, the Pipeline Masters Trials was an event almost as prestigious as the actual Pipeline Masters. The event featured 32 of the best Pipeline surfers in the world who were not among the Top 30 on the World Tour. (The Top 30 automatically qualified for the Pipeline Masters main event.) Pro surfing had grown in leaps and bounds in my decade away from the sport, and that included changes in event formats to accommodate the growth. Out of these 32 surfers, only the top 2 from the Trials would make it into the actual Pipeline Masters.

I was quite ecstatic to receive the invitation and return to the North Shore of Oahu for the first time in a decade. Who has ever done that on the world tour level? I couldn't think of anyone else, but other, more pressing matters preoccupied my mind. Like getting into prime physical condition for the Banzai Pipeline. This time, I had a known program and my gym, and I got right to work, training seriously for the North Shore. By the time I flew into Honolulu and drove the 45 minutes up highways H-1 and H-2 and through the pineapple fields to Haleiwa, turned right and headed up Kamehameha Highway—a drive that thrills every nonlocal when they return to the North Shore each winter—I was in peak condition for the dangerous and challenging wave. The training helped to give me confidence.

As it turned out, I surfed reasonably well in my return to Pipeline. By sheer determination, I had reestablished my place in that challenging lineup and highly competitive pecking order. I went on to post a good showing in the Pipeline Masters Trials, surprising myself and others that I still had passion and skill for surfing Pipeline so many years after raising my arms in victory.

I proceeded to surf in the Pipeline Masters Trials over the next three years, highlighted by my seventh-place finish in 1999. When I surfed my last heat at Pipeline in December of 2000, I joined a very small and exclusive club of surfers who competed at Pipeline in four different decades! I'd come a long way from the gung-ho California Kid of 1978 to the pastor and father of four who paddled out in 2000.

A long way.

New Year's Day 1999 arrived with the Buran family and yours truly in a far different, more enjoyable and better space than 1998. Jennifer and the kids were doing great, we lived in beautiful Cardiff and I was still working at Surf Ride Boardshop. As a family, we were involved in a local church, and I continued to guest speak regularly at churches throughout Southern California. I was able to surf most of the time and our finances had stabilized. It was a great time for all my family.

Then came another blessing and opportunity wrapped into one juicy package. During the early part of 1999, officials of the well-known surf company Billabong approached me and offered me the job as coach of the Billabong USA Junior Surf Team. I'd always liked Billabong and their truly surfer's-first approach to their business, from the way they designed clothes and board shorts to making sure the media focused more on the competitors than their brand during more than a decade of hosting ASP World Tour events in Hawaii and, more recently, Lower Trestles near my home in Southern California. This company was so surfing-centric that, on Friday mornings in the 1980s, company president Bob Hurley would hold board meetings. Nothing special about that, right? Sizable companies always hold board meetings.

However, these were truly *board* meetings. Bob and his staff paddled out to Huntington Beach Pier and, during the lulls between catching waves, covered the items on their agenda. After an hour or so, they surfed their final waves, drove back to Billabong headquarters in nearby Costa Mesa, showered in the onsite facilities, and got to work. Bob was one of the nicest guys in the industry, a great businessman and a patient, inspiring motivator. When he left Billabong in the early 1990s to start a new company ten years after Billabong first arrived from Australia and he began building the US operation by selling Billabong board shorts out of his car to Orange and LA County surf shops, it came as no surprise that he succeeded in a big way. The new company he now owned? Hurley International.

Though Bob had moved on, Billabong remained in the hands of excellent management. I saw this as a great opportunity and a wonderful experience to be regularly at the beach coaching and surfing, while also actively engaged in ongoing pastoral ministry. I enjoyed the freedom of not being the primary pastor of a church, but still being able to bless others in the capacity of unofficial pastor and "surf coach."

In due time, by the end of that year, and despite the success I was having with Billabong, I began to strongly sense that I was about to be called back into full-time ministry.

Moving upon this lead, I notified Billabong I would be stepping back from surf coaching and returning to full-time ministry at the end of 1999. I believed God showed me that I had to first resign from Billabong before He would reveal what was next. Talk about a test of faith with four small kids at home! I will never forget the response of my Billabong boss, who asked how I could let go of a sure job and paycheck to wait on the Lord for my future.

"Sometimes we have to fully let go of one thing before God can give us the next thing," I responded.

"I admire your faith," my boss said.

As we hung up from the call, I'm sure my boss also thought I was crazy, though he knew that, no matter my love of coaching, my bigger heart lay in ministering.

Shortly after that conversation, on December 15, my good friend and mentor, Brian Brodersen, called to inform me that he was moving back to the States after spending several years living and ministering in England. He was en route to California to join the staff at Calvary Chapel Costa Mesa to serve under his father-in-law, the legendary Calvary Chapel founder, Pastor Chuck Smith. He was scheduled to begin in January 2000.

He reached the reason why he picked up the phone in the first place: "Will you consider joining my team and coming on board as well?"

Join his team at the Calvary Chapel mothership? Are you kidding? "Of course!"

I accepted the invitation, wondering for an instant how my Billabong boss would react if he saw how quickly it happened. My future was clear.

What a three-year period it had been since we left Vermont and years of starting and pastoring a pair of churches to come back home. I worked at a surf shop, coached a local surf team, and then developed and coached a national promotional surf team. At the same time, I grabbed my board, trained and surfed myself back into top form, won the 1998 ASP World Masters Title, and competed for three straight years at Pipeline. It had been a wonderful personal season of surfing, an endless summer of my own.

Even so, I was now eager to return to full-time ministry. Not just any ministry, mind you, but to serve as a pastor at the legendary Calvary Chapel Costa Mesa.

16

THE WORSHIP GENERATION

What a decade, the '90s. All the moves, starting two new churches in unfamiliar places, welcoming three children into the world, returning to California, buying gas with pennies, receiving a gift at our financial lowest I can only describe as manna from above, then finding new love as a coach from the flame of my old life—surfing—and pocketing a world championship as a competitor in the process.

You can't make this up. You can't sit there with a day planner and say, "This is how my life will go."

My faith and trust in God was absolute, and the journey he sent us on was truly wild.

Now, he had something else in store for Jennifer, the kids and me: stability. Thanks to Brian Broderson's offer to work at Calvary Chapel Costa Mesa, we established ourselves in Orange County in the first half of 2000 and didn't budge for ten years.

It was the closest thing to a perfect situation. Our children thrived at the Calvary Chapel Costa Mesa school and made healthy and natural transitions into their young adult lives. Then Jennifer made a change. From the time Hannah was born in 1990, Jennifer had been a full-time stay-at-home mom. When our youngest son, Luke, started first grade after we moved to Orange County, Jennifer decided to return to the workforce. Eventually, she returned to college to finish her degree in human development and graduated with honors. That led to a career as a teacher and administrator at the same school the kids attended. I was so inspired by her determination to see it through and complete that chapter of her life she'd so willingly given up when marrying me 15 years prior.

As for the ministry, I prospered at Calvary Chapel Costa Mesa. The church was made up of about 5,000 congregants who attended the three primary services taught by Pastor Chuck on Sunday mornings. It was a new and amazing experience for me to be serving alongside so many other pastors in receiving and fulfilling the numerous and various needs of the large congregation.

A few weeks after attending and serving at the legendary church, I began to notice and realize that the majority of the congregation was older than me. In some cases, much older. Where were the younger congregants, people in their teens, 20s and 30s, like me? How could I reach them? As I considered the matter, realizing it would take a different strategy to reach coming-of-age millennials than how it worked for my generation, I began to get a heart and vision for reaching the next generation. I prayed, sensing that God was going to do something special. I just needed to trust in Him and wait on His timing.

Within a few months, Pastor Chuck presented me with a great ministry opportunity. After consulting with Brian, they decided to open up the main sanctuary to allow me to start a new weekly service, targeting the youth of Orange County. For me, it was like a dream come true! I would be teaching from the same pulpit as Pastor Chuck Smith and looking out over a sanctuary that seated almost 2,000 people. A once-in-a-lifetime opportunity? For sure. Was I nervous and excited? You have no idea. But once again, like with every previous huge leap in my life, my excitement for the potential of great things to go right superseded my anxieties and fears of what could go wrong.

I began to think about what we could call this new ministry night. God was going to do something special, of that I was sure . . . but what would we call it?

During an appearance as a guest speaker at a public high school Christian club, two words merged in my mind while sitting back and watching about 60 students singing praise songs to God: *Worship Generation.* Surfing had the popular Momentum Generation and sociologists had started tagging successive generations by different names: the Silent Generation, Baby Boomers, Generation X, millennials . . . perfect. I gratefully received the name that would define my pastoral ministry calling for the rest of my life. I observed these kids and thought, *Wow! This really is a new generation of worshippers.* My thought became a name and that name identified my ministry.

We began to officially call our Thursday night young adult service at Calvary Chapel the Worship Generation. The rest is history. A very lively history.

As soon as our ministry started, it seemed to grow a momentum unto itself. God began to connect me with numerous young, talented musicians to lead worship for these services. Among these gifted musicians was a former Calvary Chapel Bible College student from Indiana, the extremely talented Jeremy Camp. Jeremy was unheralded—but not for long. Through a mutual friend, we'd met just a few months before while ministering together at a corrections facility in San Diego. When we met for the first time in the parking lot outside that jail, we both confessed that neither one of us had done anything like this before. We were both quite nervous, but able to laugh about it and face the adventure together!

After entering the facility, door after door began locking behind us. We looked at each other nervously and smiled, like, "Whoa!" Eventually, we stood in an open courtyard with a few inmates, all of them carefully observing our actions. In their world, personal observation was a matter of survival. It was a scene right out of a movie, right down to the cold mist beginning to fall. As Jeremy began to play and sing, I looked to my left and noticed several inmates indoors watching an NFL playoff game on a TV in a large meeting room. *It's me and this guy in the rain versus pro football and the warm indoors right now!* I thought.

When Jeremy Camp hit that first chord, I knew God was going to do something special. I also realized that this young man playing the guitar was no ordinary worship leader. His first song mesmerized me as he sang to the group of about a dozen inmates who had come outside to hear us. I thought at that moment, *This guy is extremely talented, God's hand is upon him and I think we are going to become really good friends!* He sang four songs, drawing outside dozens more inmates in their matching orange suits. Some of them even started singing. Jeremy was bringing a life and joy these guys hadn't felt in ages, if ever, in that place of heaviness and sorrow.

While it was the first time I saw Jeremy perform his ministry, it most certainly was not the last. When he was done, I spoke and taught from the book of Judges about the great faith and courage of Gideon. I exhorted the inmates to move on from their personal failures and become great for the Lord. After that, Jeremy and I agreed that we should serve God together—which is what we did for the next three years.

Four months after that wet Sunday in January, Jeremy Camp became the first and primary worship leader for Worship Generation. Within two years, he had five number-one radio hits and captured his first Dove Award, the Christian music version of a Grammy. An awful lot happened in those two years, which I'll share in a minute, but I first recall a funny back and forth with another minister as we watched Jeremy begin his musical career by ministering to us and the KWVE listening audience.

"Jeremy Camp is going to be a household name in Christendom one day," I told the minister. "Bigger than Calvary Chapel is. He's going to be huge." My statement was bold; Calvary Chapel was and still is a very large church movement, with congregations in nearly all of the 50 states. But I know emerging greatness when I see it.

The minister shook his head. "He's good, but I don't see it."

"You *will* see it," I said.

Around this same time, I also became aware of Phil Wickham, another gifted teenage worship leader. I don't remember the first time I heard or saw Phil. However, after I invited him to lead the music at Worship Generation, I realized that once again, I was in the presence of another of the most gifted musicians I had ever seen. Another pastor, surprised by Phil's youth, even asked how I could use a 16-year-old worship leader for our services. "How could I not?" I replied.

Phil and I had a great friendship from the start. His focus on the quality of his music and performances reflected maturity far beyond his age. I felt like I had won the pastor's lottery with Jeremy and Phil, and I wanted more than our Worship Generation to see them. I put on my promoter's hat from my old surfing days and told anyone and everyone I knew in ministry, "Get these guys out to your churches now!" I knew from the get-go that they were both headed for greatness.

Twenty-five years later, their talent in music and faithfulness in ministry has not only earned them numerous awards and accolades, but also made them world renowned and respected. Especially Jeremy. What a blessing to myself and our early congregation of the Worship Generation, that God gave them both to us in that very first year of the new millennium.

Through the course of those first few years, God brought other gifted worship leaders to us, and I began to feature them in regular rotation as well. Jeremy was our primary worship leader, followed by Phil and then the rest of the crew. Because Worship Generation was in the sanctuary at Calvary Chapel, we were also featured weekly on live radio through KWVE locally—and nationally, on the Calvary Chapel Radio Network. My experience as a surf reporter and guest on new-wave radio stations 91X and KROQ in the 1980s certainly helped me in how I wanted to work with them. Live radio gave us such great exposure that, within six months, our audience quickly grew into the hundreds and the ministry began to take off in a great way. By the end of the year, we were drawing close to a thousand congregants weekly and building up a national audience through the radio.

In due time, we fielded numerous requests to visit other regions for church services, youth camps, and special events. In early 2001, we began to hit the road for ministry, travel to where we were invited, and take with us whichever leaders and bands were available to make the shows. Initially, it was primarily Jeremy. A fun personal moment for me came during this mission, when I participated in a youth camp in Southwestern Colorado. Remember Bill Yehling, the guy who was *that kid* athletically when I moved to Carlsbad and wanted to be the best youth athlete in town? One day, two teenage girls came up to me and introduced themselves. They were his daughters. One of them, Whitney, looked just like him! I hadn't seen Bill in 20 years, but now, through his daughters, I got to see what a great father he'd become. These types of blessings never cease to amaze me.

During our first year of Worship Generation, Jeremy, who grew up in Indiana, fell in love with Melissa Henning, a stunningly beautiful girl from San Diego County. Everything I felt from them through Jeremy, from their faith to the way they were when together, spoke one message: "perfect match." They were madly in love with each other, but there was a big catch, an obstacle no one should have to face: Melissa, just 21 years old to Jeremy's 23, was fighting cancer. Jeremy wanted to take her hand in marriage so badly, but like any young man in his position, he didn't know whether he could handle marrying someone only to see her pass away. Those of us of a certain age remember the movie *Love Story,* with Ryan O'Neal and Ali MacGraw. I first saw that movie when I was ten, and it stuck with me forever, the story of two beautiful young lovers who seemed destined for a full life together—until cancer claimed Jenny Cavilleri (Ali MacGraw). It was the first movie—or anything on a screen—that made me cry.

Jeremy and Melissa were *Love Story,* 30 years later. Only, this was very real and playing out very much in all of our lives with the Worship Generation.

In late May and early June of 2000, Jeremy and I worked and ministered at a youth summer camp in his home state of Indiana. We spent a lot of time discussing whether he should ask for Melissa's hand in marriage. He loved her so deeply—easy for me to see in his eyes, which felt like huge hearts as he poured out about her. However, he added, "I just don't know what to do. She's in remission right now ... but what if it comes back?"

Jeremy and I are about 20 years apart, so he regarded me as a close friend, big brother and minister all at once. And I saw him as one of my closest friends. What a heavy question, the weight of this young man's heart and soul bearing down on him. After we prayed on it, I said, "Let's see what happens when we get home. God is going to give you your answer and guidance on your next step shortly after you return to California."

I already had a very good idea. It was written in his eyes.

Four months later, on October 27, Jeremy and Melissa exchanged marital vows at Horizon Christian Fellowship North County in Rancho Santa Fe, a cozy town in North San Diego County. Nearly 500 people turned out, a great crowd. Jeremy was already being considered an emerging Christian artist, so some music industry people were there, too, along with members of our Worship Generation, his Bible College friends from Murrieta, and her home church. Along with their families. Rarely have I seen more love in two peoples' eyes at their wedding. Not only was it the intense outpouring of young love, but also a deep expression, from a place far deeper than their great looks and their hearts. Their love emanated from their souls through their shared faith in God.

The newlyweds wasted no time switching to honeymoon mode. They quickly flew to Haleiwa, on Hawaii's North Shore, my old stomping grounds for a decade as a professional surfer. They returned so happy and joyful, so filled with love, that everyone wanted to be around them just to feel their energy, their presence.

But something else awaited them when they flew home: physical pain. During their first week back in their new condo in Carlsbad, Melissa started feeling pain. Off they went to her oncologist, who delivered the news.

Jeremy called me, struggling to speak. "Joey, we think her cancer's back."

I didn't know what to say, to him or the congregation. We'd just shared one of the happiest moments any of us had seen … and now her cancer was back, before their marriage could even get started.

Melissa moved back into treatment immediately, aggressive treatment, but it was no match for the aggressiveness of the cancer. She slipped quickly. I visited Jeremy and Melissa more and more frequently; sometimes, Jeremy and his tight group of friends would sing praise songs. He played the guitar and sang while Melissa held up her hands in worship, despite being so feeble and frail. Through song and media, their story of love, joy, sorrow, and heartbreak unfolded before the eyes of the Worship Generation congregation as we went through their struggles together with them.

As Christmas neared, I paid them another visit. Jeremy looked at me with tears in his eyes, the sheer joy of two months before replaced by a deepening sorrow. "I don't know what to do," he said as the love of his young life fought fiercely but continued to weaken. "This is so hard."

Shortly thereafter, Melissa Henning Camp entered the hospital for the final time. While visiting with Jeremy at the hospital, he turned to me and said, "I know that Jesus wants His bride, but I want my bride too!" It pains my heart to this day.

Within hours, Melissa passed on to be with the Lord.

Jeremy suffered through a level of grief that few young people have ever experienced. He sought solace through the Worship Generation, continued leading services, and playing music. A lot of music. Then the words and melodies started pouring out. Words about Melissa, him and Melissa, the emotional ordeal of her illness, the love so powerful and magnificent that they rose above her cancer to marry . . . then his heart breaking at the end, keeping himself together by sticking to the goodness of God. Sticking to his faith after this couple's short but incredible season of love on earth. He played these songs to our congregation, in services now broadcast live on KWVE radio in Southern California . . . and people started listening. More and more people.

Eighteen months after Melissa's passing, Jeremy Camp was the most sought-after Christian artist in the land, with five number-one radio hits, all from his debut album, *Stay*, which one reviewer described as "personal experience resonate." He poured out his feelings in those songs, and they connected from coast to coast—*Stay* went gold, then platinum. And Jeremy Camp was on his way. Today, he is a happily married man to his wife of more than 20 years, Adrienne. They are also the parents of three beautiful kids.

Jeremy has won 5 Dove Awards, recorded 37 number-one radio hits, sold 5 million albums, been ranked as high as number two on *Billboard*, won 4 ASCAP Songwriter of the Year awards, and been the subject of a powerful movie, *I Still Believe*, based on his marriage to Melissa. Jeremy's role was played very well by KJ Apa, who you might remember as Archie in the popular 2010s TV series *Riverdale*, based on the Archie comics.

Like everyone else in Worship Generation, like his friends and his millions of fans, I've rejoiced in his success—but I will never, ever forget what it cost him to write those songs on *Stay*, songs that undoubtedly have helped many listeners cope with emotionally tough situations in their lives.

Jeremy and I remain great friends, though we see each other rarely. When we do see each other, two things happen: We always cry, and then we always laugh. We otherwise act like two guys who have known each other well for 25 years.

No matter how much time has passed here on earth, it's like no time has passed.

Up until the spring of 2005, and despite the background of a post–9/11 world and the emergence of personal cell phones combining to cause all too many distractions, Worship Generation thrived at Calvary Chapel. We had an incredible and memorable five-year run, reaching thousands in the sanctuary, on the radio, and in person on the road. We also produced three music CDs during that time. What an amazing and super fruitful season of ministry.

However, all things must change . . .

I concluded it was time to step back into a lead pastor role again, so I began to pray about where I should start a new church. In time, it became evident I was being led to establish a church using the Worship Generation name in the nearby community of Fountain Valley. Through our search for a facility, we ended up starting a Saturday night service in the sanctuary of the local Shoreline Baptist church. As seasons went by and then years, it became clear to me the Shoreline facility would become the permanent home of Worship Generation Church. Once again, and as always, our church family went through many different seasons. Our congregation grew older, kids grew up and became teenagers, teens moved away to college, and then on to new careers and new families of their own, often out of state.

I have found that, just as there are seasons of life for all of us, there are also seasons of life for church families. During the more than two decades since its inception, Worship Generation progressed from a youth outreach ministry at Calvary Chapel Costa Mesa to a grown-up church family meeting in the main sanctuary at Shoreline Baptist Church.

We also made a personal change after ten years of living in one home. Jennifer and I both felt the urge to live closer to the coast, so we sold our Costa Mesa house and moved our family to nearby Huntington Beach. I had competed for many years in Surf City USA, in prestigious contests held on both sides of Huntington Beach Pier, and loved the place. Its beautiful beaches, year-round surf, and outdoor activities made it the perfect community to finish raising our young adult kids and move on to our new life as "empty nesters." Over those next few years, one by one all four of our children graduated high school, moved on to college, pursued careers, eventually married—and, in some cases, moved as far away as Vero Beach, Florida, where the LA Dodgers used to hold spring training.

In a most beautiful development, my sister, Barbie, came back into our lives again. She'd suffered through years of personal difficulties, so we helped her rebuild her life. As we did, my baby sister and I restored our friendship to the place it was when we were kids, all but inseparable from each other. I learned through watching her just how inspiring she was, in sharing her challenges, but now with the lived experience and strength of overcoming them. She eventually moved to Vero Beach, where she is much beloved and supported by our entire family. She and I retain that really tight friendship and closeness those with whom we grew up in Carlsbad remember all so well.

I wasn't done working with young people. Not even close. Living in Huntington Beach enabled me to dive back into the surfing scene, and it didn't take long to realize there were a number of incredibly talented grommets ripping up the local surf from San Diego to Santa Barbara, with Huntington Beach smack in the middle of the action. As Surf City USA was when Jan and Dean sang about it in the early 1960s, as the US Surfing Championships confirmed it in the late 1960s, as the OP Pro and Katin Pro-Am Team Challenge further affirmed it in the 1980s and '90s, and as the massive US Open of Surfing made no doubt about it in the new millennium.

I spotted these young surfers, and an old vocational love circled back into my heart. Not competing—I was too old to keep up with them. But coaching. It was time to coach again, and see how far I could take these talented youngsters ... and how much I could teach and inspire them to reach their fullest potential as surfers.

17

SURF COACH

Isn't it interesting how the same themes sometimes seem to circle back into our lives? How we move on to another phase, another season, and enjoy success, but that an opportunity arises or a person from the past pops up—and suddenly, we're looking again at a world or career we used to occupy? Truly, the life journey is anything but a straight path.

Sure enough, in 2007, a few years after we'd launched the Worship Generation Church and ministry and during the height of its success, my old friend walked back into my life—surfing. I'd already returned to surfing in the previous decade, working a fun surf shop job, coaching its promotional team, winning the ASP Masters World Championship, competing again in the Pipeline Masters and working with Billabong, an industry giant. While none of these were the same as winning the Pipeline Masters or my trailblazing competitive career, they certainly were high level at that stage of my life.

Which is the thing about circling back, you have to ask: When I circle back, am I returning to the same place in which I stood before? Or am I moving forward, upward, into a higher place, one where I can utilize my lifetime of experience and knowledge?

The answer to that final question turned out to be God's next plan for me.

It began with prayer—as it always does with me. While praying during a typically beautiful summer morning in Orange County, a very clear and profound thought entered my mind: *An opportunity to return to the surf industry and beach culture is about to present itself. Yet again.*

Hmmmm. Sure enough, later that same day when I arrived at the church offices, there were two messages on the answering machine. The first was from a man I did not know, Mike Gerard, the current president of Surfing America. The second message was from well-known and highly respected former pro surfer Mike Parsons, known for not only the fine career he put together, but for riding 60- and 80-foot bomb waves around the world.

I could hardly believe what I heard on the answering machine. Both men asked me to consider taking on the position of head coach for the USA Surf Team! On one hand, it seemed like an unusual request, like a confusion of careers. How many church pastors get a call asking them to be the coach of a national surf team, let alone the prestigious USA National Surf Team? On the other . . .

Well, I couldn't help but feel excited. And laugh. I thought back to 20 years prior, when I completely walked away from the sport to follow God's next plan for me—entering ministerial work and becoming a pastor. Now here was my first calling, the surfing world, calling me up through the two Mikes and asking me to come back and coach.

Life can be such a crazy and beautiful thing, right?

I was very surprised and excited about this opportunity. Within a few days, after much more prayer and consideration, talking with Jennifer, and the encouragement and support of other Worship Generation church leaders, I decided to become the USA National Surf Team's new head coach in August 2007. I had spent the past five years building a ministry with young people, and I had a houseful of kids, so teenagers already surrounded me on an everyday basis and relied on my leadership and life experience. We'd worked together to build something really amazing with the Worship Generation. Plus, I'd enjoyed coaching the Surf Ride and Billabong promotional teams so much that when I left those jobs, I left with a very full heart and tremendous gratitude to God for giving me such an opportunity.

Now, coaching had circled back, further up the ladder. It felt right in prayer. My family supported me. And any way I could do something positive for surfing—and especially young surfers—was a way that hit home with me.

Naturally, I dove in headfirst and fully committed myself to the responsibility and tasks of the position. Prior to me becoming the coach, Team USA had finished with a disappointing fifth place at the World Junior Surfing Championships, despite guiding a talented team that, on paper and from our practices, suggested higher potential. The powers that be held great hope and expectation I could turn things around and get the red, white, and blue back on the winner's podium. So did the surfers—and as any youth sports or high school coach knows, the athletes' buy-in ultimately matters the most.

If they believe in you and that can help them meet or exceed their goals, and you will give everything you can for their direct benefit, they will move heaven and earth and jump through all sorts of walls of personal limitation to achieve success at high levels—often higher than they could imagine. Especially if the coach involves them in their own building process, it makes them feel like they helped create the success of the team beyond their own performances.

I never was and never will be a traditional coach. As I learned in my earlier coaching experiences, I can and do present advanced maneuvers and teach the finer points of them, as well as contest strategy, but I'm not an Xs and Os guy at heart. I'm an inspirer and motivator, the guy who dives into the water with the kids, feels their pain when they lose and their joy when they win, drives them to find the best of themselves and bring it out for all of us to see—and do so with smiles and fist bumps all around. While standing with anyone in empathy and support who feels disappointed or heartbroken by their result.

Lord knows that I know what that feels like.

I began to evaluate our current team and start to recruit new talent for the future. Our program included about 25 surfers, mostly from California, joined by a few talented East Coasters. As I began to review current national rankings, particularly among 12-to-14-year-olds, I decided the best thing I could do was hold open scout tryouts. In September, I began to invite junior surfers to come train in Huntington Beach with the existing team and see how they matched up.

One of my favorite experiences came from an early interaction with a mom of a girl I'd never heard of until seeing her name far down on the West Coast rankings. Like, all the way down: She was the lowest-ranked girl I had invited to train with the team. The mom and girl planned to drive down from Santa Barbara later that week after school to train with us. That's a two-hour drive—if you don't count having to navigate LA's notorious traffic. In my phone call with the mom, she said, "My daughter is way better than her ranking. You are going to be impressed!"

I'd heard similar things before from many parents. Many times. I responded to her as one would expect, like "Uh, okay, see you in the afternoon." Because of that legendary LA traffic, they arrived a bit late, walked up, and introduced themselves to me. "You are going to be impressed," the mom said again, her eyes alight, full of enthusiasm and certainty her kid was *the one.*

Uhhh, okay. "Okay, I get it," I replied. "Let's get her out in the water with these other girls and see what she's got."

The very first wave she caught was electric! She shredded it. Her surfing was athletic, fast, and aggressive. Was this a case of bottling up everything she had into a tryout just to make the team? Quickly, it became clear that was not the case. I immediately turned to her mom and said, "You are right. I *am* impressed!"

The mom was former USA Olympic swimmer Sue Peterson, who notoriously competed in the 1994 Santa Barbara Triathlon while eight months pregnant. That baby was the girl now lighting up the Huntington Beach waves, Sue's 12-year-old daughter, Lakey, and I was watching the opening salvo from a girl who would go on to become one of the greatest American female surfers of all time. Within a month, I selected her to the USA Team. In 2009, at 14, she won the NSSA Open Women's National Title, in part by pulling off the first aerial for an amateur woman in history. The following year, she was a finalist at the World Junior Championships. She jumped to the professional ranks and the World Surf League (WSL) Championship Tour, formerly the ASP World Tour, where she immediately began finishing in the Top 10, including a year-end second-place ranking in 2018.

What a career. And what an honor to see the first tryout wave on Lakey's incredible journey to world greatness. Not to mention coaching her. It paid off to realize her mom's enthusiasm was not a parent's "my kid's the best" sentiment, but the perception of an Olympic athlete who knew what she saw—and made sure to get her into our program. I can only wonder what would've happened if Lakey was *below* my cut-off line to invite kids to tryouts, rather than sitting in the final position.

Throughout those next two years, I recruited, trained, and coached the best under-18 junior surfers in America. It was a very special and trying time for me. My job with the church was full time, and like so many thousands of other sports coaches around the world, I just had to find a way to make the time to put in quality effort for our training. As an athlete, I never wanted to be in a competition situation where my opponents had out-prepared me in advance. Preparation equals performance, and I'd seen many great pro surfers with endless talent go down in heats, or championship finals, because the guy in the other contest singlet was hungrier and better prepared. Needless to say, I brought this same mindset and approach to coaching the USA Surf Team. I didn't know how good we were or were not compared to the rest of the world, but I knew what I could control: to make sure we would be the best we could be when we faced other countries.

The USA Surf Team competes annually in the International Surfing Association's (ISA) World Junior Surfing Championship events. The ISA is recognized by the International Olympic Committee (IOC) as the governing body for the sport of surfing. It was ISA that led the way in introducing the sport of surfing to the world in the 2020 Tokyo Olympics (held in 2021). Interestingly enough, two athletes I coached from 2007 through 2009, Kanoa Igarashi and Kolohe Andino, would both go on to represent Team Japan and Team USA in surfing's debut in those Olympics. Kanoa had a fantastic Olympic experience, winning the silver medal behind gold medalist and WSL World Champion Italo Ferreira of Brazil. To me, it felt like an American won that silver medal, since Kanoa has lived in Huntington Beach for as long as I know. Like tennis superstar Naomi Osaka, he has lived in the US for most of his life but competed under the Japanese flag to honor his family and heritage.

Our first big test came in May 2008. After fervently training for over six months, we traveled with our top 12 surfers to the ISA World Junior Surfing Championships in France. I was confident we could contend for team gold. As the event progressed, I began to realize that Australia and Brazil might have superior teams. Australia was not surprising to me, given their decades of dominance in professional surfing, but the Brazilian team caught me off guard. Brazilian surfers were capable and had enjoyed some world tour success, but they had never been dominant or particularly intimidating.

Well, we found out in a hurry. To put it bluntly, Team USA ran into the "Brazilian Storm." On the third day of the event, one of our top surfers was up against an unknown Brazilian kid. The Brazilian surfer was outstanding, so good I watched him perform as if I were in a trance. After the heat, the American surfer asked me, "Coach, how come they kept scoring that Brazilian kid so high?"

My only response? "That Brazilian kid is really good." I would've scored him highly too.

That 15-year-old Brazilian turned out to be none other than future three-time World and Pipeline Masters Champion Gabriel Medina. And Medina was the point of a Brazilian spear that was about to take over professional surfing on a global level. I sensed right away that my team and I were watching the history of competitive surfing transform before our eyes.

Up to that point, professional surfing had been dominated by Australians or Americans. Brazilians had appeared in tour events since I won the Waimea 5000 in 1980, but it wasn't until the late 1980s and early 1990s they began to make an impact with the dynamic duo of Fábio Gouveia and

Flávio Padaratz. Fábio and Flávio held open the floodgates, and these hungry young surfers started pouring through.

Even with that, I'd seen many of the world's best surfers at similar ages as Medina. As I watched him dominate everyone in France, and the way he competed, I also sensed I was watching someone destined for greatness. My assessment proved correct.

Unfortunately, I was a bit more underwhelmed with my overall coaching performance in France. We finished in fourth, a disappointment for me, one I kept to myself. I came home feeling that we had competed well, but never really reached our peak, and I held myself accountable for that. Never mind this lineup of Team USA had only been together six months. I believed strongly that we could've been in the Top 3, so, chastened by the results and already reflecting on how I could improve as a coach, I was determined to lead us to better results in 2009.

After another year of training, we returned to the ISA World Junior Surfing Championships, this time in Salinas, Ecuador. Once again, Team USA performed well, but for the second year in a row, we had to settle for a fourth-place finish. As we returned home, I was pretty discouraged and exhausted. The trip proved especially hard on me with the equatorial heat, so hard that I was taken severely ill and was hospitalized with food poisoning during a critical three-day stretch of the event. Thankfully, my oldest daughter, Hannah, traveled with me on the trip and ended up being my advocate, both in the hospital and during my recovery at the hotel.

Once we got home, my recovery continued. It took almost two months to fully recover physically and emotionally from the experience. Once my health was restored, I determined that continuing as the head coach of the program required more time and effort than I could commit to giving, especially with my many pastoral duties and responsibilities to our congregation.

So, with some regret but plenty of sense, I resigned from my position in June 2009. I had given it everything I had for two years, restored the respect of the US team on the international level and worked with some fantastic future stars. However, I knew I could no longer put in the full commitment and quality time to serve as both a pastor and a coach. My dreams of gold medals and world championships had not materialized and for that, I was very discouraged and disappointed.

After resigning, I jumped from surf coaching to both sides of a movie camera while also pouring my energy into my church work. A new project had arisen, one on which I'd worked in bits and pieces but could now finish. We were bringing to the big screen the story of my life in a documentary, to be entitled *Beyond the Dream*; this book draws from that title. The movie was a huge undertaking, but I was determined to see it through. With the assistance of well-known surf movie producer Bryan Jennings, I was able to improve and complete the film. Over the next few years, I traveled to Hawaii, England, South Africa, and eventually to Chile, showing the movie and then speaking both about the movie's themes and sharing stories from my dual careers as a competitor and a coach.

While traveling with the movie, and to no surprise, more surf coaching opportunities were presented to me. In the summer of 2010, I traveled throughout England and premiered the movie. On this trip, I was invited to lead a few training sessions with the local kids, some of whom were among the best junior surfers in England. I enjoyed it and everyone who participated found the experience fruitful and memorable.

And, a possible open door into their own futures.

Shortly after returning to California, I received a call from England asking if I would be willing to coach Team Great Britain at the 2011 ISA World Junior Championships in Lima, Peru. I was surprised and excited to be offered this new adventure of coaching a foreign team at the world championships. I love new opportunities, new challenges that seem difficult from the get-go. This looked both wonderful and challenging, so I agreed to do it.

In Peru, the waves were quite good. And tricky. The British team rose to the occasion, all the athletes performing close to the fullest of their abilities in the prestigious event. They adjusted well to the variety of surf and put forth the best performance relative to their skill sets of any team I coached besides the effort Team USA would deliver a few years later. However, the Peruvian team was outstanding, combining local knowledge and great surfing skill to win the team gold medal. During that competition, we watched the rise of yet another talented Brazilian teenager, future World Champion Filipe Toledo, who, like Gabriel Medina a couple years prior, surfed heads and tails above everyone else.

What I enjoyed most about coaching Team Great Britain was the sheer stoke the athletes felt for being at the event. They were so excited to make the trip, to represent their country, to be in a world championship competition. My Team USA surfers had felt it as well, but not like this. While the British athletes wanted to perform strongly, none of them felt the pressure and burden of the expectations we always felt when we represented Team USA.

That's one thing about being on Team USA in any sport, from surfing to basketball to track and field: We're *expected* to win. I dealt with this as our coach, and I didn't care for it. When we don't, many see us as disappointments—even if our teams don't have any realistic shot of winning. It's not fair, to the athletes or the programs, but it's the perception American sports carved out during decades of domination on the world stage.

However, the British surfers reminded me of something far more important than winning or placing for the sake of winning or placing: the joy of competing and representing your country, regardless of your actual result. In other words, the whole reason to participate in a sport. It was something I never forgot. It stuck, and I planned to apply it well in future coaching opportunities.

A few years later, in 2013, I headed to Chile for a few showing and speaking opportunities with *Beyond the Dream* and again got involved in regional surf coaching clinics. Followed by an invitation to coach Team Chile. Was this becoming a pattern? Had some sort of word leaked out that I could and would coach anywhere, that my love for new challenges would win me over as much as the offer itself?

The Chilean journey swung open a door of opportunity that would last for almost four years. During this time, I made numerous trips to Chile and coached Team Chile in five different ISA events. I regularly traveled and trained with yet another group of patriotic, enthusiastic and surf-stoked young wave riders in Chile while coaching them into world events in Costa Rica, Nicaragua, Ecuador and Portugal.

This was a particularly exciting time. Right in the midst of it, in 2016, we learned that surfing was accepted into the 2020 Tokyo Olympics. Individuals from Fred Hemmings to Peter Townend to REEF Brazil sandals owners Fernando and Santiago Aguerre, and leaders of our national teams and eventually Olympic committees, had been lobbying for surfing's inclusion since the late 1970s. Put it this way: When I became a pro surfer in 1978, efforts to include our sport in the Olympics were already well underway. The Olympic push had been going on for 40 years, only to be turned back time after heartbreaking time. Change comes very, very slowly to the lineup of sports in the Olympic movement, especially the Summer Games.

Regenerated by this huge bolt of great news, I was eager and excited to help Team Chile surfers pursue the Olympic dream.

We got to work. Chile is very beautiful and features hundreds of miles of scenic coastline. The ocean temperatures are cool year-round, but the surf is world class with excellent waves and locations throughout its coastline. While there are many talented surfers in Chile, historically very few have ever seriously pursued world-class competition surfing. My main challenge while serving as head coach was to build confidence in the athletes for international success. We were literally starting from scratch; there had been no previous success. I figured that the best way to do this was to bring together the top Chilean surfers and work hard on developing competition skills and strategies in real-time training situations, more so than I did with my Team USA crew.

As time went on, it became clear that among all of the surfers in Chile, two stood out as having the best chance of qualifying for the 2020 Tokyo Olympics: Guillermo Satt from Arica in northern Chile, and Manuel Selman from the central region of Vina Del Mar, near the capital city of Santiago. Both surfers were already world-class athletes with substantial world tour surfing experience. They were friends and rivals, completely different in personality. Manuel was brash and confident and spoke excellent English. Guillermo was quiet, calculated and confident as well, but spoke almost no English.

Throughout my time coaching Team Chile, I sought to give extra time and attention to these particular athletes. However, that did not diminish my commitment to the team as a whole; I poured my very best into them and they definitely appreciated it. By late 2016, though, the same feeling that seeped through me with the Team USA started to creep in . . . that feeling that it was time to go and circle back to my bigger commitments—family and pastoring. The work and future required more than I could give, and so with gratitude and peace, I resigned in early November 2016.

Those around me had a similar question, some saying it, others holding it in their thoughts: "How did you manage to still be both pastor and coach? While also traveling to a distant foreign country to do so? What was the difference between 2007 with Team USA and 2015 with Team Chile?"

The answer? Motive and perspective. With Team USA, I was motivated to win gold at the world championships, both for the team and myself. With Team Chile, I was motivated to create a positive experience for the athletes and, in so doing, provide a good testimony of faith. I'd matured as a coach, and also taken a further step within myself by making it a part of my walk with the Lord. As for perspective, I had allowed and enabled the politics of parents and sponsors to bring me down and frustrate me more than once with Team USA. With Team Chile, I vowed to myself to stay positive in every situation, regardless of parents and sponsors. Also, truth be told, the Chilean surfers and their families were, as a whole, extremely appreciative and supportive of who I was and everything I was doing for them. Team Chile worked so well for all of us because of better motives on my behalf and a better environment the Chileans presented. It was and still is my favorite memory of being a surf coach.

After I resigned from Team Chile, my good friend Magnum Martinez took over the program. Magnum is an outstanding surfer and a former ISA

Masters World Champion, but even more importantly, he is a fantastic surf coach. Under his leadership at the beginning of 2017, the Chilean surf program took off from the base we'd laid down under my tutelage. By 2020, he had the Chilean pros surfing at peak performance and fully prepared for the ISA Olympic qualifier event.

In the 2021 ISA World Surfing Games, held just a few months before the Tokyo Olympics, Magnum and Manuel Selman proved to be a great coach-athlete combination in El Salvador. Manuel clinched the 20th and final spot for the first-ever Olympic surfing experience by a Chilean athlete. I was overcome with emotion a few months later while watching these two good friends participate in Japan as the Olympic flag and its interlocking blue, yellow, black, green and red rings flapped in the breeze on the beach.

I figured I was done coaching, quite satisfied with my experiences from the journey. I was home with Jennifer, and back to serving at Worship Generation. But apparently, God wasn't done putting me into coaching situations. Little did I know my greatest chapter as a surf coach was right around the corner—this time not as a California Kid nor just as a parent, but also as a grandparent.

On the first week of 2017, Jennifer and I welcomed our first grandchild, Zippy Bradley (from our youngest daughter, Leah). I was a grandfather! During this amazingly beautiful and joyful week for our family, I couldn't imagine what could add to my happiness. Then another call came from Team USA. This time, Greg Cruse was on the line. Greg and I had been personal friends since I'd first coached the team. He needed help from someone who could serve as a program volunteer. For years, deep down, I'd carried a sense of unfinished business with Team USA, so I said, "Yes!"

Welcome back, Joey Buran, to round two as the Team USA coach. This time for the love of the sport and coaching. I would receive one more chance to build a great team, one good enough to medal, possibly a team gold—a prospect even more exciting with the Olympics on the horizon. I didn't know what to expect, but I was confident that my experiences coaching Great Britain and Chile had taught me many valuable lessons and made me a better, more mature coach who operated from a broader perspective and understanding of our true strengths and weaknesses.

American surfing has always enjoyed a tremendous amount of talent. Since Peter Townend and Ian Cairns joined forces with Chuck Allen at the NSSA in 1979, and even earlier with coach/mentors like Midget Smith, our athletes have been well developed through elite regional coaching and the innumerable events which transpire almost every weekend throughout the United States. So, for the second time, now ten years wiser, I began to organize regular team training schedules for both the West and East Coasts. Again working with about 30 elite juniors, we trained throughout the year, primarily in Huntington Beach. By the end of the summer of 2017, we had selected 12 athletes—8 young men and 4 young women (the selections didn't reach gender equality at 6 men and women each until 2018)—to surf for Team USA and compete in the upcoming 2017 ISA World Junior Surfing Championships. This time, the event would be held in late September in Japan.

Soon after I took over the reins again, we ran into an unforeseen obstacle. In late August and early September, four of our top athletes canceled and pulled out from our World Junior Championship Team for a variety of reasons. It was a challenging turn of events, but we had to respond—quickly. Within a few days, we added four alternates to replace them, and then off we went for the ten-day "grind" known as the ISA World Junior Surfing Championships.

Over the years, I have found the ISA Worlds a true test of what is required of any coach in teaching and refining surfing skills, along with the ability to lead and manage 12 teenagers toward a common team goal in a primarily individual sport. To obtain success at the event, coaches and team managers have to rise well beyond their official titles. They also need to chaperone and coach life skills, and be tireless cheerleaders and confidence boosters. The main challenge is to keep everyone positive and unified against daily headwinds of more and more surfers being eliminated from the event. Great coaching at a world junior event is often accomplished by keeping the eliminated team members engaged and cheering on their teammates and peers (normally their rivals for those 12 coveted spots, and then again in the competition itself), even after they have been knocked out of the event.

I saw one of the best-case scenarios as successfully motivating our team members to enthusiastically cheer on their teammates still alive in the event. That's the first great thing that happened in Japan. Secondly, it became clear in the water that we were getting great results, all while establishing and strengthening that all-important team unity on the beach and at our hotel. With each passing day, as we remained in contention, I could feel our team togetherness growing and growing.

When we entered the final weekend of the event, it was apparent that the Australian, Japanese and Hawaiian teams were also racking up outstanding performances. Going into the final two days, we were in a strong position to win a medal, possibly even the team gold. But as much as I wanted to go there, to relish the thought of being a gold-medalist coach, I tried not to think about it. Previous experiences had taught me to be guardedly optimistic. I knew we had a great chance.

I also knew everything could fall apart on the final day from an interference call or a fluke perfect wave popping up in the final ten seconds—and a kid from the other team catching it, racking up points by stacking up one great maneuver after another, and knocking our kid out. For us to win team gold and become world champions, we would need a perfect scenario to unfold on that final day of competition.

Guess what happened? The perfect scenario.

Everything that had to go our way did so. Our surfers came through in every clutch situation, their wave selection spot-on, their performances electric. On the beach, every team member hooted and hollered as if they were at the Super Bowl, because they were—the junior surfing Super Bowl. As I watched and cheered, the heats and results seemed like a blur. I knew I'd never be able to recall this final day in detail, but our remaining surfers elevated their games and it became evident we'd achieved the rarest of feats for any team.

We'd performed at nearly 100 percent of our potential.

Still, after the last final of the day, no one on our team knew for sure if we were in second or first. The awards ceremony unfolded, with Australia finishing in fourth, then host Japan was announced in third. It came down to Team USA and Hawaii. I was so nervous as I waited for the commentator to announce the second-place team. Then I heard it loud and clear, "In second place, winning the silver medal . . . Team Hawaii!"

Oh my goodness! Twelve teenagers and I jumped up and down, screaming in shared joy. We had done it! We had pulled together, stayed together, risen together, and somehow, with a team featuring four alternates, become world champions. The day reminded me so much of December 17, 1984, when I won the Pipeline Masters—only this time, I was riding not on my achievements, but the individual and collective achievements of the 12 surfers who made it all happen. It was our day.

Afterward, I was exhausted and ecstatic, full of God's love and joy, along with sheer happiness for these kids. Not only was it my best day ever as a coach, but it was the culmination of 15 years of coaching surfers from three different countries.

What could I do for an encore? Well, that turned out to be a journey reserved for someone else, namely Brett Simpson. I stayed on one more year as Team USA coach, adding bronze- and silver-medal results to our gold-medal effort. Finally, in December 2018, I retired with another designation and achievement under my belt: the most successful Team USA coach in ISA history.

During my final two-year run, I really enjoyed another opportunity: the opportunity to work directly with other top coaches within the USA Olympic Sports program. This was a great learning experience for me, one I will never forget. It even included three days of training at the world-famous Joe Gibbs Racing Center in Charlotte, North Carolina. Joe was an assistant coach for my hometown San Diego Chargers when I was a fledgling pro surfer, then went on to lead the Washington Redskins (now the Washington Commanders) to three Super Bowl titles. After that, he moved onto race cars—and, not surprisingly, fielded dominant teams in NASCAR and every other auto racing division.

It was an incredible conclusion to a coaching career I could have never foreseen or even imagined.

Because I was technically the head coach of USA Olympic Surfing at the time of my retirement, some have asked me why I chose to retire before having a chance to coach at the first-ever Olympic surfing experience in Tokyo in 2021. The truth is, by late 2018, I felt that yet again, the time, passion and skill required for the final Olympic push was more than I could give. Upon honest self-reflection, I knew deep inside I was not the right person for that role going forward. If I couldn't give the same 100 percent for our surfers that I'd expect of myself were I training for the Olympics, then I didn't feel right about coaching them. In that case, leading them to the Olympics would be more about *my* experience than theirs, and I'd long since graduated from that school of thought. Thirty years of pastoring, mentoring and coaching makes quite an effect when it comes to putting the focus on others.

There was no doubt in my mind that I had completed my surf coaching journey. I was at perfect peace letting go of the Olympic dream and moving on to other priorities and interests in my life, my great coaching adventure complete. I was replaced by the highly respected and capable Brett Simpson, the former two-time US Open of Surfing champion. Brett and my good friend, team manager Greg Cruse, carried the program forward and helped Team USA win the women's individual gold medal in Tokyo. This was accomplished by reigning four-time World Champion Hawaiian Carissa Moore.

Looking back, it's pretty amazing to reflect on that first day coaching a handful of young local surfers in Oceanside and where it was ultimately going to take me. What started as a coaching clinic for a local surf shop in

1997, ended up a 20-year journey around the world, culminating in becoming the World Champion Coach for Team USA.

Yet again, the God of second chances had given me another one. This time, with Team USA surfing, its ending proved not only memorable, but golden as well.

18

ALWAYS FORWARD

What comes next?

I looked in the mirror, out at the ocean and into my heart, asking that question. I didn't frame it the way others in their mid-50s might after a life full of eventful occurrences: "What do I do from here?" I easily could have gone that route, perhaps out of fear it would be hard to experience a senior moment equal to traveling the world on my surfboard, winning the 1984 Pipe Masters and 1998 World Masters Championship, starting two churches and the Worship Generation movement, or coaching Team USA to a world championship in 2017.

What do I do from here?

At first, I felt like I'd played out this question. I'd experienced feeling like I was on top of the world as a husband, parent, grandparent, minister, surfer and coach. I thought that it was going to be a lot harder to move forward and find meaning, that I'd have to turn over rocks in some desperate search for *the next thing*, the next big event in my life.

It did not turn out that way. Things seemed to come to me—especially after I fully brought Jesus into my life as my Lord and Savior. Especially after I proceeded forward on a path of God with my family. Even before I fully committed my life to God in 1987, He was bringing people and big moments to me—a big brother and mentor in Midget Smith. A come-to-Jesus conversation with a dying Chris O'Rourke. My talk at Pipeline with Adam 12. The waves that came to me, and no others, to secure my Pipeline Masters title. When I became a believer, then a minister, those answered prayers grew in so many amazing ways, creating stories and memories I shared with my wife, my kids, my youth groups and congregations . . . and now, with you. It feels inside like a dynamic back-and-forth flow, powered by prayer, belief, and also being *open to receive* the answer, the next indicated step forward—and then taking that step, in concert with God's wishes for me ...

Which requires forward thinking. I've always been a forward thinker, not listening so much to what others thought my limits were, focusing instead on what I believe I could achieve for myself. Then, as I grew into my family and ministerial roles, what I could achieve for the good of all. Along the way, I've always felt the blessing of knowing when to pump the brakes, to feel the end of a season arriving, to bow out gracefully and to move on to whatever God wanted me to do next. After coaching Team USA to our world championship, I'd arrived at that crossroads moment yet again:

What comes next?

As I refocused my energies on my family and ministry, I began to realize that I had a strong personal desire to organize my life experiences and lessons into a simple but systematic thought process. A process of principles I've learned that I could share with others to inspire and equip them in their pursuit to fulfill personal goals and life dreams. A simple, clearly stated list I could pass like a baton to others, so they also could get into the race of a successful life spiritually rooted in God. Which, I would say from my own life experience, is the best race of all, the greatest wave in the set, one we can ride forever, never leaving the glorious tube until we emerge on the other side, in eternity.

As I considered and organized these principles, I began to see them as pillars. Just as pillars hold up a building, these held me up and guided me throughout the experiences and successes that shaped and defined the legacy of my life. And gave me something new to share with everyone going into my golden years. My primary goal now is to inspire and encourage as many people as possible, especially those of future generations, by sharing these eternal truths. Truths that have served me well and guided me through my life journey.

I am convinced that my greatest character strength in life has been a desire and determination to always move forward in the pursuit of my goals and dreams, regardless of obstacles, setbacks, and perceived failures. And the endless chatter of limitations others tried to place on me; in my view, that is chatter none of us needs to listen to if we want to achieve those goals and dreams. The prevailing thought over all my pillars? That each of us must have a personal drive and determination within us to resolve, to never give up or surrender our goals and dreams unless we feel an abiding peace in our souls and with God to do so. Until then, keep going. Keep making the effort. As the late North Carolina State basketball coach Jim Valvano famously said in his final speech, shortly before dying of cancer, "Never give up. Just never give up."

That is, unless we feel that abiding peace in our souls and with God. Then we know we've lived out the full season of our dream, goal or objective, and it's time to ask, "What comes next?"

While there are many topics and principles by which we can frame or organize our thoughts for personal success, I ultimately settled on eight macro principles for my pillars:

The first pillar is **Divine Purpose**. Without a doubt, I believe the single most important truth in the human experience is for each of us to realize that every human life has value, meaning and divine purpose. I strongly believe that all humanity is created in God's image. Humanity is the apple of His eye, not just collectively, but individually as well. While there is a commonality for all of us in being human, there is also an absolute personal distinction with the divine design, set of experiences, outcomes and details, and destiny for each of us. Believing in God as our creator gives each of our lives value, meaning and eternal purpose. He is the source of our being, identity, purpose and destiny. Imagine the peace and joy for each of us when we believe that God is truly in control of our lives and guiding us in and through all that our life purposes are meant to become!

Well, I would say you don't have to imagine it anymore. You can live it.

The second pillar is **Personal Faith**. Intellectually knowing or agreeing that God created us provides a good foundation in life, but is insufficient for the dynamics of personal purpose, calling and divine destiny. I believe that God calls each one of us to the place of accepting or rejecting Him through personal faith in His son, Jesus Christ. The Bible declares that God so loved the world that He gave us His only son, Jesus Christ. When we choose to believe in and receive Jesus Christ personally in our lives, we are assured of receiving forgiveness for our sins. We are also promised the hope of heaven for our eternal future. Personal faith in Jesus puts us on track to let God do His work in and through us. Though He will send us nudges and encouragements along the way, even gifts at crucial moments, His work for each of us can only truly begin once we put our faith in Him. When Jesus is Lord of our lives, then our divine destiny operates in full force, unhindered, moving forward day by day in personal growth to a life filled with meaning and purpose, and one with a future promising hope and glory. Since this force gives you a feeling you've never before experienced, an almost superhuman feeling you can achieve and do great work for the betterment of others, beyond what you've achieved before, well, it's time to bring it in!

The third pillar is a **Positive Attitude**. In the human experience, attitude is everything. It shapes our worldview, passion for life, and our responses to all that happens to us. If we believe that our life has a purpose and that God is personally guiding us, we can feel confident that all the events and circumstances in our life are working together for good. God's promises and protection back all of His divine purposes over each of our lives. This truth gives confidence to our faith and is an endless source of encouragement to our positive mindset. My positive mindset doesn't render me immune to disappointments and heartaches, but it does help ensure I will persevere and triumph through them and be the better for it!

The fourth pillar is **Big Dreams**. Many people harbor big dreams and accomplish seemingly great things, with or without Jesus in their lives. That being said, all dreams from God are of eternal significance, value and legacy. We can be sure that, if God is the source of our dreams, He will be the guide, the power, and the fulfillment of them as well. I have long since learned that if I seek God in all things, He will be faithful in His way to make clear to me the way I am to turn and the decisions I am to make to fulfill my dreams. When God opens a door, no man can close it; when He closes a door, who could want to push it open again?! If we delight ourselves in God, He will give us the dream, confirmation, strength and encouragement to see it through. So dream big, because no dream is too big for the Lord!

The fifth pillar is **Absolute Priorities**. As we pass through our days and the journey of our timeline, we need to be clear and intentional as to what things are most important to us and stay focused on them as our life's priorities. I find it imperative that we proactively and intentionally manage our priorities, time, daily decisions, and overall life direction to keep our main things the *Main Thing*! Time is precious. It needs to be valued and redeemed, because once used, it is never regained. Every day, we walk into an exchange of time toward eternity, so our priorities must be clear, in order, and keep us moving steadily and consistently toward all that God is seeking to do in and through each of our lives. At the top of the list of priorities will always be personal faith and service to God. Our purpose is eternal, so in our short season of time on Earth, keeping God first will always be the most important thing in every day. The highest priority after faith in God is holding and maintaining loving and healthy family relationships. Faithfulness and diligence with work, careers and personal finances come next, followed by a disposition of respect for others and healthy involvement in our local communities. Life is meant to be an adventure of faith and ongoing personal growth, to be properly shared with others. If we keep our priorities in order, it will be.

The sixth pillar is **Clear Goals**. When we wake up every morning, rub our eyes, have our coffee and start thinking about the day, doesn't it always feel like we have a million things to do? For this reason, we need to match our absolute priorities with clear goals. By doing so, we establish for ourselves a good foundation by which to determine what responsibilities, ideas, and interests receive the highest priority of our time and energy. We naturally find clarity for the details of things that must be done. This also helps us identify goals. Most people often associate goals with dreams and rightfully so, but the ability to identify clear plans and the tasks we undertake that will propel us to accomplish our goals is the key to reaching our dreams and moving them from wishes to reality. Identifying clear goals, the tasks necessary to accomplish them, and the obstacles to overcome along the way are valuable life skills that can and should be learned and strengthened, whether you're a parent, coach, businessperson, minister, teacher, worker, or whatever your calling. Holding clear, detailed and realistic goals gives us benchmarks for progress toward our dreams and a clear picture of what defines successful completion of them.

The seventh pillar is **Take Action**. Our life is a divine stewardship, and our divine stewardship is about faithfulness and accomplishments. To build toward and achieve successful accomplishments, we must first begin them! All dreams are nothing more than a wish list until we take the first steps of action toward realizing them. Most of us are familiar with the idea that talk is cheap; yes it is! In the real world, action is everything, and a life lived with divine purpose begins with the first step of faith. And another. When we have absolute priorities followed by clear goals, the first steps of action become clear and attainable. Take that step. Then take another. The more action steps we take toward our goals, the stronger we become and the better we feel about ourselves. We have begun the journey to our destination! Each step forward builds up our faith, teaches us new lessons, and strengthens our resolve to see things to completion, push through obstacles and setbacks, and remain intentional and determined to reach our goals. Great things are there for each of our futures, but to reach them, we must take action.

The eighth and final pillar is **Finish Well**. On the seventh day of creating the heavens and the earth, God rested. Talk about finishing well! Likewise, when the job is done, the task is complete, the dream fulfilled and there is nothing left to be done, you have finished well! Of all the things to be valued in the human journey, almost every culture would agree that a job well done is worthy to be esteemed by all. If we can weave our lives into a pattern of successful completion of those things entrusted to us by God, we will indeed enjoy the most ideal of all lives, one at the highest level of divine purpose and destiny.

When our life becomes a daily pattern of easy things done well, little things done well, and simple things done well, it will lead us onward to a lifestyle of difficult things done well, big things done well, complex things done well—and a lifetime legacy of all things done well! To the one who has, more will be given. That is what God wants for us: to entrust us with more and bless us with more. The prize in things done well is not so much the reward at the completion of the task or goal, but who we became in the process. There could be no greater summary of our lives than to stand before God in eternity and hear Him say, "Well done, good and faithful servant!"

Ultimately each of our lives will become a legacy. Once we are gone and have moved on to eternity, our entire life and core values, what we lived for, who we shared it with, and how we treated others will become our enduring legacy here on Earth. While we still enjoy the gift of life, we continue to have the opportunity to write the story and legacy that we desire. For all I do not know or have yet to learn, this I do know: God's plans for all of us always include both a future and a hope. He has given us all things necessary to become and remain successful in this life, and He has promised us we can do all things through Jesus Christ who strengthens us.

As I look ahead to my life, a life shared for more than 35 years with Jennifer and populated by my children and grandchildren, I can say that I intend to give it everything I have in these final years of my journey, even more so now than ever before. I am committed to doing my very best going forward, not just to achieve a dream, enjoy the perfect day with my wife and family, catch a perfect wave, preach a perfect sermon, or chase new adventures in the life beyond a dream, great as each of those experiences feel in the moment. No. I am committed to doing my very best to fulfill the sheer destiny of it all, the upward call of God in Christ Jesus.

In sharing my story, I hope I have inspired you to do the same.

SURFING GLOSSARY

Surfing has its own culture, fashion sense, music—and terminology. I wanted to be sure you experienced the culture and feeling as much as possible, so I used terminology throughout the book. Here is a glossary to help you along the way:

Backside — When the surfer's back is to the open wave as s/he rides it.

Barreled — The act of riding inside a tube.

Beach-Break — Waves that break onto sandy bottoms, most often close to the shore. These tend to be fast, powerful waves and shorter rides.

Bottom Turn — The long, sweeping turn a surfer makes when s/he reaches the bottom of the wave and redirects to the open face.

Cutback — Completely redirecting the board to return to the most powerful part of the wave and regain speed.

Dawn Patrols — One of the greatest moments of any surfer's day: catching the first waves just as daylight is breaking.

Deep-Water Channel — A small river of water that forms most often in big-wave locations. It pulls water outward, allowing surfers to get outside to set waves without being impacted by incoming waves.

Dry Docked — Pulling off a surfing maneuver in extremely shallow water, and either landing or wiping out on exposed reef, rock or sand. Highly dangerous.

El Niño — A weather pattern in which the Eastern Pacific warms up, causing bigger and more frequent storms (such as "atmospheric rivers" and "Pineapple Expresses") and bigger surf.

Frontside — When the surfer is facing the open wave as s/he rides it.

Going Left — Surfing to the left side of the breaking wave. Surfers are riding to their left, and the spectator's right.

Going Right — Surfing to the right side of the breaking wave. Surfers are riding to their right, and the spectator's left.

Goofy Foot — Surfing with one's right foot forward. S/he directly faces waves breaking to her/his left and the spectator's right.

Grommets — Beach slang for kids, particularly kids who surf. Also known as "Gremmies."

Haole — Hawaiian term for a Caucasian.

Interference — When one surfer impedes another's ability to ride a wave for which s/he has priority. Interference can happen through direct physical contact, or when one rider slides in front of the surfer with priority to take off and ride the wave.

Paddle Battle — When surfers paddle furiously to get outside and catch the next wave. Paddle battles can be fierce and aggressive; hence the world tour's decision to create a priority buoy in the latter years of my career.

Peel — The act of a wave slowly breaking, either on one or both sides, revealing the open face of the wave.

Point-Break — Waves breaking offshore from points of land jutting into the sea. Point-breaks can either have rock, coral or sandy bottoms.

Priority Buoy — Used in world tour competition, the buoy establishes priority so that surfers know who has first choice on the next incoming wave.

Reef-Break — Waves that break on coral or rock reefs. Waves tend to seize upward and increase in size, as well as improve shape, when they break over reefs.

Regular Foot — Surfing with one's left foot forward. S/he directly faces waves breaking to her/his right and the spectator's left.

Sets — A succession of waves, breaking at specific intervals. Sets usually cluster in groups of three to six waves, followed by a lull, then another set.

Shore-Break — When the wave breaks directly onto the beach, with little to no water beneath it. These waves are explosive, fast and difficult to ride.

Shoulder — The open part of the wave that forms as the wave breaks. Performance surfers always seek out shoulders on which to unleash some of their moves.

Stinger Surfboard — A popular board when my career began, it features an abrupt reduction of the width in the back half of the board, allowing for sharper turns and improved flotation and planing speed.

Surf Leash — The cord at the back of a surfboard. Surfers attach it to their boards and ankles so they can retrieve their boards after falling off without having to swim to shore.

Thruster — A three-fin short surfboard. The invention of the thruster by Simon Anderson in 1980 revolutionized the sport and greatly enhanced the types of maneuvers surfers could perform.

Town and Country — A hugely important surfboard company and surf shop during my career. Also a Hawaiian geographic term: "town" is Honolulu, and "country" is the North Shore, an hour's drive away, where the legendary big waves break.

Tube — The opening in a wave when the top of the wave breaks over itself.

Waiting Period — In big-wave competitions, the time allotted for contest directors to successfully complete the event. The goal: to hold each day of the event in optimal surf.

Wetsuits — The rubber suits that surfers wear to stay warm in colder water. They range in thickness from one millimeter to five millimeters. Because of them, we can surf in water as cold as Alaska's winter waves—though I won't be promoting it!

Whitewater — The billowing, foamy water of a wave after it breaks. The whitewater carries all the way to shore, or wherever the wave fully dissipates.

THE SURFING ASSOCIATIONS

ASP (Association of Surfing Professionals) World Tour — The second iteration of the world pro tour ran from 1983 until 2015. The ASP brought in many more events, a huge increase in prize money, media coverage, sponsorships and participation.

IPS (International Pro Surfing) Tour — The first iteration of the world professional surfing circuit, the IPS formed in 1976 and continued through 1982. I was an ISA member from 1978–82.

ISA (International Surfing Association) — The official association that regulates the Olympic surfing program and administers world championships and Olympic Games events. Surfing became an Olympic sport in 2021 after a 45-year effort.

NSSA (National Scholastic Surfing Association) — The premier amateur surfing organization in the US since its inception in 1979, the NSSA features middle school, high school and collegiate competitions on all coastlines. The NSSA began rising to power during the second half of my career.

WSA (Western Surfing Association) — The predominant amateur surfing organization when I began my career, an offshoot of the USA Surfing Federation, which also includes the Eastern and Gulf Coast associations.

WSL (World Surf League) — The current iteration of the world tour has introduced solid six-figure prize money to every event and created equal prize purses for women and men since it grew from the ASP World Tour in 2015. WSL events also are held in many of the world's most prestigious and big-wave locations.

ACKNOWLEDGMENTS

With sincerest thanks to all those directly involved in the production of this book, beginning with my wife, Jennifer, oldest daughter, Hannah, and Angie Emma. Their early edits and feedback kept the project going forward and in a good direction. When the book really needed input and skills beyond me, the addition of longtime friend Robert Yehling was the perfect fit. His life experience as a writer along with his team of Erin Jenkins, Rob Weinberg and Theresa Jenkins took the project forward to much greater heights than where it had previously been. The additional edits and publisher input from Jennifer Geist were much needed along with ongoing personal encouragement from Keith Randolph and Susan Branch. Special thanks to the surf photographers who generously lent their support and resources to this project, Brian Beilmann, Allen Carrasco, Aaron Chang, Jeff Divine, Sean Evans, John Jackson, AJ Neste, Ben Reed and Brian Stephen. And finally, additional thanks to all those who were willing to read, review and endorse this project. Your feedback and encouragement have been greatly appreciated. I could never have done this project without all of you and your support. Forever grateful for all of you! May our final product inspire and bless the multitudes.

JOEY BURAN

Joey Buran grew up primarily in Virginia, where he was a multiple AAU youth swimming champion. When he was 12, the family moved to Carlsbad, California, where Joey quickly took up the most engaging local sport—surfing—and determined he would be the best in Carlsbad, then California, then the nation, and finally the world. By 15, he was one of the top amateur surfers in America; by 17, he was a professional surfer and finalist in the event he wanted to win more than any others, the famed Pipeline Masters.

After legendary ABC *Wide World of Sports* host Jim McKay tabbed him The California Kid, Joey became the spirit and face of California surfing, just as the Golden State was taking its place as the cultural, competitive and economic Mecca of the beach and ocean lifestyle—a central component of youth culture in America for the next 20 years. Two years after turning pro, he won Brazil's Waimea 500 in 1980, then captured California's grand prize, the Stubbies California Surf Trials, a year later. He firmly entrenched himself in professional surfing's Top 16 for five years, the first US mainland surfer to do, peaking at No. 7 in the 1983–84 season.

Three months after announcing his retirement from competition, on December 17, 1984, Joey won his final world tour event, the one about which he'd dreamed and focused his entire life since age 12—the Pipeline Masters.

Along the way, Joey's boundless positivity and intense love for his sport and its culture and history made him a star in the people's eyes, the subject of endless media coverage, and a household name to millions around the world. That same boundless positivity and "can do" message, combined with a storytelling style that harkens to both his Southern and ocean years, comes through in the narrative of *Beyond the Dream*. It feels once again like we're hanging out on the beach with one of surfing's greatest cultural ambassadors and storytellers.

Joey's contributions to his sport continued with another first—founding and producing the first US Pro Tour of Surfing, the PSAA. After serving as producer for one and a half years, Joey stepped away from surfing—and transformed from focusing on his own achievements to serving others.

He found his new calling as a minister in the Calvary Chapel community, first in North San Diego County, then in Orange County. His deep faith and surfing prowess were on full display in one of the most viewed surfing films of the past 40 years, *SON Riders*. He and his wife, Jennifer, and their family moved to the East Coast in the 1990s, where Joey founded churches in Virginia Beach and in Burlington, Vermont. Following almost a decade away from California, he returned to continue his ministerial work . . . and to return to the waves he so dearly missed. In 1998, he found the victory stand again, beating his former rivals—including several world champions—for the title in the World Masters Championship.

From there, Joey blended ministry, surfing and a new pursuit—coaching young surfers. He'd spent his life going from one to the other, but by the early 2000s, struck a balance that has informed his life for many years since. He founded the Worship Generation in Costa Mesa, California, which became a nationally respected and highly regarded youth ministry, and he also accepted the coaching reins of Team USA, America's national amateur surf team, as the sport was making its drive to become an Olympic sport (which it did, in 2020). He took Team USA to four Top 5 finishes in the worlds, including the 2017 World Team Championships with a crew that includes some of today's greatest professional surfers. Not only that, but he revived and built strong teams as the head coach of Team Great Britain and Team Chile between his stints as Team USA coach.

Joey lives in Huntington Beach, California, with his wife of over 35 years, Jennifer. They have four children and nine grandchildren. *Beyond the Dream* is his first book. His future plans include writing other books while continuing to serve others in the hopes of reaching their dreams—or elevating above them.

Printed in the USA
CPSIA information can be obtained
at www.ICGtesting.com
CBHW072127230824
13639CB00005B/128

9 781956 897449